Trivets & Stands

*An illustrated catalogue of nineteenth and twentieth
century trivets with emphasis on those which are American
and cast in iron or brass. The text includes notes
on the manufacture, distribution, design and dating of
trivets and stands.*

Trivets & Stands

*Rob Roy Kelly and James Ellwood
in conjunction with Shelburne Museum,
Shelburne, Vermont.*

Text by Rob Roy Kelly; edited by Robert Shaw.

Golden Era Publications,
Lima, Ohio.

Text set in 10/12 and 8/9 point Century and printed Offset on 70 pound Mead Moistrite Matte by The Walsworth Press, Inc., Marceline, Missouri.

Color separations by Walsworth Publishing Company, Marceline, Missouri.

Catalogue trivet photographs by Ken Burris, Shelburne Museum, Shelburne, Vermont.

Other catalogue and illustration photographs by Craig Smith, Tempe, Arizona.

Photographs from:

The Metropolitan Museum of Art, New York, New York.

The Philadelphia Museum of Art, Philadelphia, Pennsylvania.

Hagley Museum and Library, Wilmington, Delaware.

National Park Service, Harpers Ferry, West Virginia.

Chagrin Falls Historical Society, Chagrin Falls, Ohio.

Shelburne Museum, Shelburne, Vermont.

Book design by Rob Roy Kelly.

Production assistance by Scott Surine.

This book was made possible through research grants from Arizona State University, Tempe, Arizona, to Professor Rob Roy Kelly.

1986 Faculty Small Grant Program.

1987 Special Funding; Office of the Vice-President for Research and the College of Fine Arts.

1987 Art/Social Sciences/Humanities Grants for Tenured Faculty.

Copyright 1990 by
Golden Era Publications
A Division of Green Gate Enterprises
P.O. Box 934,
Lima, Ohio 45802.

ISBN 0-926110-00-4
LC 89-81850

TABLE OF CONTENTS

"Trivets will never die for me! I say trivets will never die."

Harry Haupt, blacksmith, Center Point, Pennsylvania, from a taped interview with Paul and Flora Harner in 1984.

This book is respectfully dedicated to:

Dick Hankenson, antique dealer from Maple Plains, Minnesota, who was a well known trivet collector. He published two small books, *Trivets, Book 1* and *Trivets, Book 2,* in the early 1970's.

William Paley of Paris, Ontario, who spent most of his adult life collecting trivets and early American lighting devices. He wrote numerous articles for antique journals about his collections. At his death, he left his collections to Shelburne Museum, Shelburne, Vermont. His trivet collection is in excess of 2,100 trivets and stands reflecting a wide variety of styles, materials, and production processes.

John Zimmerman Harner of Boyertown, Pennsylvania, who in his retirement began making reproductions from authentic old trivets. He was responsible for making patterns for approximately sixty-five trivets. Some of these designs might have been lost if he had not made new patterns.

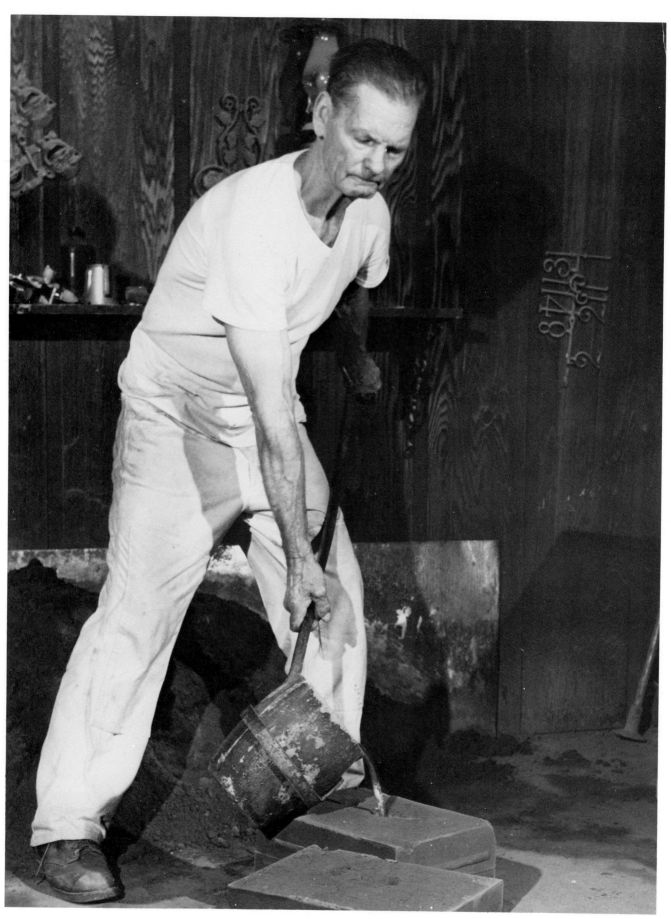

Wilton Company molder pours an aluminum alloy into a sand mold.

Acknowledgements

It is nearly impossible to do a book of this kind without the support and information provided by numerous individuals, and we are greatly indebted and appreciative for their assistance.

Ken Burris, photographer, Shelburne Museum. Ken had the enormous job of photographing the Paley collection at Shelburne Museum as well as flying to Phoenix to photograph the Ellwood collection. This book would never have been accomplished without his time and talent.

Also, special thanks to our other photographer, Craig Smith, a graduate student at Arizona State University.

Laverne Stimmel, Unicast Company, Boyertown, Pennsylvania.

Paul, Flora and Carl Harner, Boyertown, Pennsylvania.

Charles Salembier, and Hunter Earhart (deceased), Virginia Metalcrafters, Waynesboro, Virginia.

Henry Wilton, Wilton Products, Wrightsville, Pennsylvania.

Golda Dellinger, Wilton Products, Wrightsville, Pennsylvania.

Hank Ott, Etna, Pennsylvania.

John Engle, Keystone Grey-Iron Foundry Company, Pottstown, Pennsylvania.

Mortimer Spiller, Mortimer Spiller Company, Eggertsville, New York.

Larry Gilbert, John Wright, Inc., Wrightsville, Pennsylvania.

Donald Stoughton, Unicast Company, Paoli, Pennsylvania.

Julie McNamara, John Wright, Inc., Wrightsville, Pennsylvania.

Louis Pardini, Arizona State University, Tempe, Arizona.

Harry Haupt, The Art Smithy, Worchester, Pennsylvania.

Heddy Richter and Diane Portnoy, Hagley Museum and Library, Wilmington, Delaware.

Chagrin Falls (Ohio) Historical Society.

Lee Boyle, Supervisory Park Ranger, Hopewell Village National Park, Elverson, Pennsylvania.

Morrison Heckscher, Curator of American Decorative Arts, The Metropolitan Museum of Art, New York, New York.

Portage County Historical Society, Ravenna, Ohio.

Rudy Turk, Director of University Art Collections, Arizona State University, Tempe, Arizona.

Thomas Schantz, Kutztown University, Kutztown, Pennsylvania.

Carol and Jimmy Walker, The Iron Lady Shop, Waelder, Texas.

Ernest Winter, Westfield, New Jersey.

Frank Politzer and his wife Judy (deceased), Sonoma, California.

Edna Glissman, Carlsbad, California.

Dick and Marge Kelley, Oklahoma City, Oklahoma.

Susan DeCordova, Norwich, New York.

Larry Quick, Mesa, Arizona.

Margaret Suggs, Scottsdale, Arizona.

Jessie Williams, Scottsdale, Arizona.

Vi Swanson, Seattle, Washington.

Emmory Prior, Binghamton, New York.

Paul Holtzman, Philadelphia, Pennsylvania.

Special thanks to JoAnn White, as editorial consultant, and my wife, Mary Helen, for many hours of work on this book.

Shelburne Museum grounds, adjacent to Highway 7, in Shelburne a few miles south of Burlington, Vermont.

Shelburne Museum

Shelburne Museum is a vast and eclectic assemblage of American art and architecture located near Lake Champlain in Shelburne, Vermont. The Museum was founded in 1947 by Electra Havemeyer Webb, a pioneer collector of Americana and folk art. Mrs. Webb was among the first to recognize the aesthetic merit of everyday American objects from folk art to tools. Her wide ranging "collection of collections" forms the nucleus of Shelburne's holdings.

Shelburne Museum's 37 exhibit buildings, situated in a 45 acre park of rolling lawns, lilacs, roses, and formal gardens, house important collections of folk art, horsedrawn vehicles, hand and farm tools, paintings, circus posters and carvings, toys and dolls, household implements (including trivets and stands) and decorative arts. There is also a fine small collection of Impressionist art by Monet, Manet, Degas and Cassatt.

Shelburne's folk art collections of quilts, decoys, weathervanes, trade signs, cigar store figures, scrimshaw, hooked rugs, paint decorated furniture and carousel animals are widely considered to be the finest in public hands in the world. Among the Museum's historic structures are six early New England homes, a covered bridge, a general store, a country inn, a 1901 Vermont round barn, a Shaker shed (from Canterbury, New Hamshire), a lighthouse from Lake Champlain and the 220 foot sidewheel steamship *Ticonderoga,* which traveled the lake from 1906 until 1953.

Portions of Shelburne's collection of trivets and stands are exhibited in the Museum's six period homes as well as in the Shaker Shed. The Paley collection is currently in storage but is available to serious researchers by appointment.

Shelburne Museum is open to the public daily 9:00 a.m. to 5:00 p.m. from mid-May to mid-October. Inquiries may be addressed year round to: Shelburne Museum, Shelburne, VT 05482. Telephone (802) 985-3346.

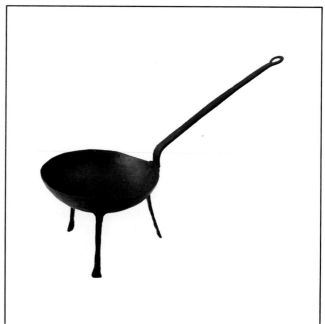

The first three-legged stands were cooking utensils with extended legs to hold them above fire and coals. Representative are the Pennsylvania German pieces shown here.

Above: Gridiron. The Philadelphia Museum of Art; gift of J. Stogdell Stokes.

Below: Rotating gridiron. The Philadelphia Museum of Art; gift of J. Stogdell Stokes.

Above: Hearth skillet. The Philadelphia Museum of Art; gift of Mrs. William D. Frismuth.

Below: Covered kettle; note loop on the handle for hanging from a fire-bar. The Philadelphia Museum of Art; gift of Mrs. William D. Frismuth.

I. INTRODUCTION

Trivet. *(triv'et; -it) (As. Trefet, fr. L. Tripes, — pedis, three-footed.)* 1. A three-legged support; a tripod. 2. An ornamental metal plate on very short legs, used under a hot dish to protect the table.

Webster's New International Dictionary, second edition.

Variously known as trivit, trevet, triplit, trivott; trivets in some form or another have been used by man for nearly as long as fire has been used in the preparation of food. Trivets have been found in every major culture, and they can be as useful today as they were when first conceived.

Trivets have evolved through three major roles in their long history. They were initially devised to serve in the cooking and warming of food. These were hand-crafted trivets used with hearths, fireplaces and box irons. In the second stage, with the advent of the iron cook stove, trivets moved from the hearth to the table, where they protected wooden surfaces from the heat of pots and pans. These cast trivets were associated with iron stoves, counters and sadirons. Most recently, there has been a revival of interest in cast-iron trivets connected with home decorating that features Early American decor. Trivets and stands are still used in the kitchen, but they are now appreciated more for the attractiveness of their design and are used as decorative pieces. Today, trivets and stands are often used as wall hangings or plant stands.

Traditional hearth stand used for cooking or warming.
The Philadelphia Museum of Art; gift of Mrs. William D. Frismuth.

Trivets were essential to hearth cooking. They remained in common use as long as an open hearth was the principal means for preparing food. Many early three-legged stands were actually skillets, pans, kettles and grills with extended legs to hold them above the fire and ashes. Trivet stands which were made for cooking could also be used to keep food warm or to set pots aside when not in use. A three-legged stand sits steadily on an uneven surface such as a hearth floor. A four-legged stand tends to wobble on an uneven surface. True trivets are three-legged; those with four or more supports are called quads or stands. Hearth trivets were individually hand-crafted by blacksmiths and thus unique in design, even though styles might have been copied from earlier models. During the seventeenth century, trivets were cast in Europe; the casting of iron trivets did not become commonplace in this country until the nineteenth century.

During the nineteenth century, American craftsmen produced a wide array of cast-iron and brass trivets and stands in various sizes, styles and designs. According to their use, they were called trivets, stands, quads or rests. The clear distinction between these different designations faded as hearths, iron cooking ranges and sadirons fell into disuse. Eventually, irons were set on kitchen stands, pots were placed on sad stands, both were used on tables and practically everything hung on walls! Today, we make little distinction between any of the various styles and functions and simply call all of them trivets.

Trivets were never a major item in the household and their utilitarian function prevented them from being especially noteworthy as objects. As a household accessory that was simple and inexpensive to produce and distributed widely in huge quantities, the history of trivets is obscure. Those who made trivets are difficult to identify, and the sources of their designs are nearly impossible to trace. A majority of trivet patterns used by nineteenth century American founders originated in England, France, and Germany, while others came from the Orient. However, there were many trivet designs using eagles, stars, advertising or other motifs which were peculiarly American.

Trivets have assumed a new importance today. Beautiful in themselves, they reflect older eras of technology and craftsmanship. Iron is strangely pleasant to view and touch in a period of chrome and plastic. Trivets induce a certain nostalgia about our ancestors and former lifestyles with open hearths and iron stoves. The old designs evoke curiosity by suggesting hidden meanings which we may no longer recognize. It is difficult for anyone who really examines trivets to resist the charm and mystery of the older designs and workmanship.

In the early 1900's, some individuals saw beauty in trivets and began to collect them. These collections were often displayed on kitchen walls where they were both attractive and accessible for use when needed. As more people collected, supplies of old trivets began to diminish even though large quantities had been produced. Because iron is brittle, many trivets and stands were broken and discarded; large numbers disappeared into scrapyards through the course of several wars; others were collected and institutionalized or secured in private collections. Many rusted away or were lost.

As more collectors became avid seekers of trivets and stands, it was inevitable that there would be trivet reproductions. Beginning in the 1930's and peaking in the 1950's, Early American furniture and home accessories became fashionable and reproductions of cast trivets in both iron and brass became profitable. Since the 1930's, many trivet reproductions have been marketed. Perhaps 80 percent of these were produced by Wilton Products, Inc., John Wright, Inc. and Virginia Metalcrafters, Inc. Traditional designs were most commonly reproduced and, with few exceptions, patterns were made from older castings. In the 1950's, when postage rates increased substantially, most manufacturers of trivet reproductions made new patterns so larger trivets and stands weighed fifteen ounces or one pound with packing.

Electric warmer, alcohol or candle warmer and wall sconce using trivet designs. Marketed by Wilton Products.

Reproductions differ from older castings in several ways. They are smaller, the feet tend to be short and stubby, and often they have four feet rather than three. The newer patterns may also include some provision for hanging which did not exist on the older designs. The feet on some reproductions are so short that the trivet may be more properly considered a plaque trivet. The short legs facilitate hanging the trivet flat on the wall. A trivet with one and one-half inch legs poses some difficulty in hanging.

The companies manufacturing reproductions used the traditional trivet designs to produce a variety of other products. Some trivets were made with a heating unit in the center so that the trivet became a warming plate. Trivets also were made as candle holders. Some were used as ornamental ends on paper-roll dispensers, while others were made into sconces, wall hooks, shelf brackets, pen holders or other decorative pieces.

The fidelity to traditional designs and the quality of reproductions, especially by the three companies mentioned, were generally good. In some instances, such as with the Rimby trivets, reproductions were remarkably close. The original had a platform which was slightly heavier, while detailing in the reproduction was sharper and the legs much shorter. There have been some reproductions produced in the past forty years that are quite remarkable in themselves, and likely some of these will become collector's items in time. The two brass versions of Rimby's *Many Tulips* and *Twelve Hearts* marketed by Wilton Products in the 1950's most certainly fall into this category.

Large numbers of trivets, copies and reproductions were imported into this country from abroad. Most recently, large quantities of iron trivets have been shipped in from Taiwan as have brass trivets from India and Thailand. In the 1930's and 1940's, China and Japan exported many iron trivet reproductions into this country. Innumerable trivets from around the world came into the United States either as possessions of immigrants or as imported trade goods.

There are also many indigenious designs, especially from Thailand, India, Israel and China, which were imported. An interesting aspect of some Indian and Chinese trivets results from the period of English colonization. The English governed India and were posted in parts of China over an extended period of time. Oriental designs brought back to England were popular with English manufacturers and the public. Also, the English took their own designs to the colonies where they were frequently copied by local artisans. Even today it is possible to find trivet designs from India based on the round table stands with paw feet so popular in Victorian England. These adaptations of European designs were usually made in brass, but the surfaces were etched in a traditional oriental manner and motif. Sometimes handles were added and platforms elevated an inch or more above the paw feet.

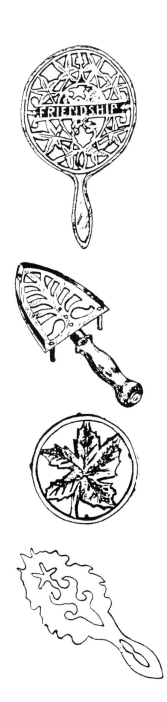

There are many private collections throughout the country, and collectors have been extremely dedicated in their search for new acquisitions. Richard Hankenson, formerly an antique dealer in Maple Plains, Minnesota, was one of these individuals. In 1972, he produced two small, spiral-bound books on his collection which were published by Wallace-Homestead. (At that time, the company was located in Des Moines, Iowa.) At his death, the extensive collection was auctioned and the trivets dispersed. Regrettably, this is the fate of many private collections.

One of the better known trivet collectors was William Paley of Paris, Ontario. Paley spent many years traveling throughout Canada and the United States with occasional trips abroad. He published a substantial number of articles on trivets in his collection. Well known to dealers and other collectors in this country and Canada, he maintained a running correspondence with them over the years. A small, unobtrusive man who lived with his mother, Paley taught mathematics in a local high school until his mother's death. Later, he quit teaching but did occasional tutoring. He traveled in an old Datsun stationwagon and usually stayed in public campgrounds where he prepared his own food and slept in his car. He died in 1983 and bequeathed his trivet and early American lighting collections to Shelburne Museum in Shelburne, Vermont.

The Paley collection has in excess of 2,100 trivets of all kinds. There are hand-wrought and cast trivets, stamped metal and tin ones, others made of wood, silver, enamel, glass, tile and a variety of wire stands. A choice segment of the collection is a group of handcrafted brass and copper trivets, mostly of European origin. Many of these are exceedingly old; they are very beautiful and rare. Through all of his years of collecting, William Paley kept a journal of his acquisitions, and typically, he listed his purchase prices in code. Every entry was illustrated with a small photograph of his own making. Often he would photograph a number of trivets together and then carefully cut around each one and attach it next to the appropriate journal entry. Curiously, in all of his published articles, he made drawings of his trivets and never used photographs.

Trivet drawings by William Paley; illustrations for articles in Spinning Wheel.

The James Ellwood collection in Scottsdale, Arizona is composed of about 1,400 trivets including iron, brass and bronze with cast and hand wrought examples. There are a few wire and stamped metal pieces, but the focus of the collection is cast-iron. Ellwood was extremely selective regarding which trivets and stands were included. The Ellwood collection is one of the best of its kind in the country.

Ellwood's collection began with about thirty trivets inherited from his

James Ellwood at home in his "trivet room."
Photograph by Craig Smith.

mother. Over the years he added new acquisitions to his mother's modest collection. In 1981, Ellwood established an antique business called *Irontiques,* and he became considerably more active in antique shopping throughout the midwest, east and northeastern parts of the United States and his collection grew accordingly. He purchased a number of collections intact including the Politzer collection of miniatures.

One lady in North Carolina collects only Wilton trivets; some collect only iron or brass rests, others have built their collections around trivets or stands incorporating hearts or initials. Dick Kelley, a retired laundryman and his wife, Marge, in Oklahoma City have a large collection of predominantly nineteenth century utensils, tools and equipment, including a large collection of trivets. These exhibits are only open by appointment. Trivets are represented in a number of museum collections, especially those institutions specializing in Americana. Trivets are seldom the focus of a display; usually they are shown as accessories in larger exhibits or period room settings. Numerous historical societies have trivets, but again, it is rare to see collections of trivets displayed. More often they are only items in a larger display. In 1979, the Metropolitan Museum accepted a collection of approximately 100 trivets from Jane Cole. Even though the collection is relatively small in number, there are some exceptional old trivets in that collection. The Prairie Museum in Minden, Nebraska has a collection of approximately 250 trivets on display.

The older hand-wrought trivets, grills, stands, footmen and fenders have been prized by antique dealers for years and values for these are well established. Antique dealers seldom know if cast trivets are old or recent. Cast trivets may be either overpriced or underpriced because so little is known

Archival photographs by Shelburne Museum staff of Paley's house.
Pictured at left is a closet, at right is the basement.

about them. It is difficult today to discover genuinely old cast trivets or stands. Most trivets in flea-markets or at garage sales are recent reproductions. Cast-iron or brass trivets may be found in attics, garages, antique shops or flea-markets; they are sold at auction and purchased as antiques or collectibles.

Traditional trivet designs remained relatively unchanged over long periods of time. The same patterns were copied many times over by various manufacturers at different times. Different castings of the same design may vary in size, detailing and finish. They also may differ in the position, number, shape and length of legs. Brass, bronze or aluminum were sometimes used in place of iron. Handles, frames, and motifs were constantly repeated in new formats. Any design that was popular with the public or caught the eye of a manufacturer was copied in its day or revived at some later date. Under these circumstances, copies may be nearly as old as originals, and it is extremely difficult without documentation to know which version of a design preceded others. This situation is further complicated by the fact that few of the older cast trivets carry any identifying marks which can be used to date them.

Today, collectors may find an incredible number and variety of trivets resulting from original castings spanning several hundred years as well as older copies and recent reproductions. There also are many old and new imports from the Orient and Europe. There are hand-wrought trivets, stands, footmen, and fenders in a range of styles and sizes in addition to cast trivets and stands. Flask casting and improved iron technologies in the nineteenth century made mass production possible. Cast-iron, brass and bronze trivets spewed out into the marketplace in incredible numbers

John Zimmerman Harner in 1957 with trivets and other iron reproductions made at Unicast Foundry.

Dick and Marge Kelley with their collection in Oklahoma City.

between 1850 and 1925. Add to this the profusion of manufactured ceramic, glass, wood, silver, wire, and most recently, plastic stands.

Manufacturers in both centuries also produced a number of miniature trivets as salesmen's samples, or as toys. Later, miniatures were produced in sets as decorative wall hangings. Collectors have included swinging trivets which were attached to iron cooking ranges and ornate parlour stoves, fancy burner trivets from early kerosene or gas stoves, camp stove grills, and almost anything which remotely resembled a trivet or table stand. Even metal letters and numerals with pegs to attach them into masonry, dishes with short legs, pipe fittings, cribbage boards with feet — all have been swept up by collectors as trivets!

Hearth trivets and fireplace furniture, especially the handcrafted pieces, have been reasonably well documented in books and articles. It is doubtful that much, if anything meaningful, has been written about cast trivets until this century. Perhaps the best known publications were the two small books produced by Dick Hankenson, *Trivets, Books 1* and *2*. These books showed a variety of designs from Hankenson's collection; each example had the author's comments and a recommended price. Hankenson gave names to many of the trivets and it is suspected that many of these were of his own creation. Being the only publications exclusively devoted to trivets, copies of his books are valued, well worn, and heavily annotated. Many of the names Hankenson gave to his trivets have become an integral part of trivet collectors' current vocabulary.

Apart from Hankenson's effort, writing about trivets has been fragmentary, usually references, illustrations or a short chapter in a larger book. Articles in trade publications such as *The Collector* or *Spinning Wheel* were mainly based on personal observations. References to factual information are infrequent, and most articles treat trivets as curiosities.

We know many trivet designs by name, but it is questionable whether early makers of trivets ever gave names to their designs. It is believed that names came about with collecting. Early advertisers illustrating trivets simply assigned a stock number to each design. Companies making early American reproductions did use names for each of their designs as a marketing ploy; it lent a touch of historic or romantic allure to the items. Some manufacturers who were unfamiliar with the common names invented their own for trivets they produced and distributed. However, there are some names that appear to have been in general use for many years and the source for these names is as much a mystery as the origin of the designs themselves. *Grapes & Scrolls, Eagle & Heart, Lincoln Drape, Dumb Dutch, Hex, Tulip, Snowflake, Butterfly, Tree of Life, Peacock* and *Urn with Fern* are representative of consistently used descriptive titles. Trivet names are useful, but they are certainly not a major factor in cataloging.

The focus of this book is American cast trivets produced in the nineteenth and twentieth centuries. It is not always clear which trivets were imported or made in this country. However, all trivets illustrated in this book, regardless of their origin, are cataloged, physically described, and have relevant information recorded. To the extent that information is available, the makers of trivets and their manufacturing operations are described. In addition, the origin of designs, symbols or motifs is examined and the sources of information regarding trivets are listed.

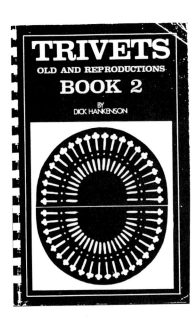

Covers of the two six-by-nine inch trivet books published by Richard Hankenson in 1972.

Even though both copies in the author's possession show a 1972 copyright, Hankenson first printed and copyrighted "Trivets, Book 1" in 1963.

Cast house reconstructed at Hopewell Village National Historic Site. Pictures below show different stages of construction and the exposed furnace. Woodwork was done by Amish carpenters in 1963-64. Photographs furnished by The National Park Service.

II. IRONMAKING IN COLONIAL AMERICA

The technology for making iron was brought to North America by European settlers. An abundant supply of wood for charcoal and plentiful supplies of iron ore were instrumental to the establishment and rapid expansion of the iron industry in America. The earliest attempt to produce iron occurred at Falling Creek, Virginia, in 1621. Because of its remote location, the furnace was destroyed, and eighty workers were massacred by Indians the following year. In 1644 iron was successfully smelted in the Massachussetts Bay Colony at Braintree, and two years later, the Hammersmith furnace on the Saugus River was built. The Saugus works went bankrupt in a very short time, and the exodus of workmen contributed substantially to the spread of iron technology to other colonies and settlements.

Diagram of a cold blast furnace.

The next major expansion of the industry took place in Pennsylvania. Between 1716 and 1776, at least twenty blast furnaces, forty-five forges, four bloomeries, six steel furnaces, three slitting mills, two plate mills and one wire mill were built in Pennsylvania (*Iron and Steel in America,* W. David Lewis, Eleutherian Mills-Hagley Foundation, 1976, p. 20). As early as 1750, England attempted to prohibit the American colonists from manufacture of iron goods or building of slitting mills for the making of nails and rods. England wanted the raw iron shipped back to its own forges where it would be made into products to sell back to the colonists. However, the British Iron Act of 1750 was never entirely successful in suppressing the manufacture of iron products in America. In 1756, the colonies actually surpassed England in the total production and processing of pig and wrought iron; there were 135 forges in England and 175 in the American colonies. At the time of the Revolutionary War, there were more than twenty-five furnaces and forges in Berks County, Pennsylvania, alone. By 1775, the American colonies were producing 30,000 tons of pig-iron a year, which amounted to one seventh of all the iron produced in the entire world at that time. Without the capability to produce and manufacture iron, the Revolutionary War might have had a different outcome. The contribution of cannon, shot and iron to the war effort by the iron furnaces and forges was essential to an American victory. At least seven signers of the Declaration of Independence were connected with the iron industry.

Iron works in colonial America included furnaces, forges, bloomeries, rolling and slitting mills and "puddling" furnaces. Forges converted pig-iron into wrought iron which could be used by smiths; bloomeries and "puddling" furnaces accomplished the same end. Rolling and slitting mills heated and rolled the iron into sheet metal which was cut to make strips that could be converted into hoop iron, rods, nails, and wire.

Colonial style iron plantations, which lasted until late in the nineteenth century, represent an interesting meld of social and industrial life. The charcoal iron plantations were usually many thousands of acres in size and located in isolated areas because of the need for huge amounts of wood. Some furnaces would burn the equivalent of one acre of wood per day.

The ironmaster was either a wealthy man, or a persuasive man, who could raise the required capital and recruit the craftsmen necessary to establish an iron plantation. Plantations were frequently established by a group of investors who put up the capital to build a furnace and hired an ironmaster who was responsible to the Board. The ironmaster needed sound business acumen and thorough knowledge of iron processing to be successful. The ironmaster had absolute responsiblity for the entire operation and all who worked for him. The history of iron-making in colonial America is riddled

Charcoal, iron ore and limestone, the principal ingredients for making iron. Photographs furnished by The National Park Service.

Diagram of wood pile for making charcoal.

Bottom picture shows a worker tending the pile while making charcoal. The process took several days to complete. Photographs furnished by The National Park Service.

with records of furnaces that quickly went bankrupt because of poor management.

Because of their remote locations, plantations tended to be self-sufficient communities. The ironmaster operated a store for the convenience of his workers. Employee purchases were charged against earnings and carefully noted in the company ledger. There were gardens, orchards, fields of grain, flax or hemp and livestock. Many horses or mules were required in the operation of the furnace; the 1830 records of Hopewell show they had eighty-four horses at the time. Additionally there were cows, swine, chickens, and often flocks of sheep. Wives and children did much of the work connected with the raising of food and crops. Ironmasters frequently encouraged tenant farmers to locate on the plantation and they provided additional grain, produce, and labor when needed. Plantations might supplement what they could not provide by purchasing supplies or labor from adjacent farmers.

The ironmaster lived in a grand house known as the "Big House" while tenants lived in less pretentious buildings adjacent to the furnace and shops. Ironmasters never lived as sumptuously as their counterparts on the Southern cotton plantations, but they often did live elegantly in the style of gentry with social gatherings, a fine stable of horses, and the traditional pack of hounds. However, they could hardly be viewed as the idle rich.

Workmen led a simple life of hard labor enlivened periodically by barn dances, cornhuskings and harvest gatherings. In the early years of iron plantations, only the children of the ironmaster and his most skilled workmen received an education. Instruction was provided either by the company clerk or a hired tutor. Religious services were performed by an occasional itinerant preacher. After 1840, schools and churches were regularly built as a part of these communities.

The furnace itself was a truncated limestone pyramid built next to a hill or bank. A covered bridge spanned the gap between the top of the furnace and the embankment. It was through this bridgehouse that fillers delivered the ore, charcoal and limestone to load the furnace. It required about one hundred and eighty-five bushels of charcoal. The amount of charcoal varied from as low as one hundred to as high as two hundred bushels. The type of wood used to make the charcoal was a factor because hard wood made more efficient charcoal. In addition to charcoal, two tons of ore, and about twelve to fifteen shovelfuls of limestone were needed to produce one ton of pig-iron. If limestone was not available, any local stone might be used. At least one authority, Frederick Overman, noted scientist in metallurgy, recommended in 1852 against using limestone. A large water wheel was used to provide blast for the furnace. At first, this was accomplished with a large bellows powered by a water wheel with counterweights. Somewhat later, the bellows were replaced by blowing cylinders.

Adjacent to the furnace was the cast house where molten metal poured into sand molds in a large pit on the cast house floor. The molten iron poured directly into a long trough which had gates on either side to carry the metal into the molds. The trough and molds resembled a sow with her sucklings, hence the name "pig-iron."

The operation of the furnace required a diversity of skills; miners dug the ore and had the responsibility for keeping the furnace supplied; colliers made the charcoal from wood furnished by woodcutters. It was normal that woodcutters represented the largest segment of workers. Teamsters did all the hauling. Ore and charcoal were hauled to the furnace. Pig-iron, bar-iron, and castings were carried to market and supplies were brought back on the return trip. Some hauling might be contracted out to independent firms or individuals. The success of the furnace was largely dependent on

Nineteenth century painting of Hopewell Plantation showing layout of buildings and roads. Artist unknown.

The "Big House" overlooking the cast house, company store, worker's quarters and other auxiliary buildings. Photographs furnished by The National Park Service.

Skillet

Mortar and pestle

Scale weight and horse anchor

Sash weight

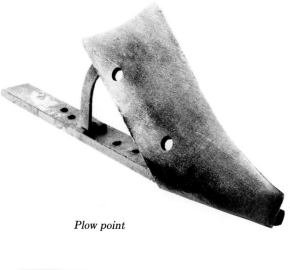

Plow point

Pig-iron

Typical products of an iron plantation. Photographs furnished by The National Park Service.

the experience and skills of the founder. It was his responsibility to keep the furnace at peak efficiency. He decided when to pour and was accountable for the quality of iron. Fillers had to charge the furnace and it is said that this was one of the most unpleasant and difficult tasks in iron-making. When the Hopewell furnace was operating at full-blast, fillers loaded about six tons a day into the furnace. Guttermen would clear away the slag and dig the channels in the cast house floor for the casting of sow and pigs. Called "potters" through the eighteenth century, molders were responsible for preparing the molds to make castings. They would prepare the molds, pour the metal, dump, clean and do rough finishing of each casting. One source stated that women and children were hired to clean castings and were paid seventy-five cents a ton for this work. However, practices and wages varied and most molders did their own cleaning.

Plantations frequently had more than the one water wheel used to operate the furnace blast. There might be grist and lumber mills, or a water wheel to power multiple trip hammers in the forge. There would be stables and a wheelwright shop because many large wagons were required to service the plantation. A blacksmith shop was needed for shoeing horses, repairing equipment or making tools. Most furnaces had their own forge where pig-iron was hammered into bar-iron. Some furnaces installed stamping mills to reclaim iron thrown out in the slag. Additionally, there were a number of storehouses, corncribs, laundry, slaughter and smoke houses, and other subsidiary buildings to serve the needs of the community.

The larger furnaces could produce between 1,000 and 1,500 tons of cast-iron per year. The principal product was pig-iron, but there were also significant quantities of bar-iron and castings. Pig-iron was high in impurities and quite brittle. Founders recognized three different grades of pig-iron; gray iron was preferred for casting; mottled iron generally was used by forges and for other processing, and white iron was infrequently produced in this country. Germany made white iron to a greater extent. White iron resulted from the smelting of sparry carbonates. It was similar to plate iron and contained more carbon than gray or mottled iron.

In the forge, pig-iron was heated, and hammered, and the process was repeated until the iron was malleable. The refined iron was called "bar-iron" or "blooms." The forging process was called "refining," and it removed many of the impurities and modified the crystalline structure of the metal to make the iron malleable so that blacksmiths could use it to make nails, tools, implements and ironware of many kinds. Refining was essentially a process of changing pig-iron grain from a polyglot structure into a parallel structure through repeated heating and hammering. It was the horizontal grain that made iron malleable. At a later date, this process was done by rolling or in a puddling furnace. Puddling was a process for making steel by heating and frequent stirring.

The making of stoves was an important operation of most early iron furnaces. At its peak, Hopewell Furnace produced about 5,000 stoves a year. Cast-iron stoves were invented in Germany near the end of the fifteenth century and brought to this country by early German settlers. These stoves were crude iron boxes constructed of five cast-iron plates with an open end which faced either the fireplace or an opening in the wall to vent smoke and gases. Somewhat later, there was a six plate stove and the ten plate stove came into use about 1765. It is believed that the ten plate stove originated in the Pennsylvania Colony. In 1836, Issac Orr of Washington, D.C., improved the box stove by installing a controllable draft and sealing the joints making the first airtight wood stove.

Early stove plates and fire backs were cast in open molds from designs which had been carved in hardwood. The patterns were pressed into the

*Early Jamb Stove. The Philadelphia
Museum of Art; Joseph E. Temple Fund.*

*Stove Plate. The Philadelphia Museum of
Art; Henry C. Mercer Collection.*

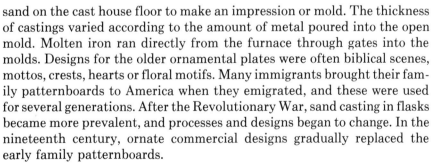

*The Hopewell waterwheel that provided blast for the furnace.
Photograph furnished by The National Park Service.*

sand on the cast house floor to make an impression or mold. The thickness
of castings varied according to the amount of metal poured into the open
mold. Molten iron ran directly from the furnace through gates into the
molds. Designs for the older ornamental plates were often biblical scenes,
mottos, crests, hearts or floral motifs. Many immigrants brought their family
patternboards to America when they emigrated, and these were used
for several generations. After the Revolutionary War, sand casting in flasks
became more prevalent, and processes and designs began to change. In the
nineteenth century, ornate commercial designs gradually replaced the
early family patternboards.

The advent of flask casting combined with improvements in iron technology
changed the design of stoves. Flask casting allowed stove plates to be
curved, castings to be more complex, and plate thickness to be controlled.
The culmination of this technology is best exemplified by the marvelous
Victorian six-hole cooking range and the parlour base burner, both replete
with fancy nickel-plated trim.

Castings made at the furnace varied from plantation to plantation but surviving
records show hollow wares, such as kettles, pots, cauldrons, dutch
ovens, fish kettles, skillets, and mortar and pestles were regularly cast.

26

Hopewell trivet.

Hopewell Stove. In 1845, the furnace produced 5,000 stoves a year. The tenplate cooking stove shown here was made in nine sizes and a number of different patterns. Hopewell also produced four styles of Franklin Stove. Photograph furnished by The National Park Service.

Also, plantations made gratings, sash weights, fuller's plates, forge hammers, sadirons, stoves, plow shares, and a great variety of other products.

Records of the Hopewell furnace show that it did market sadirons and stands in 1817-18. These stands were recorded as selling for twenty cents each; twenty-eight cents with a ball of cotton (which was used to keep the bottom of the iron clean). However, there is no indication whether these stands were cast or made in the blacksmith shop. There are no known examples of the stands today so we do not know what designs were used. Recent archaeological excavations at Hopewell have turned up two trivets, but it is not known if they were produced at Hopewell or brought in as household goods by workers. New patterns were made from these two trivets and souvenir castings are made by the Unicast Company in Boyertown. The trivets are sold in the Hopewell gift shop. *Hopewell* was embossed on the reverse of the larger design, and the smaller one was called *Wedding Rings* by John Harner who made the matchplate pattern for this design.

The one hundred years between 1750 and 1850 saw many significant advances in the making and casting of iron. The British were in the forefront of new technological developments. The move from charcoal to coke began at Colebrookdale (England) in 1709 and it was widely used in England by 1750. This was brought on in part by the growing shortage of wood in England. John Smeaton in 1762 developed "blowing tubs" which replaced the water wheel operated bellows. The invention of "hot blast" in 1828 made it possible to substitute anthracite coal for wood, but it was not until 1839 that anthracite was successfully used in North America at Pottsville, Pennsylvania. In this country, anthracite furnaces surpassed charcoal in iron production by 1855. Coke was not extensively used in this country until after the Civil War, mainly because of huge supplies of wood and anthracite coal. In America during the the latter part of the nineteenth century, charcoal, anthracite and coke furnaces were all in operation at the same time.

Transportation rather than an abundance of wood became the key factor in the location of furnaces. Steel plants and foundries clustered along navigable rivers, near railheads or in proximity to some form of economical transportation. Rivers, canals and railroads provided the most practical modes of transportation for moving coal and ore to the furnaces and hauling iron and iron products to market. By 1860, there were elaborate canal systems throughout the industrial areas of the Northeast. Although extremely slow, barge transportation was extensively used because of its relative low cost. Railroad building was a high priority during this period; tracks were laid to new markets in the West and the network of railroads in the East was enlarged by connecting lines and spurs. Locks were built on the major river routes which permitted even more barge traffic. Manufacturers employed mass production methods and the production of iron in America increased enormously. Cities grew around these industrial complexes. The Civil War put extensive demands on the iron industry which accelerated the development of new technologies connected to iron-making and casting. Following the war, the expanded iron industry converted from armaments to an incredible diversity of iron products for both domestic and foreign markets.

In the space of one hundred and fifty years, the colonial iron plantations were transformed into iron and steel mills which provided the base for tremendous industrial growth in the United States during the twentieth century.

Author's note. *Several of these early iron furnaces have been preserved and are open to visitors. Among the most notable is Hopewell Village near Elverson, Pennsylvania, now administered by the National Park Service. The furnace and other buildings have been beautifully reconstructed and visitors can easily visualize how the plantation must have been during its operative years. The "Big House," workers' quarters, and numerous auxiliary buildings are revealing of life on early iron plantations. Historic Batsto Village in New Jersey is another beautifully preserved site of early iron-making. Also, the Saugus works in Massachussetts has been restored as a historic site. Any of these are well worth a visit by those with an interest in the formative years of iron-making in America.*

Turn-of-the-century base burner.

Parlour burner, advertised by Sears Roebuck & Company in 1908.

Two matchplates made in the pattern shop of Unicast Company by order of John Zimmerman Harner. Photographs by Craig Smith.

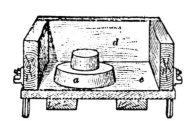 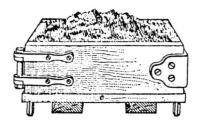 

Page 28, left to right:

1. Pattern is placed in bottom of drag.
2. Sifting and filling drag with sand.
3. Ramming the sand.

Page 29, top to bottom:

4. Top of drag is cleaned preparatory to placing bottom board.
5. Drag is turned upside down and mold board removed.
6. Cope is locked to drag; sprue-pin set.

7. Cope is rammed; shows downspout and gate to pattern mold.
8. Pouring the mold.
9. Casting with gate and downspout attached.

Illustrations from Green-Sand Molding, Part I, *International Textbook Company, 1915, 1928, 1933.*

III. CASTING AND FINISHING TRIVETS

The first trivets were most likely made of ceramic material, later they were made of bronze, and finally they were cast in iron and brass. Casting, as compared to forging, of trivets or stands reached its peak during the nineteenth century in America, but considerably earlier in Europe. There are records of cast-iron trivets made in France during the early part of the seventeenth century. A wide variety of trivets and stands were fashioned in iron by blacksmiths hundreds of years before they were cast. The cast stands resembled the hand-wrought ones only in the most basic respects. Casting permitted, if not actually encouraged, entirely new concepts of decoration. Surfaces could be modeled in relief with shape and detail posing no special problems.

The earliest American cast-iron trivets tended to be large, heavy and decorated with geometric or heart designs. The first American trivets, which can be definitely dated from the early 1840's, are attributed to William Rimby of Baltimore.

The casting of trivets and stands represents a simple form of mold-making and casting procedures. Even though there have been significant improvements in the making and casting of iron, where the product does not warrant expensive tooling the older techniques, materials and tools may be used even today. Trivets fall into this rudimentary form of casting.

The earliest mold was a simple depression in the ground, and molten iron was poured into it. This is called "open casting." These castings were crude and required considerable effort to refine and finish. Metalsmiths had been smelting, casting and shaping non-ferrous metals long before the discovery of iron. Iron required an extremely high temperature to reduce it to a molten state. Because of the high temperature, a much stronger mold was needed than for other metals. For most of the casting operations including pattern-making, mold-making, runners, vents, gates, wells, pouring basins and other techniques, the necessary tools had already been invented and refined centuries earlier by jewelers, armourers, artists and others working with precious metals, copper and bronze. When iron came into general use, most of the tools and techniques for forming it were already well-known.

Metal founders and potters were able to combine their skills early in the history of founding. It was the potter who developed the crucible, which is essential for converting iron into a molten state without contamination. Potters were instrumental in making clay molds for casting before the time of sand-casting. In the nineteenth century, it was a potter who invented the precision grinding wheel that revolutionized the metal and glass industries.

Clay molds represented the most common European means for casting iron until the eighteenth century when sand-casting was firmly established. There are some references to stone molds, most likely a pattern carved into limestone, but it is doubtful that stone molds were used extensively.

In both Europe and China, clay molds were used for hundreds of years, and the art was raised to a very high level of fine casting. A sixteenth century formula for clay molds used in Europe consisted of loam, wool clippings, and animal hair, sometimes with the addition of dry dung from horses or donkeys. All of these ingredients were thoroughly beaten and mixed with a heavy iron rod. The European founders were reluctant to replace clay molds with sand because clay gave a much smoother surface to castings. However, as higher pouring temperatures were achieved, sand was added to the loam to strengthen the mold. Conversion from clay to sand probably came about gradually.

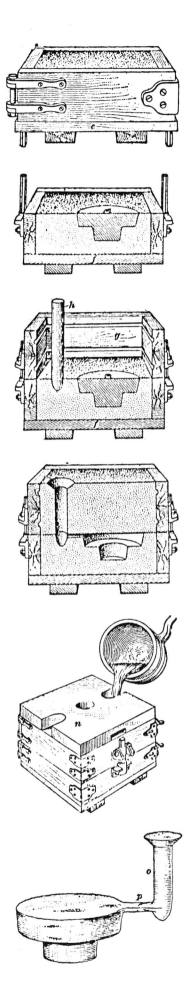

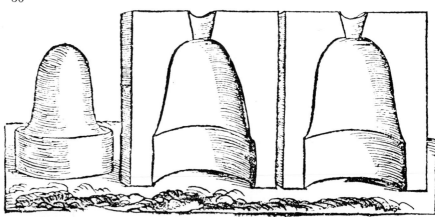

Thirteenth-century green sand mold for casting a bell. Note core on the left. From Seven Centuries of Brass Making, *Bridgeport Brass Company, 1920.*

Sand-casting began in China where it was in use as early as the sixth century B.C. Although furnace metal was found in Germany dating from 1313, cast pipe from 1455, and stove-plates and firebacks from 1490, there is evidence that the processes for casting iron were greatly refined after the trade routes between Europe and China were reopened in the sixteenth century.

Nevertheless, sand-casting was understood by Europeans long before it came into general practice. In the late fifteenth century, Leonardo da Vinci advised that to make casts rapidly and simply, river sand moistened with vinegar in a box was sufficient. Biringuccio, a contemporary of da Vinci, kept journals on metallurgy which have survived. Biringuccio wrote: "Contrary to the natural order of the art, it has been discovered how to cast in moist earth in order to avoid labor and expense. This is truly a thing that many desire and few practice because it is not as smooth a way nor as easy as it apparently seems. To do this, one part of fine-grained yellow tuff is taken, or some very fine river gravel that has been well washed and baked in a furnace. Then a third part of a young ram's ashes is taken and a twelfth part of the whole of old flour that is fine sifted. By pounding, all these are incorporated and mixed together well. Then take urine or wine and moisten it, and mold whatever you wish with moistened material in frames or wooden boxes. Having taken out your reliefs, make the gates and vents, if you did not make them at the same time that you molded the object. Then cover them with soot as usual, with the smoke of turpentine or a tallow candle. Then the molds that you made are again fitted together and are cast at your pleasure when your metal is melted." This description dating from the late fifteenth century clearly demonstrates a thorough grasp of the sand-casting techniques that were to become prevalent in Europe and America during the eighteenth century.

Sand-casting as it was practiced in this country is attributed to Jeremy Florio, an Englishman in Kingston, who devised techniques that were adopted broadly by Europeans and Americans. In this country, most iron casting was done in open pits until after the Revolutionary War when the flask came into general use.

Properties of Metals Used in Making Trivets

Most trivets have been cast in either brass or iron; others were made of bronze, and in this century, some were cast in aluminum.

Between the seventeenth and nineteenth centuries, there was always a clear distinction between trivets and stands made for use in the kitchen and those made for the parlour and bedrooms. Most kitchen trivets and stands were made of iron, either hand-forged or cast. Parlour trivets, stands

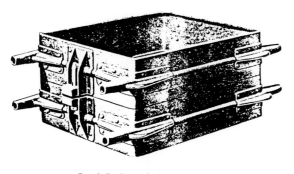

Steel flask made by Sterling Company, early twentieth century.

Top: Flask from Hopewell furnace, nineteenth century. Note pins holding the cope and drag in alignment. Photograph by Craig Smith.

Below: Early twentieth-century flask made of cherry wood with box joints, brass shim and cast-iron edges and locks. Designed for use with matchplates. Obtained from Unicast Company. Photograph by Craig Smith.

Tools of the pattern-maker.

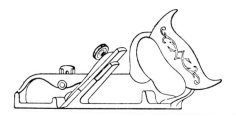

and fireplace accessories were frequently cast in brass or bronze, or constructed from a combination of parts made of iron, copper and brass. After 1885, many manufacturers of cast trivets and stands offered customers an option of cast iron or brass in most designs.

Kitchen trivets made in America between 1840 and 1870 tended to be large and heavy. The iron used was different from that used today. The older process was to make iron from ore; its impurities and additional carbon imparted a distinctive quality not seen today. Trivets made through the reduction of scrap-iron are lighter in color. Iron becomes sufficiently molten to cast at about 2,700 degrees and shrinks in the cooling process approximately one-eighth inch per foot.

Brass is a particularly good material for trivets because it is a poor conductor of heat. The color of brass, an alloy of copper and zinc, may vary considerably depending upon the proportions of different metals. A red brass consists of 90 percent copper to 10 percent zinc; true brass is 83 percent copper to 17 percent zinc; and white brass is 30 percent copper to 70 percent zinc. When casting very fine detail, lead was often added to improve the fluidity of the molten brass. A Chinese brass called Pakton, which resembles silver, fascinated Europeans in the nineteenth century. It was 44 percent copper, 40 percent zinc and 16 percent nickel. Bell metal, a reddish brass, is a combination of copper and tin, in reality bronze. The pouring temperature for brass is 1,800 degrees and it will shrink approximately three-sixteenths to one-fifth of an inch per foot.

There is considerable evidence that some small foundries, without the technology to cast iron, made brass trivets and painted them black to resemble cast-iron trivets. This is rather ironic as today brass trivets will usually sell for more than iron trivets.

Bronze was highly prized by Victorians and there were many bronze trivets and fireplace accessories made in that era. Bronze is generally 20 percent tin to 80 percent copper. It shrinks three-sixteenths of an inch per foot in cooling. During the Age of Bronze, the formula was approximately 14 percent tin to 86 percent copper.

Aluminum trivets are characteristic of this century. Aluminum becomes molten at about 1,200 degrees and shrinks about three-sixteenths of an inch per foot. Many aluminum trivets and stands, painted black, look like iron trivets, but the weight discrepancy between iron and aluminum clearly reveals the difference. The technology required to cast aluminum permitted basement and garage foundries to produce small numbers of trivets and stands using existing iron trivets as patterns. Many of these homemade aluminum trivets are extremely crude castings.

Patterns

A casting can be no better than the pattern from which it is made. Near the beginning of the fifteenth century, pattern-making became a separate operation in the casting process. Wooden patterns were used to make molds until about 1800 when metal production patterns came into general use. Sand was sufficiently abrasive to destroy detail and round the sharp edges of wooden patterns with prolonged use. However, wood continued to be used to make the master pattern from which a metal production pattern was made.

Wood for the making of patterns had to be free from knots, close and straight grained with the annual rings not too strongly developed, and soft enough to be easily and neatly worked. Cherry and mahogany made excellent patterns. However, they also were expensive hardwoods which were more difficult to work. Well cured pine was frequently used, with mahogany reserved for fine work.

Patterns had to be made slightly larger than the size of the finished casting to compensate for shrinkage as the metal cooled. Foundries used special measuring sticks that incorporated this adjustment for shrinkage. These shrinkage rules were usually about two feet long. A rule for iron casting would have a 12 and 1/8th inch measurement for each 12 inch increment. There were different measuring sticks for different metals.

All patterns were designed with a draft, or beveled edge, of approximately .007 degrees. The draft usually angled from the reverse to the face of the trivet to facilitate removal of the pattern from the drag mold. On some designs, where more metal was going into the legs than into the platform, the draft would be reversed.

Wooden master patterns were varnished or painted to protect them from moisture in the sand that might cause them to warp or split. Old pattern-makers often used a mixture of beer and black lead (graphite) to protect the wood.

Pattern-makers might "back-out" or "back-cope" the wooden master pattern when it was appropriate. Back-coping may be described as scooping out the reverse of a pattern in its thickest parts. This practice could be used to save metal or to reduce weight of the final casting. Also, castings with constant walls were less susceptible to breakage; where a thin part of a casting joined a thick section, the casting was vulnerable to breakage. Most back-coping was done with routers and the walls were quite smooth.

On the early Rimby trivets from the 1840's, there is shallow back-coping and the chisel marks are discernible. A number of trivets produced in the 1870's have elaborate back-coping. The loop handled *Stars & Braid,* signed E.R. Manley, from this period demonstrates exceptional craft in back-coping.

If an existing trivet was used to make a pattern, it was first "smoothed" which entailed cleaning, burnishing, and filing. A conscientious pattern-maker used the smoothed trivet to make a mold to cast an intermediate pattern of white metal (a combination of lead, tin and antimony). The process of smoothing was repeated. Damaged areas were built up, details refined, and any imperfections corrected. The finished white metal casting was then used to make a mold. From this mold a production pattern in brass, bronze, lead or iron was cast. To insure a good quality metal pattern, a finer grade of sand than normally supplied for production work was used. In only a few instances was the wood pattern used as a production pattern, but occasionally a trivet does show evidence of wood grain on its reverse side. Wood grain marking is usually more perceptible in brass than iron.

For some very ornate trivets, the original patterns were modeled in wax or clay or they were carved in plaster. A plaster mold was shaped from the original, and a white metal casting poured from it was used to make the production pattern. Examination of the original George Washington trivet, cast in brass, clearly reveals on the reverse that the original had been modeled in wax or clay. Today, a number of foundries are using plastic to make patterns which are lighter in weight, give sharper detail and require considerably less labor to produce.

The concept of "gated-patterns" and multiple castings from a single mold had been used with non-ferrous metals for centuries. The gated-pattern included two or more trivet patterns, runners, gates and sprue well. As kitchen, table and sad stands became smaller after the Civil War, the gated-pattern for casting trivets came into general use. Most gated production patterns were cast in either brass, lead or iron. Sometimes brass runners and well were combined with white metal patterns. This type of pattern multiplied the number of castings per mold without increasing the number of molds to be made.

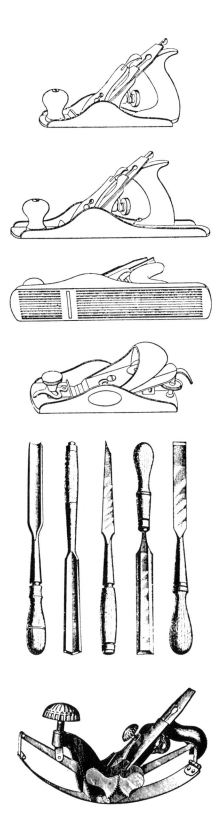

Tools of the pattern-maker.

Horace Burns, pattern-maker for Virginia Metalcrafters, preparing new trivet patterns. Photographs dating from the 1950's furnished by Virginia Metalcrafters.

Another type of pattern is the "dead-head" or "cassette" pattern. This type of pattern was mainly used for small items. It did not have runners or gates connected to the pattern; it was asymmetrical and had the trivet face on one side and the legs on the other. It was usually made as a single block of metal. (The patterns observed by the author were made of steel.) The dead-head pattern was fitted into an empty space in a sand mold being used to cast other objects, and the runners and gates were made in the sand by the molder. Another form of dead-head pattern was the cassette pattern. The cassette pattern had grooved edges so the pattern could be locked into a frame that functioned like a matchplate. A variety of small patterns were locked into a single frame, and with each mold, the number and selection of patterns could change. This gave molders flexibility in casting a variety of designs in different quantities.

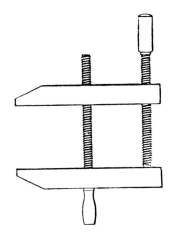

It was about 1900 that a new type of production pattern called a "matchplate" came into general use for flatback casting. This is the type of pattern commonly used today in casting trivets. The matchplate is a flat surface, three-eighths to one-half inch thick, with handles at either end. The face of the trivet and runners are on one side, and the legs and sprue-well are on the reverse, with both the front and back of the trivet in perfect alignment. Matchplate handles have holes for pins or locks to secure the pattern securely to the flask. The matchplate is the same size as the flask. Most trivet matchplates approximate 12 x 20 inches, and are made of aluminum.

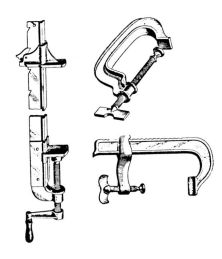

With a matchplate pattern, it is normal to have two, four or six trivets cast in one operation. With smaller trivets or stands, even more can be cast at a time. The matchplate is locked between the cope and drag; and the sand rammed into each; the wedge or sprue inserted, the cope is lifted, the matchplate removed, cope and drag locked, and the mold is ready for pouring. With the matchplate considerable time is saved, and the quality of molds is greatly improved.

It is plausible that the matchplate was developed in conjunction with the manufacture of trivets. The earliest matchplates were made of wood and metal; it was not until the 1940's that they were cast in aluminum.

Even today, temporary matchplates for limited production runs may be made of wood. Existing trivets are smoothed, the legs cut off, the platform attached to one-half inch plywood with machine screws, and the legs fastened on the reverse. The gates, runners and sprue-well are shaped in wood and secured in place with glue or screws.

Sand

In the casting operation, perhaps the most critical factor is sand. In the nineteenth century, a natural sand called "green-sand" was used. The "green" referred to the high moisture content (as with "green" wood). Green-sand was a combination of dark, usually but not always, greenish grains of glauconite mixed with 5 percent clay and water. The quality of sand was determined by the proportion of clay to sand, the moisture content, and the amount of impurities.

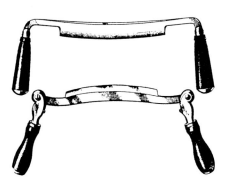

Perhaps the best known deposit of naturally bonded green-sand is the Albany deposit in upstate New York. However, other good molding sands are located in New Jersey, Indiana, Illinois, Tennessee, Mississippi and Alabama. Unbonded sands suitable for molding with additives are found in many other parts of the country.

Tools of the pattern-maker

The important property of sand used for casting is its ability to hold during the handling, pouring and solidification processes. Permeability of sand is necessary to permit gases and steam to escape. To improve molding qualities, molders have used a variety of additives. Sometimes more clay was added, corn or wood flour, cereal binders and even dry manure. Many

Reverse of the George Washington trivet suggests that the original pattern was sculpted in wax. A plaster mold was made from the wax model and a white metal casting made to produce a production pattern.

"Cutting" the sand.

Shovel styles favored by molders.

old molders had private recipes for improving the molding quality of sand, and they did not easily give away their secrets.

Sand was graded by screening into a variety of sizes. A fine grain sand was used for casting where detail and smooth finish were required. Fine sand is so sensitive that it will register the brush strokes and depth of pigment on painted china used as a pattern. Nineteenth century founders used a somewhat finer sand than that used by later founders. Where finish and detail were not critical, a coarser grade of sand was used. Porous sand is required for quality casting. When molten metal enters the mold, the clay, additives or impurities are burned out. A coarse grade of sand permits the resulting gases and steam to escape easily, but the finish of the casting will be as rough as the sand was coarse. Fine grained sand is not as efficient in terms of venting, but it does give fine detail and finish. Venting is also affected by the pressure used in ramming the sand.

The amount of clay and additives reduces the porosity of the sand. Too much moisture creates steam which causes bubbling that will usually result in imperfections in the casting; too little moisture may cause the mold to crumble when the pattern is removed. Also, excessive moisture will create steam which may result in pin-holes in the casting. The grade of sand and amount of clay, additives and moisture had to be balanced with precision to achieve fine casting. This skill was acquired by molders only after many years in the trade.

In recent years, synthetic sand or olivine has replaced natural sand. In part, this was due to health hazards connected with silicosis, as the naturally bonded sands have a high silica content. Synthetic sand is a natural sand which has been carefully cleaned to remove the impurities. The sand is graded and clays, additives and moisture are mixed with the sand in precisely measured quantities. Most of this grading is done by automation today. This process permits making sand for specific types of casting, finish or detail. It also leads to a more consistent and better quality of casting with less defects.

Casting

The molder requires a flask, sand, and a variety of hand tools for making molds. The "flask" is a box with no bottom or top which has been cut in half horizontally. The top and bottom halves are designed to be locked together in perfect register through the use of pins, latches, or clamps. The top half of the flask is called the "cope," the bottom half the "drag." Flasks were made of wood until about 1900 when steel began to be used. In the 1940's, manufacturers began making flasks of aluminum. For doing light casting, they used a small, iron flask usually not much larger than fourteen inches in width. Most flasks were named after their designer or manufacturers (for example, *Adams, Hines*).

A cast room of circa 1900 was a large open space with a number of waist high benches and piles of sand scattered around. The benches were slid to different locations as the molder moved from flask to flask. The molder would first select his flasks, depending on the type of patterns to be used.

In addition to the conventional cope-drag flask, there was also a snap flask which was used for light casting. More than likely many trivets were cast in this type of flask before the advent of the matchplate. The snap flask was hinged at one end and after tamping it was removed, leaving the mold in a block of sand. One flask could be used to make many trivet molds. Being light castings, there was less pressure on the sides and ends than there was with heavier castings. The reinforcement of flask walls was not required. Trivets would fall into this category of casting.

When using a cope and drag flask, the drag was placed upside down on a mold board and both were placed on a bench. This was called "bench casting" and it was the method most often used in the making of trivets.

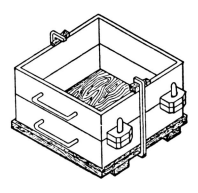

When using a single pattern, the casting technique used was "flat-back" or "follow-board." A wooden block called the "follow-board" was shaped to the contour of the trivet. It was as deep as the legs were long. Holes were made for each leg to fit into snugly. This block prevented sand from filling the space under the pattern at the time the mold was made in the drag for the face of the trivet. The drag was placed on a mold-board which fit under the bottom of the frame. The pattern (with follow-board in place) was centered in the bottom of the drag on the mold board in an upright position. The pattern was dusted with charcoal dust or some similar substance to prevent sand from sticking to it. If sand stuck to the pattern it would damage or destroy the mold when it was removed.

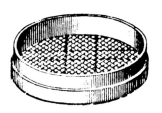

The molder filled his "riddle" (a round sieve) with sand and sifted the sand over and around the pattern by a swinging motion, hitting the rim of the riddle repeatedly with the heel of his hand. When the drag was about half full and the pattern well covered, he shoveled sand from the floor, filling the drag.

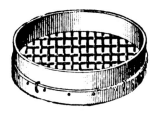

Using the wedge end of his "bench-rammer," the molder tamped the edges and corners firmly; using the round end of the rammer, he tamped sand in the center of the drag. Tamping is a critical step in making the mold as blotches may be formed if the tamping is too far away from the pattern. Scabs may result when the tamping is too close or actually strikes the pattern. The rammer should not come closer than two inches to the pattern.

He then leveled the top of the drag and carefully cleaned the edges of the drag. Placing the bottom board on top, he carefully turned the drag upside down and removed the mold board and follow-board. The bottom board usually had two runners so when the drag was turned upside-down, it was raised above the surface which facilitated picking up or turning the flask. Any sand which had sifted under the follow-board was blown out with a hand bellows. He was likely to take his finger and trace around the pattern to create a trough. The trough around the pattern permitted the cope mold to overlap the drag mold, eliminating the seam and thereby reduced the chance of finning.

The top of the drag mold and exposed underside of the pattern were dusted with charcoal or some similar substance. At an earlier date, molders often used burnt sand to make the parting but finely ground bituminous coal was also used. Later, a gray silica powder came into general use. Today, most molders use a release spray which may be purchased from any foundry supply house. Release spray is usually some combination of benzene and wax.

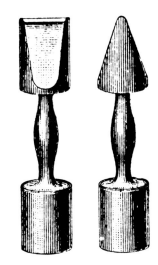

The cope was attached to the drag and the molder repeated the process of sifting, shoveling, ramming and cleaning the edges. The tapered "sprue pin," or "wedge," was set before the tamping was begun. The sprue created the funnel through which molten metal flowed into the mold. Completing the ramming, the molder tapped the sprue or wedge, breaking it away from the sand so it could be removed without damaging the pouring spout.

Lifting out the sprue pin, he used a "strike bar" (a straight bar of wood or iron) to smooth the surface of the cope. The cope was lifted and set on its side. With special tools, he cleaned out the pouring spout to insure clear passage for the molten metal.

Tools of the molder; flask, riddles and hand rammers.

Before removing the pattern from the drag, the molder wet the area around the edge of the pattern to set the sand so that the mold would not crumble when the pattern was removed. To do this, he used a "swab" or "quill." The

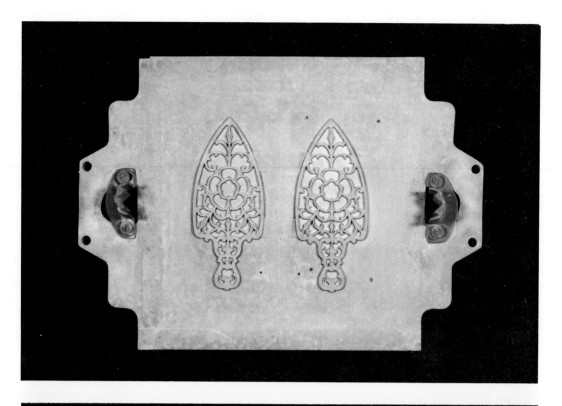

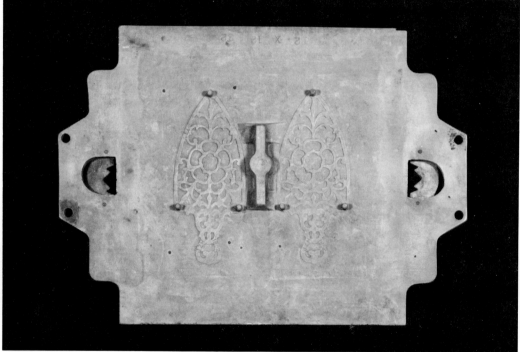

A modern aluminum matchplate; top of the matchplate shows the face of the trivets; pouring basin, legs and bottom of the trivets are below on the reverse of the matchplate. Photograph by Craig Smith.

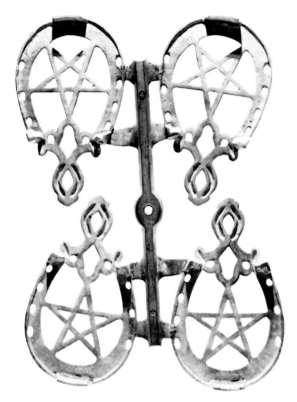

A loose gated-pattern used to make trivets before matchplates. This trivet pattern was made of white metal; sprue-well, or lift-plate, and gates were brass. Center hole was to insert draw-screw and remove pattern from mold.

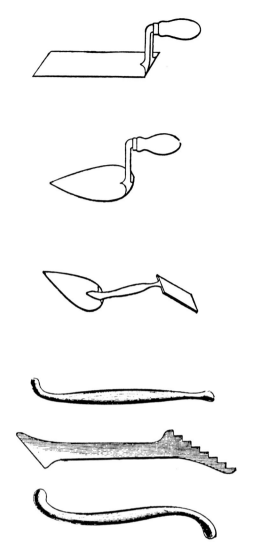

Hand tools of the molder.

swab was fibrous material such as hemp or flax, soaked in water and gently squeezed around the joint with care to prevent the sand from becoming too wet. The quill was fibrous material with a wire extending through it. When the wet material was squeezed, water ran down the wire to the joint, giving the molder more control in directing the moisture.

Next he gently removed the pattern from the drag using a "draw-pin," "draw-hook" or "draw-screw." The draw-screw usually had an eye at the lifting end. Some gated patterns had a "draw-plate" attached to the pattern with a threaded hole to receive the draw-screw.

After removing the pattern, the molder made any necessary repairs to either the cope or drag molds. He had to be very cautious in patching or smoothing the surface of the mold as this tended to bring clay to the surface which might adhere to his tools and damage the mold. Overworking the mold surface could cause scars.

The cope had the mold for the bottom and supports of the trivet and the drag contained the mold for the top of the trivet. The cope and drag were reassembled, locked and put on the floor ready for pouring.

A dead-head, or cassette pattern.

To give a fine finish to a casting and preserve detail, molders might spray the completed mold with "molasses water." After spraying, the mold was baked. The result was a smooth, tough finish to the mold. This type of casting was used in making iron toys. Among the old patterns from the Mount Joy Grey Iron Company in Pennsylvania, (now in possession of John Wright Company) was a complete mold for a toy horse and wagon which was a molasses treated mold. This mold was at least fifty years old; it had been moved around, and piled in boxes with other items, yet it was still in perfect condition. Molasses molds were sometimes made as a pattern

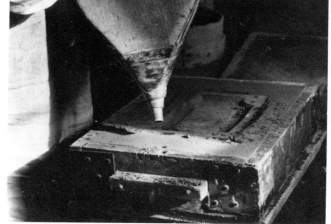

Above: A flat, wooden "mold board" was first laid on the molder's bench as a base. The drag, or bottom half of the flask, was placed on the mold board and the pattern put inside the drag. After dusting the pattern to keep sand from sticking to it, the molder sifted a fine, damp sand over the pattern with a "riddle."

Below: He then filled the drag to the top with unsifted sand and "rammed" the sand, first around the edges with the wedge end of the rammer, and then in the center with the broad end.

Above: The excess sand was then cut away with the "strike."

Below: A bottom board was held or clamped on top and the drag turned over. The mold board was removed and loose sand cleaned from the edges with a bellows. The top of the drag and pattern were dusted with fine charcoal or coal dust; today it is sprayed with release spray. This insures a clean parting when the cope is rammed and then separated from the drag preparatory to removing the pattern and pouring.

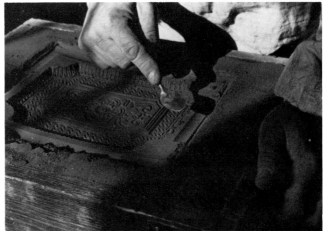

Above: The cope, or top half of the flask, was attached to the drag, more sand was riddled over it. Then a wooden wedge or sprue, the "gate," was inserted to form a hole, or "downspout," that allowed entry of the molten iron. Sand was rammed around the wedge or sprue.

Below: The excess sand was again cut away with the strike. After the wedge or sprue was removed, the drag and cope were separated and the pattern was carefully removed with a pair of "lifters."

Above: The impression was touched up with a "spoon" and the downspout was cleared.

Below: The drag and cope were fastened together with clamps or a lock to prevent the liquid metal from lifting the cope.

Molten iron was poured into the mold space through the gate made by a wedge or sprue.

After the iron had cooled, the flask was separated, the casting removed and the attached gate was broken off. The casting was readied for market by filing the rough edges and brushing off the burnt sand.

All photographs furnished by The National Park Service.

Hand tools of the molder.

Molder's tray with tools, riddle, hand rammer and bellows.
Photograph by Craig Smith.

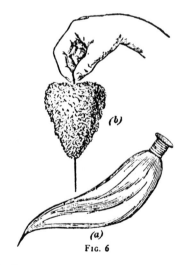

Quill and swab.

to make a matchplate because of the exceedingly smooth surface. They were also used as loose patterns when a limited number (thirty or forty) castings were made. It is conceivable that this process could have been used in making trivets.

A variation of the flat-back process was a pattern without legs. This eliminated the need for a follow-board. The drag was rammed in the same manner as with a follow-board, the cope attached and only the sprue pin was rammed. When the cope was removed from the drag, there would be a slight impression of the bottom of the trivet in the cope mold. Using this impression as a guide, a pattern for the legs or feet could be punched into the cope mold using a peg with some form of adjustable gauge so that all supports would be uniform in length. After punching in the supports, removing the pattern and making any necessary repairs, the cope and drag were locked and ready for pouring. This technique only worked for three-legged trivets or stands.

The process for preparing the mold was essentially the same for a gated-pattern. Flat-back, follow-board and gated patterns were all referred to as "loose-pattern casting."

The molder might use a "sprue-pot" or "button," which was a turnip shaped tool to enlarge the top of the downspout, making a funnel for pouring the molten metal. In the case of large trivets, which were usually single castings, the downspout went directly into the reverse of the pattern. With gated-patterns or matchplates, the downspout went into a sprue-well where the metal flowed through runners and end-gates into each mold. The gates

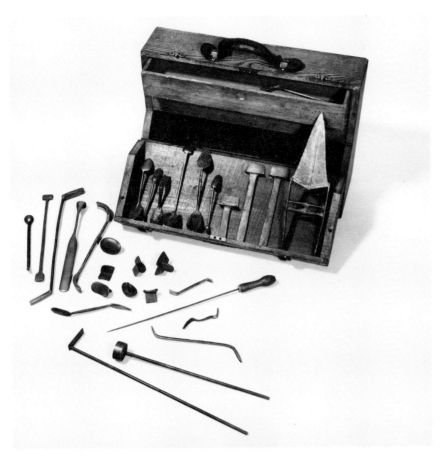

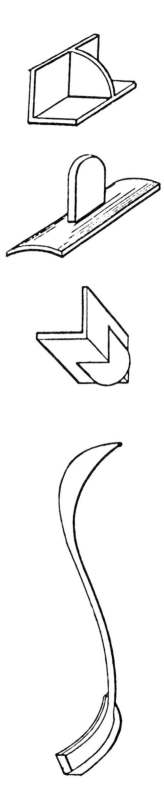

Molder's tool box. Stamped tin strip on the cover says "J. Robertson." Top is oak, ends and bottom are pine, and sides are mahogany. Some iron tools were hand forged; some spoons and other tools were brass. Photograph by Craig Smith.

were on the edge of the platform or handle. Those poured through the rim show gate-marks after casting. A casting made with a single pattern normally has a sprue or wedge mark on the reverse of the platform. The downspout was formed with either a "wedge" or "sprue-pin." The wedge would be made of either metal or wood; it would taper from a square or rectangular head to a narrow rectangle at the bottom. The smallest end would be placed against the pattern or sprue-well. After pouring and solidifying, it could easily be broken off at its narrowest point. The sprue-pin originally was a solid, tapered, cylinder that worked on the same principle as the wedge. The size of the wedge or sprue was determined by the size of the casting and how fast the metal had to move into the mold. Generally, a tapered sprue poured faster than a wedge. The proper size and type of wedge or pin were crucial to a good casting. After the introduction of mechanized ramming, a hollow brass sprue was used to cut a downspout after the cope had been squeezed by an automated rammer. The downspout was formed by rotating the hollow sprue to cut the sand down to the pattern.

Hand tools of the molder.

With mechanization, an improperly filled flask could cause a solid sprue to be driven into the pattern, destroying the mold and possibly damaging the pattern. Today, the downspout is made by a hard rubber sprue which is built into the platen of the mechanical squeezer.

In the nineteenth century, the molder did all the jobs connected with casting. He would come early in the morning and cut his sand, replenishing the additives, and adding water. "Cutting" describes how the molder used his shovel to mix the ingredients. When the sand was ready for molding, he began to lay his molds for the day's casting. In the early afternoon, the iron would be ready to pour and it was distributed to all the molders. Each would ladle the molten metal into his molds. After the metal had solidified, the molders would "shake out," or dump, the molds. Gates were broken off, excess burnt sand sticking to the castings was removed, and rough edges, where the gates had been broken away from the castings, were smoothed with a hand file. Molders were paid by the piece (they still are), and each casting had to be approved by the superintendent. Scraps of metal, runners, wells and defective castings were separated from the sand and heaped as returns to be reduced and used again. Because the sand was hot and dry, it would be shoveled into a pile and splashed with water so it would be somewhat moist and ready for cutting the next morning. At a later date, it became customary for a night crew to come through and remoisten the sand and do some cutting. Molders worked long hours at the foundry, at least ten to twelve hours a day. Generally about seven and one half hours were spent in making molds, and another two and one half hours were used to pour, shake out, clean and prepare for the following day.

In the making of trivets using loose patterns, a good molder could make about fifty molds or 50 to 200 trivets a day depending on whether there were one, two or four trivets per mold. With modern overhead sand delivery, machine squeezing, and matchplate patterns, a molder today can make about two hundred and fifty molds, or in excess of 1000 trivets in an eight hour day. In a mechanized foundry, the molder does nothing but make molds; others pour, shake out, and finish the trivets.

Author's note: *In researching this section, it became apparent that terminology varied considerably from one region of the country to another, and from one time period to another. In the text, I have followed what seemed to be the most logical terminology, using that which came from the most reliable sources.*

All the procedures described here were not followed by every molder. My principal difficulty was obtaining information about practices before the turn of the century from those in the iron industry today.

Finishing

After the castings had solidified and the flask was dumped, excess metal was removed from the castings. With iron, gates were broken away; with brass, they were cut away. Today, the molder may use either a chopper, which is a hand tool for cutting gates, or a cut-off wheel, which is a bonded grinding wheel that (with pressure) cuts through gates and risers. The trivet had a coating of burnt sand when dumped from the flask. Even after the molder brushed the casting, additional cleaning was required.

The old method for removing sand was to put the casting into a tumbler with either coarse gravel or cast-iron stars called "tumbling jacks." Sand was removed through tumbling or vibrating action. The method most often used today is to hang trivets in special cabinets where they are shot-blasted with steel pellets at a high velocity. This blasting can also be done in a machine that tumbles the trivets in an action similar to a cement-mixer. The surface of iron is sufficiently abrasive that small particles of steel shot adhere to trivets giving them a silver lustre. A silver finish is a clue to modern iron casting.

Finishing requirements depended on production processes; molds made from loose or gated patterns often had fins to be removed. Finning was caused by a shifting of the pattern in the mold during ramming of the cope. During pouring some metal might extrude at the joint where the drag and cope molds met. This excess metal on the outside edges was removed with

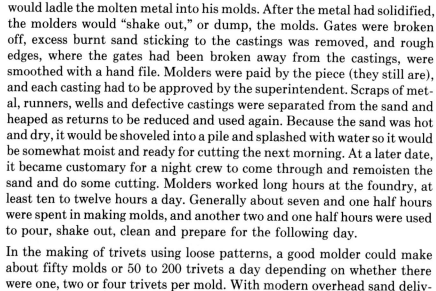

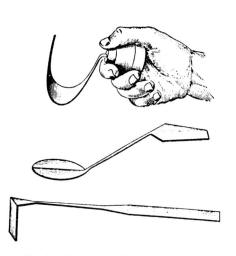

Hand tools of the molder.

From the left: Wooden wedges, hollow brass sprue and cast-iron wedge with a lifting ring in the top. Photograph by Craig Smith.

a flat file and on the inside edges by a rotary file. Finning depended on the skill of the molder; a good craftsman could make perfect castings from loose patterns. Trivets cast from matchplate patterns tend to be exceedingly clean; the joints where legs meet the platform, and the openwork, are normally sharp and without fins. There is a minimum of finishing required with matchplate castings except for grinding the gates.

Before 1890, it was not customary to completely remove gates, only the sharp edges were smoothed with a file. The older finishing process was to burnish iron trivets. It was common practice to put iron trivets into a tumbling machine with either corn-cobs or walnut shells and agitate them for several days. This resulted in a beautiful, soft burnished surface.

Brass trivets, after cutting away the gates, were put into vibrator tubs which were about ten feet in diameter and three feet deep. The first tub was filled with water and rocks; a second tub with water and smaller rocks, and the last tub with water and corn-cobs. In recent years, plastic nuggets have been substituted for the cobs. The three stage tumbling process gives a matte finish to the brass, and some trivets are marketed with a dull finish. A more common practice is to bring the surface to a high polish using buffing wheels.

Brass trivets are generally marketed with no further treatment. Iron trivets may be sprayed with a satin black paint or hand-decorated in bright colors after the fashion of Pennsylvania German tole decoration.

Between 1885 and 1920, trivet manufacturers regularly advertised trivets and stands in a variety of finishes. Electroplating was patented around the middle of the nineteenth century, and copper or nickel-plating became popular. Occasionally, trivets were advertised as bronzed or brass-plated but these were in less demand than nickel or copper. Nickel finish is susceptible to corrosion and not durable over a long period of time.

In examining the Paley Collection, it was interesting to note some trivets where the nickel finish had worn away; the iron was more corroded than on trivets that never had a nickel coating. This was due to the acid bath that was part of the nickel-plating process. In examining a number of trivets and stands that were nickel-plated, the removal of gate-marks and fins was more thorough than on unplated trivets.

During the revival of Early American decor between the 1940's and 1960's, only John Wright experimented with copper-plated trivets. The company marketed six designs — *Distelfink, Tassel & Grain, Doppel Adler, Grape, Eagle,* and *Dumb Dutch* (in miniatures also); these carried John Wright stock numbers in the 200 series. Wright has done no more plating since that time.

Japanning was in style throughout the same years as electroplating. The name is derived from the Japanese practice of using high lacquer finishes. Mary Earle Gould in her book, *Antique Tin & Tole Ware*, states that the art of japanning was brought from China by Englishmen and introduced to Europe in 1780. The Western process was achieved by a combination of asphaltum and varnish fired to harden into a brilliant and transparent coating. There are brass trivets from around the turn of the century which appear to have been gilded and have a japanned finish applied over the gilt paint. The result is an unusual, rather tawdry glitter which seems to be characteristic of the period.

A modern electric furnace used by Virginia Metalcrafters for reducing non-ferrous metals to a molten state.

In the seventeenth and eighteenth centuries, Europeans frequently applied baked enamel or ceramic coating to iron stands. The French produced enameled ironware earlier and more extensively than anyone else. In the Paley Collection, there are many examples of old, heavy, cast-iron, French table stands which are enameled. Many of these have large wedge-marks on the reverse which testify to their age.

In America, a few stove manufacturers began to enamel trivets in the 1930's about the same time that baked enamel exteriors were becoming popular on kerosene and gas stoves. A few sad stands made in both England and America had either an enameled or ceramic finish, but it was not a common practice. Some *Order of Cincinnatus* designs were made by Virginia Metalcrafters in the 1960's with a mottled glaze in either yellow, orange or blue. Apparently these did not market well and the practice was discontinued.

Early twentieth-century cast room.

Left: A modern casting operation with overhead sand delivery and automated squeezer.

Middle: Workman pouring molds which ride on a conveyor belt to another workman who dumps the casting, breaks off gates, and removes defective castings.

Right: A worker polishing a brass casting on a buffing wheel.

These photographs were made in the cast room at Virginia Metalcrafters, Waynesboro, Virginia.

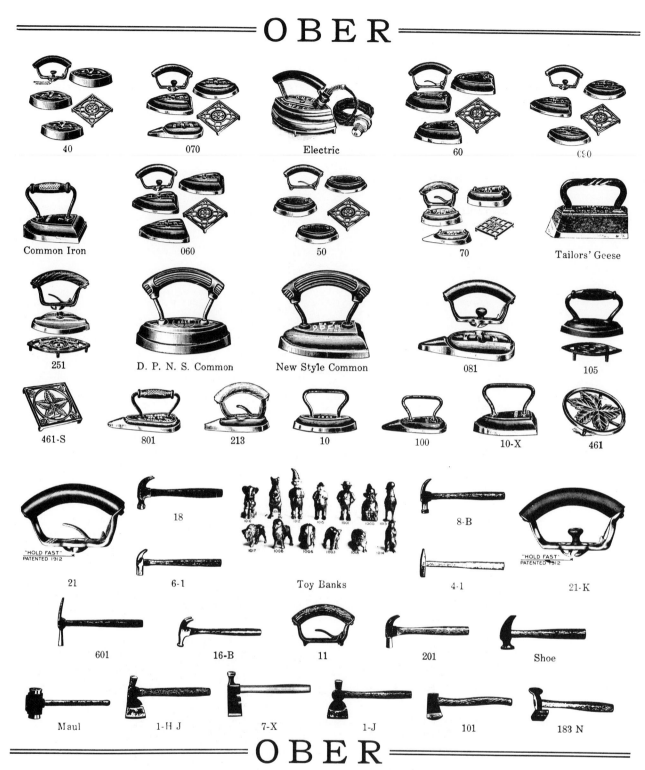

OBER

40	070	Electric	60	090
Common Iron	060	50	70	Tailors' Geese
251	D. P. N. S. Common	New Style Common	081	105
461-S	801	213	10	100	10-X	461

21	18 / 6-1	Toy Banks	8-B / 4-1	21-K
601	16-B	11	201	Shoe
Maul	1-H J	7-X	1-J	101	183 N

OBER

THE FIGURES UNDER THE CUTS ARE THE CATALOGUE NUMBERS.

Please notice the neat designs of the above goods. They are nicely finished and are sure to give the best of satisfaction. Samples will be furnished free of charge on application. Write for complete Catalogue and Price List. Why not get in line with the "OBER" goods and be assured of satisfied and permanent customers.

THE OBER MFG. CO., Chagrin Falls, Ohio, U. S. A.

10-5-14-20m

Ober Manufacturing Company catalogue page dated October 14, 1914.
Courtesy of Chagrin Falls Historical Society.

IV. TRIVET MAKERS AND DISTRIBUTORS

Production of trivets and stands was never the exclusive activity of a manufacturer or foundry. Trivets and stands were always minor items and represented only a small part of much larger casting operations. At the turn of the century, trivets were produced in huge quantities, which can be established by marketing materials from the latter part of the nineteenth century. Trade catalogues published by manufacturers and distributors from that period advertised that trivets could be purchased singly, either a half or full dozen to a box, by the gross, or by the barrel. A barrel might contain six to eight gross or nearly one thousand trivets or stands!

"Sad iron stand."
Reading Hardware, 1885.

As the nineteenth century progressed, the technologies connected with the making and casting of iron made great advances. With improved capability to produce trivets, the number and variety of designs increased substantially. With greater productivity, marketing became essential to maintain or increase sales. The growth of the printing industry following the invention of wood pulp paper in the 1860's gave further impetus to marketing through a profusion of printed flyers and catalogues. Marketing led to intense competition, which in turn placed emphasis on improving products, and developing new styles for sale. All of these conditions led to incredible numbers of trivets and stands being produced and marketed between the 1870's and 1920's.

Manufacturers of housewares sold large numbers of trivets and stands in conjunction with their other products. Several houseware companies, such as Griswold, Wagner and General Housewares, began in the nineteenth century and have continued into this century. Both Wagner and Griswold were absorbed by General Housewares, which is still in business.

During the nineteenth century, hardware companies operated their own foundries and made a wide variety of kitchenware in addition to conventional hardware. Most of these companies showed a few trivet designs as part of their line of merchandise. Manufacturers of iron stoves, especially cookstoves, made trivets that were sold or used as advertising premiums. This practice continued with the development of coal-oil, gas and electric stoves. Almost every foundry, large or small, kept trivet patterns on hand from which they would periodically cast an inventory of trivets or stands. Foundries generally held on to their patterns if they had storage space. When trivets came back into style during the 1940's and 1950's, some foundries dug out these old patterns (which might not have been used in fifty years) and began marketing trivets made from the old patterns.

"Sad iron stands; coffee pot and plate stands."
Reading Hardware, 1886.

The eighteenth century American iron plantations incorporated all the steps of smelting iron, manufacturing, and marketing. In the nineteenth century, each of these became separate industries. There were mine operators, coke producers, and a variety of specialty mills and foundries. The first independent foundries began operating around 1820, and by mid-century they were firmly established. In the beginning, foundries were concentrated in the Northeast and down the Eastern seaboard, but they quickly spread to all industrial areas of the United States. These foundries were known as "gray-iron jobbers." They might subcontract to manufacturers, make castings for distributors, engage in light manufacturing on their own, or do all three.

There is strong evidence that independent foundries cast the majority of trivets and stands produced in this country since the Civil War period. They used patterns of their own making or patterns furnished by a distributor or manufacturer. As a jobber, or middleman, they rarely indentified their own work with a signature other than a stock or pattern number.

"Coffee pot and sad stand."
Grey Iron Casting Company, Mount Joy, 1889.

"Coffee pot stands."
Reading Hardware, 1885.

"Good luck tea or coffee pot stand."
Wing Manufacturing Company, c. 1888.

Trivets or stands cast by a jobber were more likely to carry the name or stock number of the contractor. It is nearly impossible through examination to tell when and where trivets were made if there are no markings or identification.

Throughout the same years that the iron industry was developing, a number of brass foundries were in operation. These companies specialized in a variety of products including plumbing fixtures, hardware and ornamental brass. In the early years, the brass industry was centered in the Northeast, principally in Connecticut. Brass foundries specializing in ornamental work sold brass trivets and stands. During the nineteenth century, brass trivets were made and marketed in Waterbury, Connecticut, by Benedict and Burnham, The Waterbury Brass Company, Brown and Bros., and Holmes, Booth & Haydens (*Antique Collecting for Everyone*, Katherine Morrison McClinton; McGraw Hill Book Company, New York, Toronto and London, 1951). New England brass companies regularly advertised their trivets as being representative of "the latest English styles."

Any small foundry could easily reproduce trivets in iron or brass using an existing trivet to make a pattern or mold. Many of these improvised castings did not begin with a sharp pattern so the result was often crude, scabbed or pin-holed. These poor quality trivets were sporadically cast by small non-commercial foundries. A good commercial foundry would never permit such shoddy work to leave the plant.

With few exceptions, trivet designers and makers were anonymous craftsmen and their identity will probably never be known. We are left with cryptic initials, marks, stock numbers or nothing at all to tell us who made a particular trivet. Many of the individuals, companies, or foundries which made trivets during the last century have completely disappeared.

The history of manufacturers has been better recorded than that of foundries. By looking at company histories, we have clues to the production and distribution of trivets before the turn of the century. By reviewing the history of companies and foundries which have continued into this century, we gain insight into earlier production and business practices.

Beginning in the 1930's and peaking in the 1950's, public interest in Early American decor created a substantial market for trivet reproductions. World War II interrupted the production of iron novelties, but business revived with gusto following the conclusion of the war. As previously mentioned, the three principal producers of iron and brass trivet reproductions were Wilton Products, Virginia Metalcrafters, and The John Wright Company. Virginia Metalcrafters concentrated heavily on brass reproductions of all kinds, including trivets. There were other companies such as Griswold, Wagner, Dalecraft, Portland Stove Foundry, and B & P Lamp Supply concurrently marketing trivets; and distributors such as Robert Emig and Iron Art; but none on the same scale as Wilton, Wright and Virginia Metalcrafters.

Iron Art and Emig were perhaps the two major distributors, and they contracted with independent foundries for their castings. Both owned patterns for many of their designs, but they also relied on various foundry patterns. Many of the reproduction patterns made by John Zimmerman Harner at the Unicast Company were used by Emig, Art Smithy and Iron Art. Robert Emig seemed to be the distributor most willing to experiment with new designs. He scouted this country and abroad for unusual patterns which he put into production.

Because Wilton, Wright and Virginia Metalcrafters are still in business, it is possible to trace their history. Company records, patterns, tools and old equipment still remain on the premises and are available for examination, which provides insight into the firm's operations over a period of time. For companies that went out of business years ago, there is only fragmentary information available, and much of it is inconsistent or even contradictory.

The following notes on a few of the companies making trivets are in no way complete, but taken as a whole, they shed light on what were probably typical production and marketing practices around the turn of the century. At best, the story of early trivet designers and makers can only be fragmentary and speculative.

Wilton's Susquehanna Casting Company, early twentieth century.

Wilton Products, Inc.; Wrightsville, Pennsylvania, 1935 to the present.

Wilton Products was one of the first companies to begin manufacturing Early American reproductions. They have consistently produced high quality products. The Wilton Manufacturing Company was founded in 1911 by Ralph Preston Wilton. Prior to that date, the company had operated as The Susquehanna Casting Company. The Wilton Company was listed in the 1914 edition of *Great Industries of the United States* as a manufacturer of brass faucets.

In 1935, the business was reorganized. A new marketing company called Wilton Products, Inc. was formed. The foundry was operated as a separate business called The Susquehanna Casting Company, and at a later date, The Wilton Company was formed in conjunction with the foundry. Wilton Products and The Wilton Company were each headed by a different son of Ralph Wilton. Henry Wilton was president of Wilton Products and Bud Wilton managed The Susquehanna Casting Company and The Wilton Company.

Today, The Wilton Company specializes in Early American reproductions and novelties made in an aluminum alloy which resembles pewter in color and finish. It is marketed under the copyrighted brand name of *Armetale*. The Wilton Company never distributed trivets. Wilton Products dealt mainly in iron, some brass and small amounts of aluminum. The castings for Wilton Products were done at the family foundry until the 1960's when The Susquehanna Casting Company converted entirely to aluminum and alloys.

The Wilton Products line consists of Early American reproductions of sconces, trivets, matchsafes, kitchenware, doorstops and Pennsylvania German folk figurines cast in iron and hand painted. Henry Wilton is

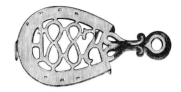

"Horseshoe sad stand."
Grey Iron Casting Company, Mount Joy, 1889.

"Crown tea or coffee pot stands."
J. Jacob Shannon & Company, 1889.

"Trevet."
Wrightsville Hardware Company, c.1918.

"Tea or coffee pot stand."
Central Stamping Company, 1889.

"Standard tea pot stand."
Hamblin & Russell Mfg. Company, 1914.

The following designs were produced by Wilton Products.

28. Plume   20. 1894

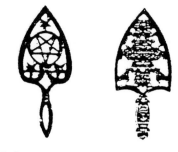

32. Star   *76. Hearts & Flowers*

21. Military   *29. Rosette*

30. Heart   *122. Distelfink*

Hex   *Dutch Tulip*

Roosters

known to be partial toward traditional German tole decoration, and it is believed that he was the first to market hand decorated trivets. In the 1950's, hand painting of trivets and figurines was done by local families whose wives and daughters would spend evenings doing piece-work. (John Wright offered customers the option of plain or decorated trivets, but Virginia Metalcrafters never followed this practice.)

Wilton Products was one of the first companies to recognize the market connected with growing public interest in early American ironware. The company ceased manufacture of its regular items during World War II and was sustained through government contracts. It resumed its normal line of business in 1946 with two employees. By 1950, the company had grown to 100 employees with a new West Coast division in Santa Barbara, California. Wilton Products was the largest business of its kind in the United States at that time.

In the 1947-48 catalogue, Wilton Products illustrated its first three trivets, *Sunburst (Order of Cincinnatus), Grapes & Scrolls,* and *Eagle & Heart.* The growing popularity of trivets is clearly shown by examining the 1953 catalogue illustrating 32 different trivet designs and one extra large *Hex* pattern. Most of these were available in either iron or brass. The iron trivets could be purchased either in flat black or decorated with hand-painted folk designs.

According to Henry Wilton, most of the patterns used by Wilton Products were made directly from authentic antique trivets. Two exceptions were *Bellows* and *Prism* which he thought were designed by company employees. (In the Paley collections at Shelburne, there is a trivet very similar to the Wilton *Bellows,* but it is obviously much older than the one produced by Wilton Products.) During the 1950's, Wilton produced some oversize versions of the traditional designs *Eagle & Heart, Family Tree,* and *Rings.* These were in scale with the reproductions of Rimby's *Many Tulips* and *Twelve Hearts.* A workman's comment about these oversize trivets was that because there was a good market at the time for larger trivets, they simply enlarged several of the popular traditional designs. On January 19th, 1984, Henry Wilton's rare and beautiful collection of antique trivets, that he had gathered as a source for patterns, was totally lost when his home was destroyed by fire.

During the 1950's when Wilton Products operated its West Coast distribution center, it used the Unicast foundry in Boyertown, Pennsylvania, to do extra castings for that division. After the family foundry ceased smelting iron, Wilton Products mainly relied on Unicast for their foundry work. The Keystone-Grey Iron Company in Pottstown, Pennsylvania also did some casting for Wilton. Wilton Products owned all the matchplates for its designs, and all trivets it marketed were cast from its own patterns. Finishing, painting, packing and shipping were done on the premises of Wilton Products in Wrightsville.

Wilton trivets are of good design and excellent quality. The company produces about forty different trivet designs altogether and displays all designs produced by the company on its reception and showroom walls. Of special interest are two large eagle trivets which were never illustrated in the Wilton catalogues (see page 90). The last Wilton catalogue was published in 1976. Most, but not all, trivets are stamped WILTON on the reverse; the company never used stock numbers.

Listing taken from Wilton catalogues for 1947, 1948, 1949, 1950, 1951, 1953, 1954, 1955, 1956, 1957, 1958, 1959, 1961, and 1976. All catalogues owned by the company.

Wilton also marketed a number of motto trivets or wall plaques.

22. Peacock   40. Tulip in Motion   25. Butterfly   7. Eagle   77. Rings

15. Dumb Dutch   23. Family Tree   6. Sunburst   5. Grape   18. Grain & Tassel

33. Snowflake   31. Dewdrop   19. Horseshoe   75. Bellows   24. Hex

26. Cupid   79. Dutch Tulip   16. Cathedral   34. Lance   27. Heart in Hand

78. Prism   39. Traditional   36. Star Wheel   35. Lace   41. Round Eagle

CW Cypher Trivet

Carters Grove

George Washington Cypher Trivet

All designs copyrighted by Virginia Metalcrafters.

Virginia Metalcrafters, Inc.; Waynesboro, Virginia, 1938 to the present.

Virginia Metalcrafters is an outgrowth of The W.J. Loth Stove Company founded in 1890 by William Loth. The Loth Company was an independent manufacturer of iron stoves until 1928 when it was purchased by General Electric Corporation and merged into its stove division. The Loth Stove Company developed the Hot Point electric stove, and this prompted General Electric to purchase the company. At the time the company manufactured water heaters, percolators and electric irons in addition to electric stoves. However, because of poor management, the General Electric plant was closed in 1932.

In 1933, Richard Clemmer purchased the company from General Electric and reorganized it as Rife-Loth Corporation (Rife-Ram hydraulic pumps). To promote his business, Clemmer produced a unique calling card, a miniature iron skillet with his name and the company title cast into the surface. He and his wife enjoyed traveling and visiting historic landmarks. He had seen small brass cooking utensils painted black at General Lee's home and this inspired his calling card. The manager of the Princess Anne Hotel in Fredricksburg saw these small skillets and asked Mr. Clemmer to make some for the hotel with *Princess Anne* engraved on the reverse.

In 1938, Clemmer and his wife began to produce metal novelties, mainly miniature cooking utensils cast in iron, which were marketed nationally under the name Virginia Metalcrafters. Late that year, the company installed a reduction furnace for brass and non-ferrous metals. A major step in the development of a gift line also occurred in 1938 when the company entered into a joint promotion with Dennisons, a Fifth Avenue department store in New York City. In this venture the company made sadiron stand reproductions. Trivets were fast becoming one of its best selling gift items.

Prior to World War II, Virginia Metalcrafters began manufacturing gift and decorative accessories in brass and iron for Colonial Williamsburg under an exclusive license. This production was suspended during World War II and the Korean conflict, but business was resumed in the 1950's.

About that time, Richard Clemmer suffered a serious illness and in 1953 he sold the company to Charles Eckman. In the same year, Virginia Metalcrafters was incorporated and purchased all assets of Rife-Loth corporation. In 1955, the Rife-Loth hydraulic pump division was sold to The Rife Hydraulic Engine Manufacturing Company in Millburn, New Jersey. In 1955, Eckman purchased from the E.T. Caldwell Company all the patterns and drawings for Colonial Williamsburg chandeliers. In 1956, Virginia Metalcrafters acquired The Harvin Company of Baltimore with its patterns for candlesticks and fireplace equipment, and in the same period the assets of Riteway Stove Company were purchased. Riteway stoves replaced the Loth line. In 1959, the brass operations were moved from the River Road foundry to the company's present location on Main Street, Waynesboro, Virginia. In 1966, Virginia Metalcrafters bought the framed picture and picture frame molding businesses from The Paul B. Victorius Company of Charlottesville. In 1971, the old iron foundry at the River Road location was dismantled and reassembled adjacent to the brass foundry on Main Street.

Beginning in the 1960's, Virginia Metalcrafters expanded its souvenir contracts to include Old Sturbridge Village, Historic Newport, Mystic Seaport, Old Salem, Historic Charleston, and brass, iron and print reproductions for The Smithsonian Institution, and The Metropolitan Museum of Art. Most recently, the company has been licensed to do historic reproductions for the Thomas Jefferson Memorial at Monticello. Virginia Metalcrafters also has been very active in the production of commemorative trivets for a variety of organizations, businesses and events.

Virginia Metalcrafters made most of its patterns from old trivets, but it has created more designs of its own than any other company making trivets. The Clemmers retained the services of Calvin Roy Kinstler, a sculptor, who produced a number of original designs for the company. He produced a carving of Citation, the famous race horse, and several other animal carvings which are still in the line. Among the trivets, *South Seas, Sailfish, Dogwood Blossom, George Washington, Carters Grove, Newport Pineapple, King's Arms, Confederate Seal, Queen Anne Cypher, King George Cypher* are representative of original designs.

According to Hunter Earhart, who has been with the company since 1946, the foundry made its first sadiron stand reproduction in 1931. It was not until 1944 that Virginia Metalcrafters began to manufacture and distribute trivets in large quantities. The company purchased a number of old trivets to use as patterns and many of these are still in its possession. Among the old patterns was an early American design stamped on the reverse *China.* This design was authentic and it illustrates how convoluted the perpetuation of designs became, in this instance, from Europe to America, to China and back to America.

In 1946, Virginia Metalcrafters employed a pattern-maker named Horace Burns who carved wooden trivet patterns, a few of which have survived. Some patterns were taken from original castings; others were made from photographs or art. The latter were modeled and cast, or carved in plaster, from which white metal castings were made, finished, and used to make an iron production pattern or aluminum matchplate. Some of the original patterns for the cypher trivets were made from mahogany using a scroll saw.

The company has continued to expand and today it produces historic reproductions in brass, iron and Silvertone (white bronze). In addition to trivets, it markets giftware, chandeliers, lamps, fireplace equipment, picture frames, sconces, desk accessories, as well as yard and patio pieces such as sun dials and doorstops. Virginia Metalcrafters has consistently produced superb, quality castings in all its products.

The trademark of Virginia Metalcrafters is a Betty Lamp with the initials V and M. This symbol is frequently used as part of the trivet signature with a stock number. Some carry only the symbol; others the name of the trivet, symbol and stock number. A number of Virginia Metalcrafter designs are registered; there is a notice of copyright on these designs. Trivets made under license usually have a patent notice, the trademark of the customer, and the Betty Lamp symbol.

Virginia Metalcrafters designs, stock numbers and trivet names:

Stock number, name, dimensions and weight; iron, brass and Silvertone. (si) sadiron (c) copyright

9-1	*Heart (si) 9" x 4½" x ⅞" 1 lb.*	
9-2	*Grape 9" x 4¼" x ⅞" 1 lb.*	
9-3	*Eagle 9" x 6" x 1" 1 lb.*	
9-4	*Fern Stella 9" x 4½" x ⅞" 1 lb.*	
9-5	*Rosette (si) 9" x 4¼" x ⅞" 1 lb.*	
9-6	*Cathedral (si) 8½" x 3¼" x ¼" 1 lb.*	
9-7	*Family Tree (2 sizes) new 7¾" x 5¼" x ¾" 1 lb.*	
	old 9¼" x 5¾" x ⅞"	
9-8	*Dew Drop 9" x 4½" x ⅞" 1 lb.*	
9-9	*Peacock 9" x 4½" x ⅞" 1 lb.*	
9-10	*Tassel & Grain (2 sizes) new 9" x 4½" x ⅞" 1 lb.*	
	old 8¾" x 5⅜" x ⅞"	
9-11	*Fleur-de-Lis (si) 9" x 4½" x ⅞" 1 lb.*	

Anne Regina Cypher Trivet

GR Cypher Trivet

William and Mary Cypher Trivet

Thomas Jefferson Cypher Trivet

All designs copyrighted by Virginia Metalcrafters.

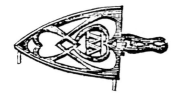

"Sad iron stand."
Dover Stamping Company, 1869.

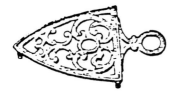

"Sad stands."
Perin & Graf Manufacturing Company, 1876.

"Tile tea or coffee pot stand."
Hamblin & Russell Mfg. Company, 1914.

"Tile tea or coffee pot stand."
J. Jacob Shannon & Company, 1889.

9-12	Plume (si) 9" x 3¼" x ¼" 1 lb.	
9-13	Tulip in Motion 10½" x 6¾" x 1½" 1 lb. 11 oz.	
9-14	Red Riding Hood 11¼" x 6¼" x 1" 1 lb. 9 oz.	
9-15	Pine Tree (si) 6¾" x 3¾" x ¾" 8 oz.	
9-16	Flaxwheel 7⅝" x 3⅝" x ⅝" 7 oz.	
9-18	Doodlers Dream 8" x 6¼" x ½" 1 lb.	
9-19	President Adams (si) 9" x 4½" x ⅞" 1 lb.	
9-20	Horse Shoe (dated 1889) 7¼" x 4¾" x ¾" 12 oz.	
9-21	Lyre & Pineapple 7⅛" x 3⅞" x 1" 11 oz.	
9-21	Lyre (si) 9" x 4½" x ⅞" 1 lb.	
10-50	William Rex 7¼" x 6" 1 lb. 3 oz.	
5-21	Old Sturbridge (si) 10¼" x 4¼" x ¼" 1 lb. 9 oz.	
5-22	1829 11" x 6½" 1 lb. 8 oz.	
5-23	Sturbridge (Seven Hearts) 6¾" x 4½" 12 oz.	
10-7	Leaf 5" x 5" x ¾" 10 oz.	

10-1, 2, 3	Sailfish	4" x 4½", 5" x 5½", 6" x 6½"	
		6 oz. 8 oz. 13 oz.	
10-4, 5, 6	Man-O-War	4" x 4½", 5" x 5½", 6" x 6½"	
	Silvertone only	4 oz. 5 oz. 8 oz.	

9-34	Cupid 8" x 3⅝" x ¾" 10 oz.
9-35	Good Luck 7¼" x 4¼" x ⅝" 11 oz.
10-8	Starwheel 5¼" x 5¼" x ⅝" 12 oz.
3803	Leaf & Vine (pair) 8½" x 4½" 2 lbs. 8 oz. (brass).
10-9	King George (c) 3¼" x 5" 6 oz.
10-10	Queen Anne (c) 9" x 10½" 2 lbs. 3 oz.
10-11	William & Mary (c) 6" x 8" 1 lb. 2 oz.
10-14	Colonial Williamsburg Cypher (c) 6" x 6" 14 oz.
10-15	Thomas Jefferson (c) 5⅝" x 6¼" 13 oz.
10-17	King's Arms (c) 6" x 6" x 1" 1 lb.
10-18	Confederate Seal (c) 5¼" x 5¼" 12 oz.
10-19	Spread Eagle (c) 8" x 9" x ¾" 2 lbs. (pair).
10-46	Newport Pineapple (c) 6" x 6" x 1" 1 lb. 4 oz.
10-12	Dogwood Blossom (c) 5" x 5¾" 8 oz.
10-13	George Washington (c) 9⅛" x 4⅛" x ⅞" 12 oz.
5-24	Sturbridge Cypher 6¼" x 6" 13 oz.
9-36	Jamestown (c) 9" x 4½" x ⅞" 1 lb.
10-26	James Monroe Cypher (c) 9" x 6¾".
10-30	Charles II Cypher (c) 6" x 5⅜".
10-55	Monticello Trivet (c) (pair) 7½" x 7".

Listing made from Virginia Metalcrafter catalogues for 1940, 1946, 1949, 1950, 1956, 1957, 1964, 1972, 1981, and 1984. Catalogues owned by the company.

Virginia Metalcrafters constantly adds new designs to its line, and it has done innumerable custom designs for clients to be used mainly as commemoratives.

John Wright Company, Inc. (A Division of Donsco Corporation); Wrightsville, Pennsylvania, 1947 to the present.

John Wright Company is located on North Front Street next to the Susquehanna River and across the street from Wilton Products. John Wright Company was formed as a branch of Riverside Foundry, a company established in 1906 by Harry Smith, Charles Shultz, and Harry Kerr. The foundry was built on the site of the older Wrightsville Foundry which had been erected in 1847. For many years, Riverside Foundry operated as a gray-iron jobber specializing in light hardware casting.

In the 1940's, Ed Musser came to Don Smith, son of Harry Smith (then president of the company), with a proposal for an iron novelties business. Musser was an artist and pattern-maker who later created many of the designs marketed by John Wright Company. In 1947, the two men became partners in the John Wright Company, which was named after the Colonial ferryman who founded the town of Wrightsville. The company produced inexpensive iron trinkets and a line of Amish souvenirs.

Riverside Foundry also owned York Metalcrafters, a company which manufactured mugs and dinnerware from an aluminum alloy polished to look like pewter. In 1968, Riverside purchased The Grey-Iron Casting Company of Mount Joy which had been marketing light hardware and making cast-iron toys, miniature stoves, wheel toys and mechanical banks since 1881. This purchase also included Wrightsville Hardware which specialized in light hardware. Both the Mount Joy foundry and Wrightsville Hardware had extensively marketed iron trivets and table stands in the years around the turn of the century. In 1973, all these holdings were incorporated as Donsco Corporation.

After World War II, the rising price of iron and labor made it unprofitable for John Wright to continue the production of iron trinkets and souvenirs. The company moved into Early American iron and brass reproductions, and the business expanded. By 1963, the Wright catalogue listed more than 850 items.

Wright trivet patterns include those acquired in the purchase of the Mount Joy foundry, Wrightsville Hardware and new patterns made from authentic old trivets purchased by the company. Most recently, Wright has copied several designs from the Paley Collection at Shelburne Museum. The originals were French enameled iron platter trivets. Wright produced them in iron with a black satin finish. John Wright has produced approximately fifty or sixty different trivet designs which were made available in flat black finish or hand decorated. The Wright Company regularly issues new trivet designs.

Most Wright trivets today are marked on the reverse, JOHN WRIGHT, and most show a stock number. At an earlier date, Wright wholesaled some trivets which carried only a stock number.

John Wright Company, Inc. designs, stock numbers and trivet names:

Stock number and dimensions; iron, brass and aluminum, (si) sadiron.

244	Family Tree 5½" x 8½".
245	Dutch Hex 4½" x 9".
246	Cathedral (si) 4" x 9".
247	Butterfly 6" x 9".
248	Distelfink 5" x 8".
249	Cupid 4½" x 7½".
250	Lyre (si) 4" x 7".
252	Rosette (si) 3½" x 8".
254	Tassel 5" x 7½".
255	Rooster 5½" x 9".
258	Eastern Star 4½" x 7".
260	(si) 4" x 8½".
262	Peacock 5" x 10".
264	Grape 4¼" x 7¼".
265	Oak Leaf 6" x 6" (aluminum).
266	Eagle 5½" x 8½".
267	Masonic 4" x 6½".
268	Horseshoe (good luck) 4¼" x 7".
270	Pin Wheel (tulip) 6" x 9".
272	Star 6" x 6".

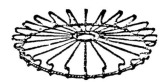

"Wire coffee stand."
Dover Stamping Company, 1869.

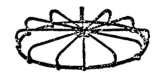

"Crown stand."
Hamblin & Russell Mfg. Company, 1914.

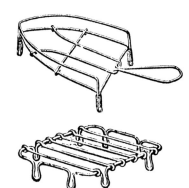

"Sad iron stands."
Hamblin & Russell Mfg. Company, 1914

"Sad stand; bronzed" (marked "Griswold.")
The Central Stamping Company, 1889.

"Sad iron stand."
Lisk Manufacturing Company, 1911.

280   Dewdrop (si) 4" x 8".
281   Openwork (Lantz No. #2) 5½" x 5½".
298   Sunburst (Cincinnatus) 5" x 9".
299   Dumb Dutch 4½" x 9".
300   Mask (Urn with Fern) 5½" x 7".
150   Amish Boy 4¾" x 8".
151   Amish Girl 4¾" x 8".
210   Antique (French Turtle) 9½" x 5".
230   Eagle Gold 5¼" x 7½".
231   Eagle Gold 5¼" x 7½".
2850   Jumbo Rooster (right & left).
1590   George Washington.
55-010 Historic Charleston Cipher 6¼" x 6¼".
33-285 Circle & Star 8" x 8".
33-260 Heart 8" x 8".
33-280 Heart & Star (Rimby 12 hearts without handle) 8" x 8".
26-522 Brass Round 8" x 8".
33-286 Cast Iron Round 8" x 8".
33-305 Oval 11".

In 1970, Wright added an "0" to stock numbers and a "4" to indicate which trivets were hand-decorated. The system changed again in 1983 when a prefix of "33" was added.

Listing made from Wright catalogues for 1960, 1969, c. 1972, and 1983. Catalogues owned by the company.

Wright marketed a large number of motto, or plaque, trivets, but these were discontinued in 1987.

J.Z.H. (John Zimmerman Harner 1872-1965) Union Manufacturing Company; Unicast Company; Boyertown, Pennsylvania, 1894 to the present.

John Z. Harner was born in 1872 at Monocacy Hill in Amity Township, Pennsylvania. He was the descendent of carpenters and wheelwrights. As a young man of 24, he became an apprentice pattern-maker at the Reading Scale and Machine Works in Reading, Pennsylvania. This company built and repaired scales and large, horizontal, power return tubular boilers. It also did blacksmithing, general jobbing and gray-iron castings. After three productive years, John moved to Kutztown Foundry & Machine Company as a pattern-maker. In 1901, he worked briefly for the Baldwin Locomotive Works in Philadelphia but soon returned to the Kutztown Foundry.

In 1910, he went to work for Union Manufacturing Company in Boyertown as superintendent. This company, founded in 1894, made cast-iron stoves, kitchen ranges, sadirons and general castings. In 1920, John Harner proposed that the Board of Directors increase his pay; they responded by suggesting that he purchase the company. So, with the assistance of a local banker, John Harner bought Union Manufacturing Company.

In 1932, his son Paul joined the firm. By 1944, John Harner was semi-retired, and his son Paul was managing the family business. This was during World War II when large amounts of scrap-iron were being collected and reduced down for reuse. John Harner was poking through the scrap pile looking over what had been brought in for reduction. He noticed an old Pennsylvania German trivet from which he decided to make copies for his own satisfaction and to give to friends. Here was a seventy-five-year-old man, highly skilled as a pattern-maker, knowledgable of all aspects of founding, who had access to a foundry and all its resources, and was interested in making cast-iron trivets. Mr. Harner took his old German trivet to the pattern-shop and had the workmen there make him a matchplate.

"Coffee pot stand."
Lisk Manufacturing Company, 1911.

On the back of his first trivet, he inscribed, *J.Z.H. 1944 A.* This clearly revealed his intention to reproduce other trivets. He began to collect trivets at auctions or wherever he could find them. Occasionally, he would borrow a trivet from a friend from which to make a pattern. From the originals, molds were made which were used to make a white metal casting. These castings were filed, scraped, and built-up where necessary. Details and lines were sharpened before making the production pattern. To ensure that his castings would not be confused with originals, he continued to put his initials, the year, and an alphabetical or numeric code on the reverse of the platform. In time he went through the entire alphabet and moved into a numbering system. The trivets reproduced by John Harner were all made between 1944 and 1958.

Mr. Harner kept his trivets in baskets in the basement of his home and when friends came to call, they were invited to choose a souvenir from his assortment. During the 1950's, when Early American reproductions were most popular, Unicast made aluminum matchplates from six of Mr. Harner's designs and marketed the trivets for a few years. Robert Emig and Iron Art also purchased castings of Mr. Harner's designs from Unicast for marketing through their own outlets.

John Zimmerman Harner is unknown to antique dealers and collectors, but he made a substantial contribution to the history of trivets through his many reproductions. He perpetuated designs which might otherwise have been lost. Every trivet he used for a pattern was an old casting. The patterns were true to the original and castings were of excellent quality. Each pattern was made from an authentic model; he was not in the business of marketing trivets so his designs were unaffected by considerations such as shipping costs or marketability. John Harner was responsible for approximately sixty-five or more different trivet patterns. It is almost certain that his A to Z trivets will in time become collector items. John Harner died in 1965 at the age of ninety-two.

In 1966-67, Union Manufacturing Company was merged with Fashion Hosiery Mills. The company was reorganized as Berkmont Industries, Inc. The hosiery mill was the Fashiondale Division; the foundry became Unicast Foundries Division, and Union Manufacturing Company produced stoves. In 1981, the Harner family sold Unicast Division. It is now The Unicast Company, maker of cosmetic quality gray-iron castings.

As a jobber, using matchplates of its own, or ones furnished by customers, Unicast makes trivets for Wilton, Iron Art, Art Smithy, Robert Emig, Hopewell Village and others. Unicast added new patterns to those made by John Harner, and today it is estimated that it has approximately 80 to 90 different patterns in stock. There are probably more trivet patterns at Unicast than anywhere else in the country. Unicast has consistently made fine castings and the quality of the work is unexcelled.

The original Union Manufacturing Company marketed sadirons and produced several different sadiron stands, identified by the name of the company on the face of the stand.

John Harner designs marketed by Unicast may or may not carry initials, but some have the name of the trivet and a combination letter and number identification. Most trivets produced for distributers such as Emig and Iron Art have a code letter identifying the distributor as well as the distributor's name. Many of the Unicast trivets carry no markings at all or only the name of the contractor.

"Coffee pot stand and sad stands."
Grey Iron Casting Company, Mount Joy, 1889.

The alphabet series of trivet reproductions which John Zimmerman Harner ordered made at Unicast Company between 1944 and 1955.

A. *7⅞ inches, 1944.*

B. *7 inches, 1944.*

C. 7½ x 5⅝ inches, 1945.

G. 13 x 8 inches, 1948.

K. 6⅝ inches, 1948.

D. 7½ x 5 inches, 1945.

H. 6¼ inches, 1955.

L. 8⅜ x 4¾ inches, 1955.

E. 8⅞ x 4½ inches, 1945.

I. 5¼ inches, 1949.

M. 8¾ x 4 inches, 1948.

F. 10⅛ x 6½ inches, 1945.

J. 6½ inches, 1948.

N. 7½ x 8½ inches, 1946.

61

O. 5 ¹¹/₁₆ inches, 1948.

S. 9½ x 4⅜ inches, 1948.

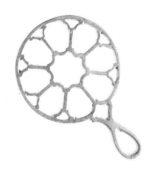

W. 8 x 5¼ inches, 1948.

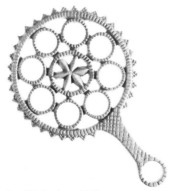

P. 9 x 5⅞ inches, 1948.

T. 10½ x 5½ inches, 1948.

X. 7½ x 4 inches, 1948.

Q. 6⅞ inches, 1948.

U. 9 x 5⅛ inches, 1948.

Y. 10¼ x 5 inches, 1948.

R. 9 x 4 inches, 1948.

V. 8 x 3½ inches, 1948.

Z. 5¾ inches, 1948.

Keystone Grey-Iron Foundry Company; Pottstown, Pennsylvania, 1936 to the present, (formerly The Prizer Painter Stove Works, Reading, Pennsylvania, 1918-58).

The Prizer Painter Stove Works purchased holdings from a sheriff's sale and established the company in 1918-19. It operated its own foundry in Reading until 1936. At that time the Reading foundry was closed because of labor problems, and space was rented in Pottstown where a new foundry was established as Keystone Grey-Iron Foundry Company. The Prizer Painter Stove Works had loose patterns for eight different trivet designs and the patterns were moved to the Pottstown foundry. In 1958, these patterns were purchased by Keystone foundry when The Prizer Painter Stove Works became defunct.

Keystone has cast trivets for Wilton, Robert Emig and Iron Art using their respective patterns. There is no Keystone identification, other than a stock number, on any trivets produced by the foundry.

Keystone Grey-Iron Foundry Company designs, stock numbers and trivet names:

Stock numbers (common names are given).

101. Hex   105. Oddfellows   117. Lincoln Drape

103. Grapes & Scrolls   102. Order of Cincinnatus   106. Star

104. Tulip   118. Eagle & Heart

Mortimer Spiller Company; Batavia, New York, 1944 to the present.

In 1943, Mortimer Spiller began to produce cast-iron newstand paperweights in an old plow factory at Batavia, New York. In 1944, he cast iron trivets as premiums and salesmen's gifts. These were never sold at retail. General Electric distributed some of the trivets in connection with stove sales. Only four designs were cast and the matchplates were made by Eastern Pattern Company of New York City. The trivets were finished in flat black only and were stamped on the reverse, SPILLER BATAVIA N Y.

The designs were *Family Tree, Lincoln Drape, Eagle & Heart and Tulip.*

Griswold Manufacturing Company; Erie, Pennsylvania, 1865-1957.

In 1865, Matthew Griswold entered into a partnership with John Card (J.C.) and Samuel Selden to operate a small business known locally as the "butt factory" because the principal product was a separable door hinge. The company was built around a foundry, finishing shed, store rooms, and an engine and boiler room. It was located on the corners of 10th and Chestnut Streets in Erie, Pennsylvania. It began by making small castings, hollow wares of special sizes and finishes, home furnishings, utensils and stove trimmings; a short time later, it added cuspidors with rollers and tobacco cutters to the line. In 1873, the company was reorganized as Selden & Griswold Manufacturing Company. There were appproximately twenty employees.

In 1884, Matthew Griswold bought out Selden's interest; and in 1887, the company was reorganized and chartered as Griswold Manufacturing Company. At this time there were about 100 employees. Undergoing considerable expansion, Griswold Company soon added to its line long griddles, waffle irons, kettles, dutch ovens, roasters, grid-irons, and a blank cartridge firing burglar alarm. In 1889, Griswold began manufacturing aluminum cookware; its first product was a tea kettle.

In 1903, the original site was abandoned when the company purchased and moved into the Shaw Piano Company building on the corner of 12th and Raspberry Streets. The company was further expanded, and by 1909, Griswold occupied the entire area bordered by Cascade, 12th, Raspberry Streets and the railroad tracks. In 1905, Matthew Griswold stepped down as president, and his son, Matthew, Jr. assumed leadership of the company.

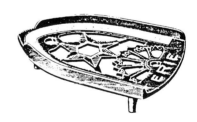

During the 1920's, the Griswold company peaked as one of the most respected brand names in cookware. The company added electrical appliances to its line of cast-iron and aluminum ware. There were Griswold distributorships both in this country and overseas. Griswold cookware represented some of the finest ever made. But there were labor problems in the 1930's that impacted on production; and during World War II, the making of nickel and chrome coated cookware was suspended. After the war, the entire Griswold line of kitchenware was introduced to the public through mail order catalogues.

Wagner Manufacturing purchased the Griswold kitchenware division in 1953. The restaurant division was purchased by McGraw Edison about the same time. The Griswold plant closed for good on December 7th, 1957, and its assets were dissolved.

Trivet styles shown by the Griswold Mfg. Company at the turn of the century.

Finding Griswold catalogues proved to be difficult, and without them it is impossible to have a complete inventory of trivets produced by the company. However, Griswold was making trivets in large numbers during the period before and after the turn of the century. Using its older patterns, it produced a number of designs in the 1940's and 1950's when reproductions were popular. The Griswold trivet castings found have been of excellent quality, and a number of designs were unique to the company, most notably cereal trivets and table stands.

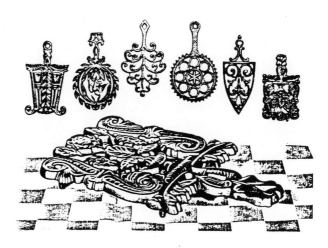

GRISWOLD
TRIVETS
Early American Trivet Assortment

THESE TRIVETS HAVE A DISTINCTIVE COLONIAL
BLACK FINISH AND ARE ATTRACTIVELY PACKED IN
INDIVIDUAL GIFT BOXES

Trivet Assortment

Set No.	Boxes Packed in Carton	Weight Carton Pounds	List Price Set
16	6	7	$6.00

(Slightly higher West of the Rockies)

Wagner Manufacturing Division; Sidney, Ohio.
Division of General Housewares Corporation; Terre Haute, Indiana, 1881 to the present.

Wagner Housewares was founded in 1881 by Mathias Wagner, who operated a retail store in Sidney, Ohio. He specialized in cast-iron cooking ware. In 1953, Wagner Company purchased the cookware division of Griswold Manufacturing Company. In the same year, Wagner was taken over by Randall. In 1969, *Wagner by Randall* was purchased by Textron Corporation and the company was later sold to General Housewares of Terre Haute, Indiana.

The public relations office at Wagner could not find any records of the company producing trivets prior to 1960. However, the company was a major producer of cast-iron housewares such as kettles, pans, pots, and other cookware. It seems likely that it also would have made trivets as its competitors marketed them during the same years. Wagner did make and market a few cast-iron trivets and iron rests in 1960. A promotional flyer c. 1960 illustrates six designs for cast iron trivets and iron rests that Wagner by Randall marketed.

Wagner by Randall designs and trivet names:

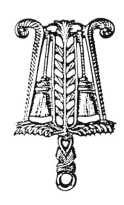

1005. Tassel & Grain 8″ x 5¼″.

1003. Arrow Head 8¾″ x 4″.

1006. Family Tree 8¾″ x 5¼″.

1007. Spike 9¼″ x 5¾″.

1004. Star 8″ x 5¼″.

1009. Grape 7½″ x 4⅜″.

Note. *These same designs were shown by Griswold shortly before it was sold to Wagner, and very likely Wagner used the Griswold patterns.*

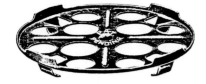

"Pressed steel sadiron and pot stand."

"The Royal sadiron stand; polished and nickel plated."

"Japanned."

The A.C. Williams Company, c. 1920.

Some of the distinctive stands marketed at the turn-of-the-century by the Ober Manufacturing Company.

The A.C. Williams Company; Ravenna, Ohio, 1844 to the present.

John Wesley Williams first operated an iron furnace in Chagrin Falls, Ohio in 1844 as the Williams Foundry & Thimble Skein Sadware Factory. The company was located on an old sawmill and furnace property next to the Chagrin River. It had a small one ton cupola, one molder and a few helpers. The company made pump wheels, spouts, and plow points. Somewhat later, the company acquired patterns for an elevated oven, wood-burning stove called "The Empire." Shortly after beginning stove production, the company expanded to include hand-wrought axles, old style short wagon boxes, and boxes for axles and sadirons in several styles. During the Civil War, the company made cannon carriages under contract with the government.

In 1865, John Williams' son, Adam Clark Williams, began working full-time in the family business and the name of the company was changed to J.W. Williams & Son. In 1886, on the occasion of his father's death, Adam took over the business and the company name was changed to The A.C. Williams Company. At this time, the company had five molders and a total of fifteen employees. In the same year, production was expanded by adding a line of sadirons with wooden handles. The company foundry was twice destroyed by fire, once in 1889 when it was rebuilt at the same location; and again in 1892, after which the company moved to Ravenna, Ohio, where a new foundry was built. The company poured its first casting at the new foundry on May 1, 1893. It was a sadiron.

By 1893, the demand for sadirons had considerably diminished and The A.C. Williams Company looked for new lines of merchandise. Over the next thirty years, the company became the world's largest producer of iron toys. Horse-drawn, wheel toys, automobiles, tractors, airplanes and several hundred styles of cast iron house and animal banks were made and distributed by The A.C. Williams Company. The company also made trade and kitchen tools and a number of trivets. Most of these items were discontinued in 1937-38.

The A.C. Williams Company remained in the family for six generations. In 1905, the company incorporated. In 1977, the company was purchased by Robert E. McCoy, but it still operated as The A.C. Williams Company. Corporate offices were moved to Akron, Ohio, and a new iron foundry was built. The iron works in Ravenna was replaced by aluminum and magnesium production. Products are marketed under the name of The Lite Metals Company, a division of The A.C. Williams Company.

Ober Manufacturing Company; Chagrin Falls, Ohio, 1873-1950's.

The company was founded by George H. Ober and his brother John in 1873. They moved from Newbury, a small farming town about ten miles east of Chagrin Falls, Ohio. Ober Brothers Company made broom and axe handles, and it was responsible for the invention and manufacture of the Ober Eccentric Lathe that could turn out axe and hammer handles in the ovoid shape. The manufacture of the lathes peaked around 1890, and the machinery was marketed around the world.

When the company began, the Ober brothers operated a retail lumber yard and made wood handles for tools, but with a growing scarcity of wood, it established a foundry and began the manufacture of iron products. The company marketed sadirons, sadiron handles of its own design, trivets, hammers, hatchets, toy banks, meat tenderizers, and other household items. After the turn of the century, Ober marketed electric irons.

In the latter part of the nineteenth century, Chagrin Falls was the flat iron capital of the nation. During those years, Ober published catalogues in four languages, but it is not clear if the catalogues pertained to irons or only to the lathe. J.C. Williams & Son Company and The Chagrin Falls Manufacturing Company were also producing a large amount of iron products.

Archie M. Ober, the son of George Ober, took over management of the business in 1882 and the firm was renamed The Ober Manufacturing Company. George Ober died in 1903. When Archie died, his son, Gale, operated the company until his death in the 1950's. The Ober foundry was discontinued in 1916 but the business continued on a small scale until the firm dissolved in the fifties.

An Ober catalogue of October 5th, 1914, illustrated a number of different sadirons and trivets. Trivets were priced from forty-five to seventy-five cents per dozen and advertised as being suitable for either an iron or a teapot. In 1893, Ober began to make miniatures of its irons and stands as salesmen's samples and a Detroit buyer quickly recognized the potential for these as toys. Ober soon became one of the largest manufacturers of toy irons and stands in this country ("Trivets Stand Up To Heat", Joan Hale; *Antique Week*, Vol. 19 No. 40, January 12, 1987).

The Ober grid and leaf stands are unique to the company. It appears that Ober never reproduced any of the traditional designs. Ober trivets were generally identified on the reverse by OBER, a monogram of OMC, the letter O, or by the company name.

Note: *Virginia Metalcrafters has distributed a reproduction of the Ober small, round, leaf stand.*

Gray's Foundry; Middletown Springs, Vermont c. 1855 to the present.

The Paley Collection includes two trivets which are marked on the reverse, *Gray's Foundry, Poultney, VT.* The *Hex* design is cast in brass and painted black; the *Family Tree* is cast in iron. Examination of the trivets suggests they were cast within the last forty years.

Child's Gazetteer and Business Directory of Rutland County (1881-82) lists a Eugene W. Gray as proprietor of a steam operated saw and grist mill with an iron foundry. The company was described as a manufacturer of agricultural implements, plows, cultivators and cheese presses. The foundry also marketed cider, cider jelly, and annually produced 300 to 500 gallons of maple syrup. Gray also farmed and had a holding of 200 acres of spruce timber land. This diversification was probably typical of small foundries at that time.

Note: *The man-hole covers used on the Shelburne Museum grounds are marked as products of Gray's Foundry, Poultney, Vt.*

T. 13.

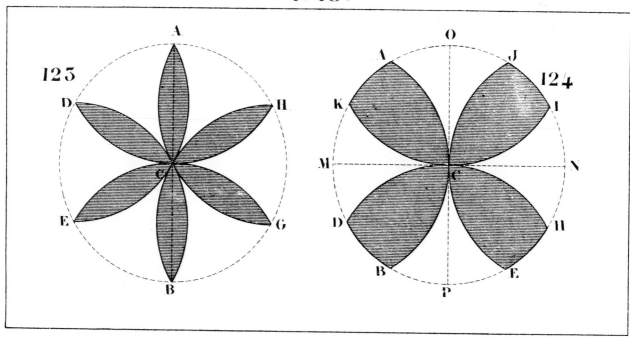

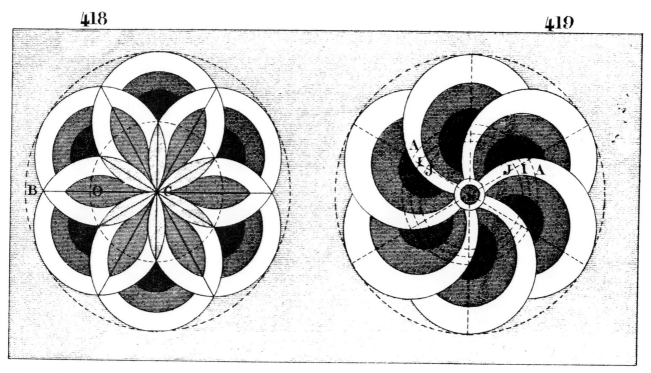

Illustration from Dessin Lineaire, J.P. Thenot; Paris, 1845.

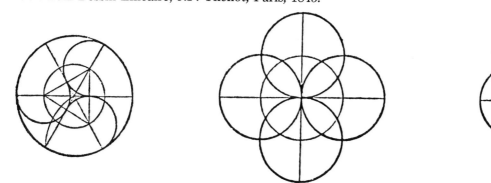

V. TRIVET DESIGNS

American cast trivets and stands date from circa 1840 to the present. Sources for early trivet designs were extremely diverse. Often the designs reflected conditions and styles of the period. The majority of motifs and symbols used to decorate pre-Civil War cast trivets originated in Europe. Most were associated with the Victorian era which pertains to the reign of Queen Victoria of England from 1837 to 1901. However, styles seldom begin or end abruptly, rather there is a period of transition into an era and and then styles slowly fade away at the end.

Some trivet designs associated with the Victorian era were actually exceptions to prevailing concepts of decoration. Religious groups, such as the Mennonites and Shakers, used symbols peculiar to their beliefs and for them decoration served a different purpose. Other trivet designs from this period reflect cultural diversity ranging from Nordic to Oriental influences. Later in the nineteenth century, advertising and marketing practices impacted strongly on the design of American trivets.

The Victorians

Victorians were fascinated by decoration. They equated ornamentation with quality and admired embellishment in almost any form. By the time of the Victorians, industrial technology had advanced to a point that allowed ornamentation to be stamped, cast, printed or formed by machines.

Until the time of the industrial revolution and machine-made products, ornamentation was done by hand and aesthetic values were imparted by the talent and skill of craftsmen. It took a great deal of time to accomplish and it was unique. As such, it was a standard of quality, and status was associated with its ownership.

With machines, ornamentation became effortless and could be cheaply produced in great quantity. John Ruskin observed in reference to machine goods, ". . . done without the difficulty which gives it honor." He lamented the stamped wood and metal, cast-iron, artificial gemstones, and imitation wood and bronzes. In 1835, Alexis de Tocqueville commented on machine produced goods, ". . . cheap imitations which give an object a look of brilliance unconnected with its true worth, and this enables its owner to appear as something he is not." (*Democracy in America*)

Victorian manufacturers responded with exuberance to rapid development of mass production. Industrial productivity led to expanding markets resulting in the manufacture of an enormous variety of goods characterized by a lack of restraint in design. Decoration was lavish, but indiscriminate; ornamentation and motifs were drawn from the past or borrowed from exotic sources. Novelty was substituted for style. Even in its own day, much of Victorian applied art was regarded as vulgar.

A number of architects, artists and intellectuals of the period were greatly concerned about prevailing conditions in the applied arts. Men such as Ruskin, Morris, Redgrave, Pugin, Wornum, Semper and others spoke for the arts and crafts movement arousing a powerful, critical reaction to the way industrialization was impacting on society. Members of the movement were concerned with the industrial influence on prevailing aesthetic values. They were also concerned about how it affected the quality of life for workmen. Ruskin commented, "I do not mean work in the sense of bread, I mean work in the sense of mental interest."

Trivets based on compass designs.

In this period of transition from hand-crafted to machine made products, many followers of the movement looked to the past for a solution, and advocated a return to the old ways and values. Some felt that nature was the

Variations of compass flower, and trivet showing compass flower motif.

perfect source for artistic inspiration. Ruskin even expressed an opinion that anything not drawn from nature must therefore be ugly. Others felt that imitation of nature was a vice, especially when used inappropriately. A gas jet in the form of a flower or similar translations of nature into man-made objects exemplified Victorian *kitsch*.

Concerns of the arts and crafts movement survive even today. Reproductions of trivets shipped in from Taiwan, traditional trivet designs converted into plate warmers, sconces, hooks, or trivets cast in plastic are anathemas to the dedicated trivet collector.

Romanticism was typical of Victorian times and many advocates of the arts and crafts movement indulged in a belief that the *folk* were unsullied by industrialization. Folk art was regarded as ideal because peasants, living a simple life close to nature, were viewed as being more pure in their values. Followers of the arts and crafts movement turned to vernacular, rustic, and folk art themes for inspiration.

Followers of the arts and craft movement attempted to organize, define, and rationalize decoration. Their attempts often led to controversy if not contradiction. However, idealistic principles such as "truth in materials" and "the relationship of function to form" emerged from the arts and crafts movement. The Bauhaus incorporated a number of these concepts which have strongly influenced the definition of design in this century. While Victorians used machines to reproduce older ideas of applied decoration, Bauhaus aesthetics focused on using new materials and machines to express the creed of "form follows function."

Victorian decoration was grounded in eclecticism and often was generically applied. The same motifs were used by architects, wood workers, weavers and metal workers. It was a matter of choosing ornaments and materials. Creativity was often measured by application of existing ornaments rather than by originality in making new ones.

The Victorian point of view did not reflect a lack of creative ability; it expressed an attitude toward decoration. The Victorians were incredibly inventive and the period is marked by energetic endeavor and many technological advances. Even in their everyday implements, Victorians were constantly devising new ones, or combining several functions into one tool. *Patent Applied For* or *Patent Pending* so common to this era reflect the energy and ingenuity of Victorians.

Victorians treated decoration and function as entirely separate concerns. Consequently, we have the irony of technologically advanced machinery being constructed and embellished with highly decorated surfaces. The functions of the machines might be progressive, but their appearance was traditional. New design today is usually reflected by product appearance. The Bauhaus creed of "form follows function" was a natural, and logical, reaction to the Victorian notion of separating function and form. The Bauhaus, to some degree, was able to resolve the Victorian dilemma of handcrafts versus machine-made products by creating aesthetics based on machine capabilities and new materials.

Victorian imagery was drawn from a body of decorative motifs referred to as "design elements." When these elements were applied, they were called "decoration." The individual elements themselves were borrowed from diverse sources. The nineteenth century was a period of intense archaeological exploration and much of the imagery connected with new discoveries found its way into the decorative repertory of the Victorians. Ornaments or devices taken from ancient Greek, Roman, Moorish, Assyrian, Arabic,

Byzantine, Egyptian and Chinese civilizations were regularly shown in pattern books of the period.

This was also the time of European colonization and world trade. Many exotic forms of ornamentation were brought home and incorporated into the growing body of decorative elements. In the eighteenth century, Oriental influences were introduced to Europe, mainly from China and India. In 1754, Edwards and Darley in their *New Book of Chinese Designs* showed a round trivet with the sides pierced in a pattern of *Chinoiserie* ("Trivets and Toasting Forks," Alice Van Leer Carrick; *Home Beautiful,* April, 1928). Japanese art exerted an enormous influence on Europeans in the nineteenth century. A specific example of borrowing a design may be found in the pineapple motif brought back to America by Yankee traders from the Caribbean where the pineapple was a symbol of hospitality to the Carib Indians. Hospitality trivets incorporating the pineapple motif were soon common in New England.

The Victorians were particularly fond of "Antiques," or the Classical periods, as they believed them to be the most lucid and beautiful. They drew from the Romanesque, Gothic and Renaissance periods as well as from the Medieval, which they labeled the "Age of Decadence." Ruskin and Morris were especially partial to the latter period. Victorians further classified ornamentation as to period and nation, i.e., 18th century French.

Victorian concepts of decoration also were shaped by new possibilities inherent in mechanical production, and consequently, by reaction to machine-made ornamentation. Victorians looked to the past for models, focused on designs derived from nature and borrowed from folk art. Also, they incorporated imagery gathered from exploration and trade. A major embodiment of applied arts from the Victorian period was collected and displayed at The Museum of Ornamental Art, founded in 1852 in London. At a later date, the institution was renamed The Victoria and Albert Museum. It is now an important repository of Victorian design.

Trivet designs from the Victorian period represent some of the most typical examples of decorative work to come from that era. This is especially true of trivets cast in this country, regardless of where the designs originated. The heart and geometric designs associated with the Pennsylvania German communities around the Civil War period are representative. These trivets are functional, with perfectly flat surfaces, and the designs are of superb quality. Details such as the supports were considered in scale to the frame, and legs were shaped and often beautifully tapered.

Many of the English, French and German trivets from the same period are encrusted with ornamentation in relief on top of the platform which creates an uneven surface. On some, the function of the handle is lost for the sake of decoration.

The English round stands from the Regency period are functional and decorative, but in many of the English commemorative trivets, ornamentation interferes with function. Trivets cast in America seldom relied on decoration to the same extent as European ones, and function was rarely neglected in the design.

Pattern Books

Because of the generic quality of Victorian design elements, there were a number of pattern books available to artisans in all areas of craft and industry. Pattern books were compilations of ornaments, usually from one source. There were pattern books that only dealt with ornaments and these might be quite specific, i.e., *Ornaments from Pompei, Egyptian Motifs,* or *18th century Italian Architectural Details.* In addition to these pattern

Arabesque from a pattern book.

Two trivets showing arabesque.

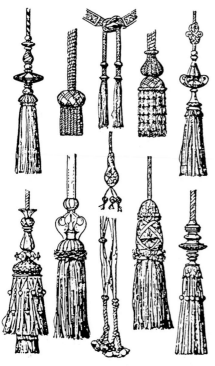

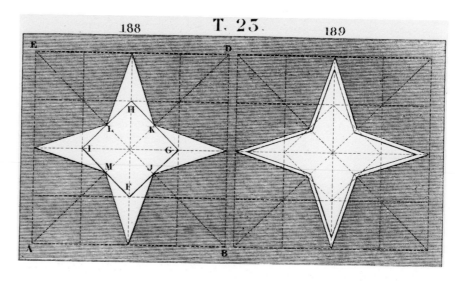

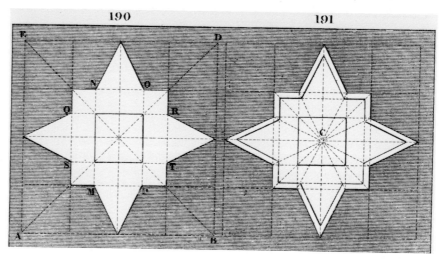

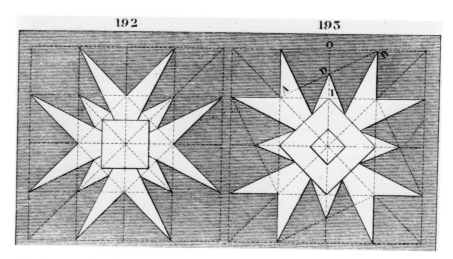

Illustration from Dessin Lineaire, J.P. Thenot; Paris, 1845.

Tassels from a pattern book, stylized tassel drawing, and "Lincoln Drape" stand with tassel motif.

books, there were portfolios with plates of ornamentation, often in color, with a small amount of text. The use of pattern books was commonplace in France during the 18th century. By the 19th century, their use was widespread throughout Europe and America.

Handbooks were directed toward the trades or specific skills such as those showing architectural plans. One reason that so many small New England frame churches look similar is that the plans were taken from the same architectural handbook. There were handbooks on signpainting or fine handwriting, woodcarving, metal work, and almost every other craft or trade. These were "how to" books with instructions dealing with technical aspects, plans, materials, tools and designs. Usually there were samples of finished work, styles, techniques and recommended ornamentation.

There were more comprehensive handbooks on design outlining the theory and organization of decoration. One of the earliest, and perhaps the most significant handbook, was *The Grammar of Ornament* published by Owen Jones in London in 1856. This was followed in 1862 by Christopher Dresser's *The Art of Decorative Design*, attempting to rationalize, and organize, the elements of decoration. Dresser subsequently published a number of books on design. There were countless other books about ornaments, decoration, design principles and organization published well into the twentieth century. All of these pattern books or handbooks were in general use and could be employed by anyone for any purpose.

In addition to handbooks, there were textbooks for correspondence courses to be used by apprentices intending to advance in their trades. These textbooks or manuals provided technical information, but they also had chapters illustrating commonly used ornaments. These textbooks were similar in many respects to the handbooks, except they were in a lesson format and contained extensive technical information.

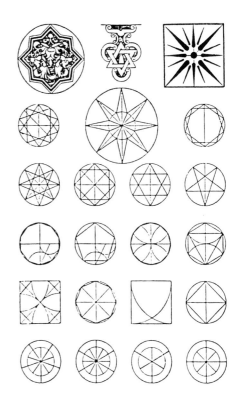

Victorian Concepts of Decoration

In Victorian language, the narrow definition of ornament was a design adapted from natural foliage. A broader definition was any decorative element. When merely drawn on paper and not applied, the foliage motif was considered in the abstract as "ornament." When applied to beautify an object, it became an "element of decoration."

The decorative elements were grouped into three main bodies; inorganic (geometric), organic (natural) and artificial (man-made). These elements were used in combination, and modified as the artist saw fit. The elements were ingredients to be mixed and applied according to accepted recipes which were called "principles."

Geometric

Geometric designs are by far the oldest known to man. Cross-hatches, zigzags, circles, squares and triangles date back to prehistoric times. Geometric designs became refined and more systematic with the development of geometric principles. Abstract geometric designs had broad application in all cultures. Geometric designs were of three types: borders or bands, panels or enclosed shapes, and patterns without beginning or end, now called all-over patterns.

A substantial number of trivet designs were literal copies from early nineteenth century pattern books based on compass and straight edge configurations. These handbooks were a culmination of prior work that can be traced back to antiquity.

The compass "flower" based on overlapping circles was used again and again in trivet designs. A flower might have three, four, five, or commonly,

Geometric drawings from a pattern book, and two trivets using geometric designs.

74

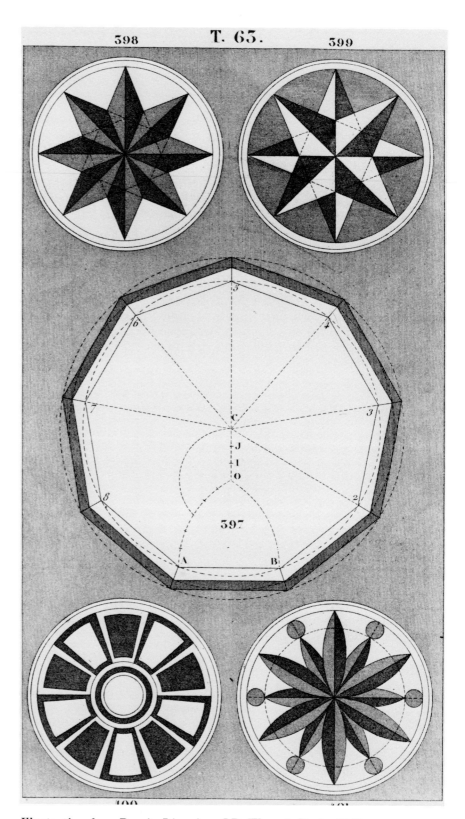

Illustration from Dessin Lineaire, *J.P. Thenot; Paris, 1845.*

six petals. Sometimes the compass construction can be seen, and at other times, only the flower is visible. Star constructions were used almost as often; Americans were partial to five-pointed stars while Europeans favored six, eight and ten-pointed ones. Trefoil, triangle and circle elements frequently were used in geometric trivet designs.

Organic

Organic designs were drawn from nature and included references to plants, birds, animals, insects, and the human form. However, this category also included what were called "inorganic models" such as snowflakes or other crystalline structures. Also, there were "natural phenomena" represented by clouds, waves, mountains and similar subjects.

Many of the foliated designs were based on organic forms such as leaves and vines, but derived from the artist's imagination. These were referred to by Victorians as "artificial." These designs were extremely stylistic and formal. The acanthus and laurel leaf designs are typical of these transformations.

The laurel leaf motif was used in several trivet designs, and often as a decorative rim. It was one of the elements which was used interchangeably on different trivet designs. Perhaps the most widely used motifs applied to trivets were plant and geometric arabesque patterns.

There were some architectural ornaments used by Victorians which were similarly applied to trivets. Scrolls, perforated crests, and capping ornaments such as the *antefix* and *akroter* were often used on trivet handles.

Birds and animals were used occasionally but were relatively uncommon in trivet design. The human figure was also a part of this category, and it was used in either a descriptive or allegorical context.

Artificial Objects

The third grouping of ornaments, "artificial objects," incorporated all things made by man. These ranged from artifacts to architectural elements that were borrowed from art, technology or science. Classified under artificial objects were a number of images described as "inventions of man's mind" including a multitude of symbols. These were religious, folk, magical, commercial, professional, fraternal and allegorical symbols. Mythical creatures were also part of this category, as represented by designs of mermaids, centaurs, the sphinx, phoenix and similar creatures.

Symbols

Symbols are non-representational and conceptual. When the beliefs that people gave to symbols change or die out, the meanings of the symbols are lost. Symbols may cease to be used, acquire new meanings, or simply survive as decorative elements. In examining symbols of the Victorian era, it is important to know whether they have religious or secular significance. The secular symbols tended to be decorative, while religious symbols were more likely to be allegorical.

Many symbols in widespread use throughout Europe during the eighteenth and nineteenth centuries were imported into this country and are characteristic of Victorian imagery. Hearts, grapes, leaves, roses, tulips, stars, tassels, sunbursts, birds of paradise, swastikas, beehives, serpents and floral or geometric designs were commonly used. The sources for much of this imagery, among religious groups were holy scriptures and other devotional literature including hymns. Many of the symbols evolved over a long period of time (in some cases, centuries) as folk art.

The symbols found frequent application in a wide variety of materials and

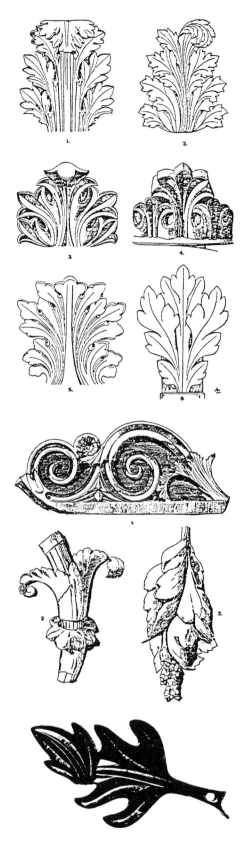

Artificial leaves from pattern books, and example of a leaf trivet.

Designs from Handbook of Geometrical Wood Carving, *Gustaf Larsson; New York and Chicago, 1895.*

Since most master patterns were first made in wood, trivet designs were greatly influenced by wood carvers.

objects in Victorian times. Furniture, weaving, jewelry, pottery, architecture and many other applications shared the same decorative motifs. It is difficult to know if artisans borrowed motifs from one piece and applied them to another, or used designs derived from a common inventory of elements. Because there is such a marked similarity between trivet designs and other decorative treatments, the practice of borrowing is extremely likely. For example, there is a high degree of similarity between trivet designs and some Pennsylvania barn signs.

Barn signs were a late development of Pennsylvania German folk art. They were first used around the middle of the nineteenth century. The signs, in addition to their decorative quality, were a means of identifying the religious beliefs of the people living there.

Many ornamental horse brasses resemble trivets in design. Hugo Darmstaetter commented on the fact that there were definite similarities between motifs carved in wooden ware imported from Holland and many of the older Pennsylvania trivet designs ("Cast and Wrought Iron Beauty," *The Spinning Wheel*; September, 1950).

The heart has a special place in trivet decoration because of its longevity as a symbol, frequency of use and myriad associations. As a universal symbol of secular and religious love, courage, friendship, hospitality, fertility, loyalty and fidelity, the heart at one time or another in Western civilization has graced almost every object made by man. The earliest known heart shape was found on an Egyptian sarcophagus dating from around 1400 B.C. It is thought that this symbol was transmitted to Europe from Egypt. Most early civilizations and many primitive peoples believed the human heart to be the source of intelligence, thought, will, feeling and consciousness.

In twelfth century Europe, the heart signified love of God and was often used as an architectural detail in the great cathedrals. The sacred heart has been associated with generations of Christian theology and by many denominations. With the development of playing cards in France and the creation of four suits representing different strata of society, the heart symbolized the ecclesiastical class. The Gothic period was followed by the age of chivalry when the heart was associated with fair maidens and romantic love. In the Renaissance, the heart was identified as the center of emotions. In eighteenth century folk art, the heart became a symbol of fertility and Mother Earth. This was often represented by flowers growing from the heart; it also became a symbol for Spring. In the nineteenth century, the heart expressed courtship and romantic love.

The heart was brought to America by the English and European settlers and was used during the Colonial period on samplers, tombstones, furniture, weathervanes, and of course, trivets. In America, the heart was frequently used as decoration on household items.

After 1820, the heart image became increasingly sentimental, moving away from the traditional and allegorical meanings. An exception to this was the use of the heart by the German *folk,* especially those of strong religious persuasion. To them, the heart symbol held religious significance. The heart symbolized the heart of God, heart of Christ or the heart of man. The eclectic and secular taste of the Victorians led them to borrow heart symbols from all sources and periods and to use them in new contexts regardless of the original intent or meaning.

The heart was often used in conjunction with other symbols to communicate specific meanings. In addition to the previously mentioned Mother Earth symbol of a heart with flowers growing out of it, there are numerous variations. The heart in hand, still used by the Odd Fellows Lodge, symbolizes "the friendship of an unselfish giver whose hand is always extended to a brother." The heart was used as an element in heraldic emblems on family crests, banners, shields or as a mark of ownership. There were hearts with flames, hearts surrounded by a crown of thorns, hearts with inscribed initials or messages, and hearts combined with other pictorial or symbolic elements. In recent times, the heart with cupid's arrow through it signifies being smitten by love. The tradition of the heart continues today through the popularity of substituting the heart symbol for the word "love" on bumper stickers, signs or T-shirts as in "I love New York" or similar messages. (For more on hearts, see *Folk Hearts,* Shaffner and Klein.)

As a decorative element on cast trivets, the heart was used singularly, butted next to each other in a continuous border, repeated in a pattern or overlapped in a configuration. Hearts were frequently used as handles, or on handles; often intertwined or as a heart-shaped opening in the handle. The shape of hearts varied considerably from wide and fat to narrow and elongated and some even had tail-like appendages. Sometimes hearts were outlined; others were solid shapes, embossed, incised or painted. They may have interior or exterior embellishments. Hearts are extremely popular with collectors today and often become the focus for an entire trivet collection.

On a number of cast trivets the swastika or fylfot in several styles, has been used as a decorative element. The swastika is perhaps even older than the heart and it is a universal symbol which has been used by primitive peoples over a wide geographical range. Used throughout Europe and the Orient for centuries, it probably reached its greatest notoriety in our day as the emblem of the Nazi movement in Germany. In addition to the conventional right-angled version of the swastika, a popular folk variation has four curvilinear arms with rounded, bulbous, terminals tapering to the center. One source referred to this as a "Chinese swastika." In fact, this variation is a Buddhist symbol which most likely came from India and was introduced to Europe by early explorers. In some versions, additional arms were added, creating a pin-wheel design frequently found in folk art.

Religion is perhaps the most pervasive source for symbols regardless of culture or period. The more common Christian symbolic associations are the circle which represents eternity and three over-lapping circles, or most any three segmented design such as a trefoil, which symbolizes the holy trinity. Many different forms of the cross, such as the Maltese, Cross of St. George, and Celtic are representative of Christianity. Interlocking hearts stand for eternal love, and the eight-pointed star represents heaven. The peacock (from pagan religions) was a symbol of immortality; the eagle represented renewal; the nightingale was a symbol of humility; the dove symbolized man seeking the savior or a messenger from heaven; the phoenix and bird of paradise were most associated with Christ, and the sun, or a sunburst, represented the sun of life, sun of righteousness or the Lord is a sun and shield. Numerous other symbolic associations are dependent on place, time and culture.

Flowers are a common motif on cast trivets. Although there were many exceptions, the English favored the rose, the Germanic peoples the tulip and lily, and the French the iris as represented by the *Fleur de Lis*. The English tended to be literal in their interpretation of the rose, but the tulip and lily had many variations. It is sometimes difficult to identify the difference between the lily and tulip in folk art as they were so highly stylized.

Horseshoe motifs are most identified with English and American designs. The sunburst was a fairly common motif, usually placed centrally with the design radiating out from it. The English and French were partial to grapes as a design motif. American trivet makers externalized their patriotism;

Triskelon and stylized tulip, with trivets illustrating their application.

Pineapple hospitality trivet.

eagles, five-pointed stars, flags, presidents and the national shield were common designs for trivets made in this country.

American eagle trivets are of particular interest as the interpretation of the eagle evolved from period to period. The eagle used in the eighteenth century resembled a sick buzzard or turkey; the eagle depicted in the first half of the nineteenth century looked more like an eagle, but a very benign one. In the period following the Civil War up to 1900, the eagle became increasingly fierce with flashing eyes and large talons and was usually presented in a predatory or threatening posture. In the twentieth century, the eagle became static, stately, and extremely dignified as it is today on our national seal. The period of origin for eagle trivet designs can often be determined by the style of eagle.

Reputedly, the eagle trivet with a laurel leaf rim *(Eagle & Heart)* was made in the Zoarite community in Zoar, Ohio, around the 1860's. In recent times, it has been one of the most frequently reproduced designs. On the original casting, the head of the eagle does not touch the laurel leaves. On more recent castings, the head and leaves are joined to make a stronger casting. Only Virginia Metalcrafters and Harner made reproductions similar to the original. Wilton made two eagle castings which were never shown in their catalogues. The style of the eagles suggests their date of origin as nineteenth century. Henry Wilton states that he commissioned these two designs sometime during the 1950's. However, the treatment of design on these trivets appears too authentic to have been recently conceived. They may have been copied from older models, but it seems improbable that the designs themselves originated in the 1950's.

The Germans occasionally used the imperial eagle as a motif, but the design is clearly distinguishable from American styles.

Pennsylvania Designs

In America during the early nineteenth century, the iron industry was mainly based along the Eastern seaboard, in New England and Pennsylvania.

In the eighteenth century, immigrants brought trivets which were copied and sold in the New England colonies. Merchants imported many trivets which were regularly marketed as representative of the latest European styles.

Some early cast trivets were regional in design. The elongated heart design with a curling tail is associated with New England. Most trivets using this motif were made by blacksmiths. Cast pineapple design trivets also have been identified with New England, although the use of the pineapple as a symbol for hospitality was widespread in America. In the South, it was customary to have a Hospitality Board, which was a decorative table centerpiece carved in wood with a pineapple motif. It is said that when a guest came to breakfast and the hospitality board was missing from the table, the guest knew the welcome was over and it was time to leave.

Pennsylvania produced an even greater variety of trivet designs than New England. Before 1840, there was a heavy concentration of German immigrants moving into the rural areas of central and southeastern Pennsylvania. They included Germanic peoples from Alsace, Silesia, Moravia and the Palatinate of Switzerland. The immigrants settled together in communities, retained the old customs, perpetuated their native folk arts and preserved their language and heritage. To this day, in German-American communities, there are annual German festivals where crafts are exhibited and the old ways are celebrated.

The Germans were referred to as Pennsylvania Dutch. This is a misnomer.

Dutch immigrants did settle in Pennsylvania, and it may be that the term "Pennsylvania Dutch" was used indiscriminately because of language similarities, or simply "Deutsch" (which means "folk") was shortened to "Dutch" through common usage by outsiders. Whatever the basis for "Pennsylvania Dutch," the term is resented by many people of German descent who still live in that region.

Pennsylvania Germans produced an endless variety of folk designs including pottery, quilts, Fraktur, toleware, iron, tin, woodwork, samplers, wallpapers, tools, furniture, and trivets. The work may be identified by style or motif with this particular area of Pennsylvania.

The German population in Pennsylvania was divided between the church Deutsch and the plain Deutsch. The church Deutsch were likely to be Lutheran or German Reformed Lutheran and the plain Deutsch were often Mennonites. The church Deutsch tended to be lavish with decoration; the plain Deutsch were restrained in the use of decoration. All Pennsylvania folk art is strongly based in religious beliefs.

Mennonites are a religious group founded in the sixteenth century in Europe. It has been characteristic for the Mennonites to splinter into many different branches and often the segments differ in their views. The Mennonites (of Germanic extraction) and the various splinter groups, mainly the Amish, were concentrated in Pennsylvania. There were other settlements in various parts of the United States.

Some Mennonite groups were ultra conservative and rejected all outside influences, while others were more progressive. Their simple life styles were conducive to developing craftworks of exceptional quality which are highly prized by collectors. The people drew from their own cultural and religious traditions for their motifs, and they preserved older styles and symbols over a relatively long period of time. People within the conservative or fundamental groups tended to resist outside influences because of religious constraints and therefore their symbolism remained true to its origins.

Even though Pennsylvania folk art expressed religious ideas and beliefs, the symbols themselves had been drawn from various sources. Concepts and images came from Persia, India, Palestine and Nordic sources among others. The same symbols found both religious and secular application, but only those used in the religious context had allegorical meanings. The extensive use of symbols by the Mennonites was consistent with their belief in individual piety and humility where indulgence in self-expression was regarded as egotistical and contrary to their way of life. Consequently, their folk art was never representational; it was always used allegorically. Each image could be interpreted in different ways according to the context in which it was used. Symbols in conjunction with scriptures, verse, music or other written forms were common.

Evolution of the American eagle, 1776 to 1890.

Shakers (followers of Ann Lee, the English woman who founded the sect) also were found in Pennsylvania. Shakers were widely distributed throughout New England, New York, Pennsylvania, Kentucky, and neighboring hill country. Of all the Pennsylvania religious groups, the Shakers were the most austere in the use of decoration. Shakers are better known for their use of materials and simplicity of form than for surface decoration.

Trivets cast or fabricated by Pennsylvania Germans are characterized by the use of hearts, fylfots (the bulbous version), pin-wheels, tulips or lilies, doves, stars (six, eight and ten-pointed), flower shapes (geometric constructions formed by overlapping circles), bird of paradise, rod of Aaron, and sunbursts. Cast-iron trivets incorporated a wider variety of symbols with more detail than those fabricated by blacksmiths.

Chasing as decorative element on cast trivets.

Fraternal and trade designs.

Paley included a number of Scandinavian trivets in his collection. These were most likely brought here by immigrants. It is interesting that the designs differ from those found in England and central Europe. For the most part, the Scandinavian trivets in the Paley Collection are simple floral or geometric patterns with a plate finish. There were several references from other sources to trivets imported from the Netherlands, but there are no trivets specifically identified from that source.

A number of the American cast trivet designs incorporated surface decorations similar to those made by a blacksmith, such as chasing, recessed scrollwork, or other surface treatments easily made with a blacksmith's tools. Few trivets from England or France utilized these decorative effects.

The eclecticism of Victorian trivet design is well demonstrated by Rimby's *Twelve Hearts,* an early cast-iron piece. Most collectors today would identify this trivet as being Pennsylvania Dutch. The platform is formed by a border of twelve adjacent hearts. The heart came from Egypt. Inside the hearts is a ring with a five-pointed compass flower which came from a pattern book of geometric constructions. The ring at the end of the handle incorporates the bulbous swastika which is the Buddist symbol for the four winds of the earth. The shank of the handle is an English floral design based on thistles. The rim of the platform is decorated with chasing similar to that done by blacksmiths.

In summation, the single largest grouping of American trivet designs has come from the Pennsylvania region. It should be noted that origins for designs common to Europe came from diverse historic and exotic sources. Most trivet designs produced in this country came from Europe. The designs were commercially introduced into this country or brought in by settlers, and the decorative motifs and styles were repeated over a long period of time.

Lodges and Other Fraternal Organizations

In nineteenth century America there was considerable status connected to being a member of fraternal organizations such as lodges, guilds or secret societies. This was particularly true of the middle and working classes. These fraternities were created for mutual aid and social enjoyment. Aside from status, another incentive for membership was health insurance and retirement benefits. Fraternal organizations frequently provided medical and death benefits. Retirement homes, hospitals, and charities are still sponsored by fraternal organizations.

One way of letting membership be known to others was to display an emblem of the organization. A substantial number of trivets were designed with such emblems as the primary motif. The Masons, Odd Fellows, Knights of Columbus, Eastern Star, Sons of Cincinnatus, Foresters, and Daughters of Union Veterans are among these lodges and societies. See Plaque and Motto trivets as these were devoted almost exclusively to lodges and fraternal orders.

Sometimes trivets were based on trade guilds or professions. Firefighters, soldiers, blacksmiths, or other occupations occasionally had trivets designed.

Souvenir or Commemorative Trivets

A number of trivets were made as souvenirs of special places or to commemorate famous people or events. The George Washington brass trivet reputedly was made as a souvenir for the 1876 Grand Exposition in Philadelphia. President Adams also was commemorated by both a sad stand and a multi-purpose trivet. A group of souvenir trivets bearing the Triskelon motif was associated with the Isle of Man. The *Jenny Lind* trivet commemorated "The Swedish Nightingale's" tour across America in the mid-nineteenth century. *Lincoln Drape* marked the assassination of Abraham Lincoln. Ironically, few people today identify this trivet with Lincoln. Modern reproductions are often called *Tassel & Grain* by manufacturers or collectors. In the original design, the tassels symbolized death and the wheat stalk represented Illinois, an agricultural state at the time of Lincoln. The British practice was to strike trivets marking events connected with royalty such as coronations, births, deaths, anniversaries, and jubilees. In this century, Virginia Metalcrafters has issued special designs for *Man-O-War, Amtrack,* and numerous historic sites. These are either souvenirs or commemoratives.

Marketing and Trivet Design

Following the Civil War, commercial symbols began to replace older concepts of decoration, in particular, the religious motifs. Also, representational images (illustrations) became more prevalent in decoration. The commercial symbols are directly attributable to marketing practices which have continued to increase in recent times.

With the growth of industrialization and commercial competition, the design of trivets began to change. Ironing stands changed in design more than table stands or multi-purpose trivets. This was a result of commercial competition. In the post-Civil War period, trademarks, company names, monograms and illustrations became commonplace. There was greater use of letterforms as manufacturers began the practice of putting slogans, company names, or addresses on the face of trivets. At the same time, manufacturers began to issue iron stands for each size and model of iron compared to the earlier practice of producing stands which would accommodate any size or type of iron.

As the century progressed, there also was greater attention paid to cost and function in the production of ironing stands and the more expensive decorative treatments began to disappear. There were a number of stamped metal stands, with steel and aluminum substituted for cast-iron, but brass was rarely used. Many of the ironing stands produced in the twentieth century had little aesthetic value. When manufacturers of reproductions began to make castings in the 1930's, they only copied the older generic sad stands and rarely bothered with the commercial ones.

Impact of Technology on Trivet Design

The characteristics of iron, in particular, its brittleness and the ease with which it would break if dropped or struck created limitations on trivet designs. Some early trivet designs were particularly vulnerable to breakage, and founders redesigned some of the patterns to reduce this fragility. Two good examples are *Eagle & Heart* and *Urn & Fern*. Early versions of the eagle trivet separated the head of the eagle from the laurel leaves. By joining these elements, the casting was made stronger. The older versions of the urn trivet separated the leaves from the rear of the platform making them extremely fragile and susceptible to breaking. The later versions of this design joined the leaves with the rear of the platform to make a stronger casting.

Changes in production techniques used in the making of trivets affected the size, finish, detailing and legs of trivets. The earliest trivets usually were cast one at a time. Following the Civil War, gated patterns were frequently used and several trivets were cast at the same time. With the introduction of matchplate patterns around 1900, four, six, or more trivets were made at a time and castings were extremely smooth, thus reducing the finishing work. As technology improved, design did not change as much as the quality of casting.

Above: Commercial designs.

Below: Functional and cost effective designs.

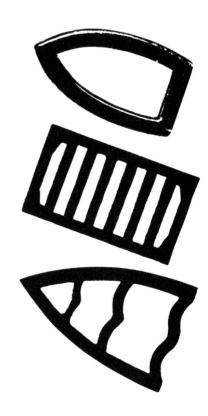

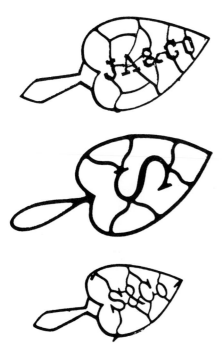

Examples of exceptionally light iron castings.

Three trivets using a laurel leaf rim.

In the latter part of the nineteenth century, founders had achieved a high degree of proficiency in casting iron. Trivet platforms were made very thin, one eighth of an inch or less, and detailing became extremely fine. Some iron trivets designed for this technology were delicate, lacy, and only weighed a few ounces. These castings look more like heavy wire constructions than cast-iron. They represented a *tour de force* in fine casting. Many of the round table stands with paw feet produced in this period revealed the same expertise in casting and finish. Never had casting been so delicate and the open-work so clean. Most of these table stands were traditional patterns but some new designs were even more refined. The finish on trivets produced in this period was smooth. Founders formerly used a finer sand for casting than is commonly used today. In many respects, the best quality cast trivets ever made date from 1870 to 1918.

Later, with all the improvements in casting, hand work began to disappear. The long legs of early trivets were too easily damaged by mechanical finishing devices and so legs became thicker and shorter. As the cost of iron, labor, and shipping went up, trivets generally became smaller. In this century, as trivet usage evolved from functional to decorative, some traditional designs were modified for hanging them on the wall. The more recent castings of *Grapes & Scrolls* illustrates this practice.

Handles, Rims and Interchangeable Parts

Another variation of traditional designs occurred when designers or founders combined elements of several older designs into a new one. The same handles, rims or symbols may be found in a variety of trivet designs which use different combinations of parts. While there were many different trivet handles, some distinct handle types were repeated in many designs. The handle called "pan" was a solid handle ending with a round, or geometric shape pierced for hanging the trivet on the wall. This same style may be seen in an illustration from *The Story of Housewares* showing bronze cooking utensils discovered in the excavations at Pompei. Another popular style was the "loop" handle, which in most instances was an extension, pinching at the rim and then swelling out into an open loop handle. If the open loop touched the rim and rolled out again, it was called a "scroll" handle. Handles with an open circle at the end and the sides of the handle either concave or convex were also common. It is not unusual to find trivets of the same platform design with different handles. On the trivet called *Cupids,* one version has the handle on one end and another has the handle at the opposite end. Scalloped, geometric and laurel leaf rims also found their way into many different designs. The laurel leaf rim of *Eagle & Heart* is the same one used for the *Odd Fellows* trivet.

A number of trivets made as advertising premiums were designed to accommodate an interchangeable center panel. The panel was a separate form that could be inserted into the pattern. The founder could use the same trivet design and change the advertising message. Many sad stands were designed for similar variations of message. The small lead letters were removed after casting and a new message was put onto the same pattern. There are examples of one trivet design with five to ten different typographic messages. A similar practice in making sad stands modified a basic design slightly for different production runs. The most common device added a perforation into the design, usually on the edge of the platform. There are sad stands which have one to nine holes along the edge marking different production runs of the same design.

Traditional Designs and Names

Because new patterns could be made from an existing trivet, American

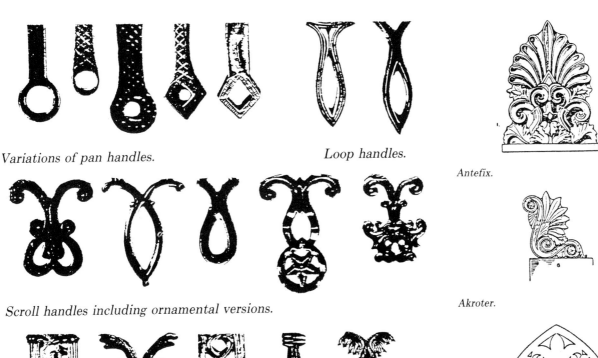

Variations of pan handles.   Loop handles.

Antefix.

Scroll handles including ornamental versions.

Akroter.

Examples of ornamental handles.

Pierced crest.

foundries were more likely to copy an existing trivet or combine elements from several designs than to create an original one. A founder could purchase a trivet, bring one from home, or borrow one from a neighbor to make a pattern. One important factor regarding the use of existing trivets is that the casting would be slightly smaller than the original because of shrinkage during the solidification process. The fact that any trivet could also be used as a pattern has contributed to certain designs being perpetuated for a hundred years or more with only slight variations.

The turtle design recently imported in large numbers from Taiwan illustrates this point. The origin of the turtle design was an early seventeenth century iron casting with a ceramic coating in France. While the design does vary from the Taiwanese reproduction, it is essentially the same design. *Grapes & Scrolls, Urn & Fern, Hex, Tulip* and other old designs are all traditional designs that have been reproduced over one hundred years with little change in the basic design.

Other founders were not content to merely perpetuate the traditional designs. Harry Haupt, an elderly blacksmith with a colorful personality is from Center Point, Pennsylvania. His home, which is also a museum and gift shop, is called *The Iron Master's House.* The museum is an outgrowth of his interest in the history of iron and iron utensils and his love of communicating this history to others. His interest in iron also includes trivets. He

Top: American casting of the turtle.

Below: Replica of early seventeenth-century turtle with a ceramic coating.

uses several foundries to do casting for him in connection with the giftshop. He also has designed a number of trivets. In an excerpt from a taped interview, Haupt recounts:

"Most of my trivets are made from an existing piece and include a story. I took this old Victorian cookie mold in the shape of a chicken and made a pattern from it and modified it to make a trivet. You see, I would have three legs on a cookie which in iron is a trivet, and that is how I was able to produce a chicken trivet."

"Now, some of my other trivets that I have were made from an antique carving or wood thing which I bought. Like this turkey I took from a door panel. It was a wood carving on a door and it is a nice wild turkey. So I took that and simplified it and planed it down thin enough, and put three feet on it. Now I have a turkey trivet. This is the way I made my trivets."

All line illustrations from Handbook of Ornament; a grammar of art; industrial and architectural designing in all its branches for practical as well as theoretical use. *Franz Sales Meyer, New York, Paris and Berlin, 1910.*

Dessin Lineaire *and* Handbook of Ornament *photographs and Xerox copies from Hagley Museum and Library, Wilmington, Delaware.*

VI. DATING THE TRIVET

To date a trivet with no markings is at best to make an educated guess. Hankenson expressed the opinion that, "On old trivets, the finish is usually very worn; dirt and corrosion will be embedded in the corners of the pattern." He further suggested, "Look for wear on the feet and on all points that touch when placed on a flat surface." Dealers and collectors state that old iron is much darker in color than iron cast in this century; some believe that "fins" or "flashings" on trivets are indications of age. Other plausible opinions are based on designs, length of legs, thickness of castings, or similar criteria. Some of these criteria are based on fact, but others are entirely circumstantial; none is completely reliable by itself.

Foundrymen concur it is nearly impossible to tell how old a trivet is by the color of iron or the casting, because these factors depend entirely on technology and practices which varied from foundry to foundry.

Trivets may be signed by an individual or company, they may be initialed, dated, bear a trademark, or only show a stock number. Most trivets will have no markings at all. Unless it is signed, dated or otherwise authenticated, dating the trivet is exceedingly difficult. There are clues that may point to an approximate date of manufacture for a particular trivet, but these clues are not infallible. A company engaging in substantial production of trivets or stands may have employed processes different from those of a smaller plant doing a limited production of the same item.

Signed Trivets

The most reliable means for dating or identifying a trivet is by a documented signature or company name. Rimby in the 1840's and Harner in the 1940's signed and dated their trivets. This practice was not generally followed. There may be either a date or a signature, but rarely both. Company names, trademarks, or stock numbers were commonly placed on the trivet reverse. The years that a company was in business usually can be verified, and the trivet can be dated within that time span. If stock numbers or trademarks can be definitely traced to a company, the same time span method for dating can be used.

Another form of signing is a patent number, "Patent Pending" or "Patent Applied For" with a date. Trivets and stands with a patent number can be traced through the Patent Office in Washington, D.C., and for a small fee, a copy of the patent papers can be obtained. Trivets marked "Registered No." are English. English designers appear to have created more new designs than Americans. This is demonstrated by the number of English trivets which have Registered Numbers compared to the number of American trivets which are Patented. This suggests that designs were better protected under English law than American patents.

Casting and Finishing

There are qualities to old iron which are distinctive but difficult to describe. Examine some iron that has been authenticated as being old. This provides a basis for recognizing the special qualities of old iron as compared to the reduced scrap-iron used today.

Darkness in iron also may be the result of oxidization. Old iron that has naturally aged develops a black powder coating of oxidized iron. This kind of surface erosion is called ferric oxide. Unfortunately, ferric oxide corrosion can be induced under specific conditions, and it is conceivable that an unscrupulous person could artificially create this dark coloration. The more common form of oxidization causes a ferrous oxide coating which is bright orange and indicates a recent rusting of the iron.

Sprue-mark. Photograph by Craig Smith.

Wedge-mark. Photograph by Craig Smith.

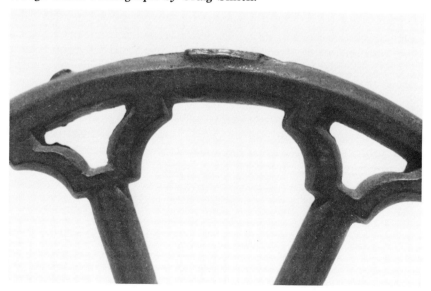

Gate-mark.

Finning; an irregular, thin, extrusion of iron from the mold at the parting-line where drag and cope met. Caused by a shifting of the pattern during tamping; characteristic of a loose pattern casting.

Iron smelting and foundry practices radically changed between 1840 and 1900. Knowledge of the changes in the casting process can approximately reveal how and when a trivet was cast. Many early kitchen trivets and sad stands were quite large, weighing two pounds or more. These heavy iron trivets and stands frequently have a cast-mark on the reverse.

A cast-mark may be either round or rectangular, depending on whether a sprue or wedge was used to make the downspout. The cast-mark is the result of breaking off the downspout after the metal solidified. Most sprue-marks are about five-sixteenths to one-half inch in diameter. A wedge-mark is about one-eighth inch in width; the length varies from three-quarters to one inch or more in length. The amount of iron poured dictated the size of the cast-mark, so that a large and heavy trivet has a more pronounced cast-mark. A cast-mark indicates that the trivet was made as a single loose pattern casting using the flat-back or follow-board process. Such a casting probably predates 1865.

Trivets poured through the rim had characteristic gate-marks. Most of the time there would be at least two, but there sometimes were as many as seven gate-marks. As described in the section on trivet casting and finishing, molders worked on a piece-work basis and were paid according to the number of acceptable castings they could produce in one day. Consequently, they made little effort to remove the gates and only filed down the rough edges. Trivets having pronounced gate-marks, with only the sharp edges filed, probably predate 1890.

It is extremely rare to find cast-marks on either brass or bronze trivets and stands. With these metals, the downspout or gate was cut rather than broken off; and since the metals are much softer than iron, it was easier to remove all traces of the gate.

In casting trivets or stands that had a great deal of openwork or very thin channels, it was necessary to quickly get the molten iron into the design so it would not solidify in the smaller parts of the mold before the entire mold was filled.

Bracket device for attaching trivets to a cross-bar. Photograph by Craig Smith.

The pouring temperature of molten metal was a factor. Prior to the Civil War, most founders could not pour at the high temperatures that were possible later. When pouring an open-work design, they usually used a sprue because it would permit a more rapid flow into the mold, and they would pour directly into the reverse of the trivet mold.

After the Civil War, improved technologies made higher pouring temperatures possible so molders could pour two or four molds at the same time through gates on the rims. Round table stands, which Hankenson identified as "Lantz," are representative of these open-work designs. Lantz trivets with cast-marks on the reverse are older trivets than those with cast-marks on the rim.

Most sad stands, except the large ones, were cast in multiples of two or more. Gated-patterns were first used for multiple casting and matchplates were used later. Sad stands made from gated-pattern molds normally showed prominent gate-marks. Patterns with elaborate open-work required two or more gates to insure a complete casting of the design. If the gate-marks appear only on the side of the stand, the casting was probably done in multiples of two; if the gate-marks are at the rear and side of the stand, the casting was probably done in multiples of four.

Another characteristic of flat-back, follow-board or gated-pattern casting is the tendency for castings to have fins. This resulted from the cope and drag molds shifting as the cope was being rammed. Flashings are rare with matchplate patterns, which came into general use around the turn of the century. Therefore, trivets with fins most likely predate 1900.

Typical filing serrations.

Characteristic machine grinding grooves. Photographs by Craig Smith.

Until late in the nineteenth century, all grinding wheels were made of natural stone. In the 1860's, potters began trying to make synthetic grinding wheels. Bonding emery grains with lacquer, glue, or cement was tried, but the experiment was unsuccessful.

Swen Pulson, a Swedish journeyman potter, was one of the men searching for an effective grinding wheel. He worked in Worchester, Massachusetts for a small pottery owned by Frank Norton and Frederick Hancock. The company produced household crocks and jugs; also it was doing some development work on grinding wheels. Swen Pulson had an idea for a grinding wheel of emery bonded with clay and fired in a kiln. After many attempts, he finally found a way to make emery wheels. His invention revolutionized the metal-working industry by replacing metal-cutting with precision-grinding.

In 1885, the Norton Emery Wheel Company was formed, and in 1887, the first factory was built. The use of Norton grinding wheels rapidly spread throughout the metal and glass industries. The adoption of precision grinding wheels throughout the industry was almost total within five years. For the first time, it was an easy matter to economically and quickly remove iron gates or flashings. Soon the finishing operations became separate from the work of the molder.

As a consequence of new technologies and division of labor, trivets and stands no longer retained the characteristic gate-marks. The grinding wheel leaves a distinctive pattern of deep parallel grooves, either vertical or slightly diagonal. File marks usually were at several angles and not as pronounced as the serrations made by a grinding wheel. Trivets and stands with machine ground grooves postdate 1890. Trivets with file marks are older.

As mentioned in the section on casting, molders using the flat-back process punched the feet into the cope mold. This method was practical when only three supports were used. Although the procedure was imprecise, three legs of uneven length could steadily stand on a flat surface. Punched in supports often resulted in legs which were not symmetrically placed, and had a slight variance in size, diameter or length. Also, the casting of the legs might not be clean, especially at the juncture of the leg with the reverse of the platform. This process of making legs is an older method, and it is doubtful that it was much used after the development of matchplate patterns. An exception would be a foundry making a limited number of castings using an existing trivet as a pattern.

Following the Civil War, founders made some of the finest trivets ever produced. The trivets and stands had extremely thin platforms and delicate open-work. The castings demonstrated fine detailing and a number of patterns were precisely back-coped. Some beautiful round stands with paw feet were made in this period. There were castings which had channels scarcely larger than a heavy wire. Most castings were smooth, suggesting that a finer sand was used than is used today. This era of fine casting took place between 1870 and 1918.

In multiple castings, many founders used a code to identify each mold. If defective castings were repeatedly produced, the molder would know which pattern to check. Sometimes the code was numerical; other times it was a number of small round depressions or dimples on the trivet reverse. This practice is of fairly recent origin; the presence of codes would suggest a recent casting.

Supports

There are some old trivets and stands cast without legs. The supports were riveted or screwed into the platform in a separate operation. These generally predate 1850. A few trivets have the two rear legs cast, and a front leg riveted to the platform.

Many brass and copper multi-purpose trivets from the eighteenth and nineteenth centuries were made with shaped supports riveted to the platform. These supports were either separately tooled or cast. On cast-iron stands with riveted supports, the legs were untapered, but they might end in ball or round-headed feet. Riveted or screwed on supports, tooled or shaped legs, or attached ornamental feet are suggestive of an old trivet predating the Civil War.

While legs an inch or more long are associated with older castings, shorter ones are not proof of a recent casting. Many old stands were designed with short feet, one half-inch or less. The function of the stand tended to dictate the length of the supports.

It is reasonable to assume that any trivet or stand platform an inch and one-half above the surface is old. Trivets and stands were made with legs in excess of one inch until at least the 1920's. During the early years of trivet-making, finishing was a hand operation. Due to mechanization of the finishing process in the 1930's and 1940's, the majority of newer reproduc-

Styles of ornamental pre-made supports which were screwed into or riveted to hand fabricated brass and copper trivets.

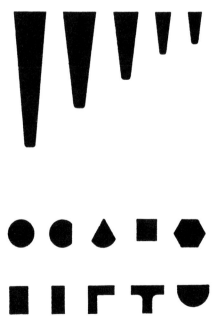

Sample leg tapers and cross-sections.

Two William Rimby designs reproduced in brass as well as iron by Wilton Products.

The Wilton Products eagle trivets which were not shown in the company catalogue.

tions have round, stubby feet from one-half to seven-eighths of an inch in length. The older designs with long, thin, tapered legs were too vulnerable to breakage by modern mechanical devices used in the finishing process.

Almost as important as the length of legs is their shape. On older castings, the legs or feet have distinctive shapes or cross-sections (shape of the support when cut at a right angle to its length — the diameter). Older trivets have legs which are beautifully tapered and somewhat smaller in diameter than those made today. Tapering may be found on short supports as well as long ones.

Half or quarter-round, square, and T-shape leg cross-sections date from earlier periods. The majority of reproductions made since the 1930's tend to have round supports without distinctive shape or cross-sections. Trivets with shaped legs or unusual cross-sections probably date from 1840 to 1890.

There are a few trivet designs, mainly iron rests, which were cast with a single leg located on the bottom of the platform. This single leg was designed to fit into a bracket that could be clamped to an ironing board or counter top. These same designs were usually made with the conventional three or four supports. Both the Paley and Ellwood collections have some trivets which have thirty to sixty or more supports. The bottom of the trivets look like coarse curry-combs. The design and casting of these trivets suggest that they are extremely old. The function of the numerous supports is not clear.

Size

Larger trivets, with designs that have been repeated over more than seventy-five years usually are older. In most instances, longer legs go with larger platform sizes. Particularly in the category of kitchen trivets, size changes have occurred as different founders repeated the design and modified the pattern. *Dutch Tulip, Grapes & Scrolls, Lincoln Drape,* and *Urn & Fern,* are examples of trivet designs where size has varied over time with different founders. A brass version of *Grapes & Scrolls* in the author's possession, dating from circa 1840, measures $8\frac{1}{2}$ x $4\frac{7}{8}$ x $1\frac{3}{8}$ inches and weighs one and one half pounds; a modern reproduction of this design is approximately $7\frac{1}{4}$ x $4\frac{1}{4}$ x $\frac{7}{8}$ inches and weighs slightly less than one pound. Size variation applies to a number of designs. In each case, the larger size usually is an older casting.

Two exceptions are a group of designs distributed by Wilton in the 1950's. The large size trivets were selling so well that Wilton selected several designs and made them larger. These enlarged designs were *Rings, Eagle & Heart,* and *Family Tree.* Other exceptions are a few designs made as reproductions of some early large trivets. Two popular designs were Rimby's *Twelve Hearts* and *Many Tulips.* These both have handles with platforms measuring approximately seven inches in diameter. Wilton and Harner made these reproductions, and Wright made *Twelve Hearts* without a handle. *Twelve Hearts* was called *Hex* by Wilton. Harner made two versions of *Twelve Hearts,* each with a different handle. One handle was the same as used by Wright and Wilton and the other was the same as found on *Roosters.*

Roosters, which is about the same size as other large trivet reproductions, was a design produced by Wilton (cast by Unicast) and Wright. It is unusual because there were two separate castings with the roosters facing opposite directions. The legs are extremely short on these trivets, and it is obvious that they were made for sale as a decorative pair to hang on the wall. Henry Wilton states that he commissioned the *Roosters* design sometime during the fifties (at the same time as the two previously mentioned eagle designs). An employee of the John Wright Company expressed the view that Ed Musser created the *Roosters* design. It is almost certain that if either Wilton or Wright actually commissioned this design, they would not have permitted the other company to produce and market it. *Roosters* appears to be an authentic German design, although it is not Amish because it is representational. Some *Roosters* trivets are marked "Bird" on the reverse. Bird was a principal distributor of Wilton products.

Harner made two other large trivets which were not reproduced by any other company. One had a short square loop handle, and the other had six small hearts inside a round frame with three on either side leaving the center open. This was designed to have interchangeable panels used in the open space in the center of the platform. The handle was the same as used on *Roosters.*

In the 1950's, Wilton produced *Hex* and *Twelve Hearts* in brass, and these are exceptional castings. Virginia Metalcrafters marketed two oversized versions of *Tulip* and *Family Tree;* the latter was discontinued in the 1950's. Additionally, there were a few unidentified brass castings of older designs, but they were not produced in large numbers or by commercial foundries. The quality of these brass castings is crude, and it is obvious that they were done by an amateur. In particular, there were copies of Manley's *Braid & Star,* done in brass and in iron, which do not favorably compare with the original casting.

Rooster trivet reproduced by Wilton, Wright and Harner.

Period Style

Style does not indicate when a trivet was cast, but it may reveal approximately when a particular design was first made. It is helpful to be able to recognize styles characteristic of the eighteenth and nineteenth centuries, especially furniture styles. For instance, the paw feet on English round stands are characteristic of furniture from the English Regency period. Period furniture styles such as Chippendale, Eastlake and Stuart found interpretation in trivet ornamentation. Familiarity with characteristic motifs from the Georgian, Regency, and Victorian periods proves useful in the identification of designs or motifs.

Handles

Wooden or amber glass handles were commonly used on European fireplace trivets in the eighteenth and nineteenth centuries. With the advent of cast trivets, the English continued to use wooden handles for some multipurpose trivets and iron rests. In America, a few manufacturers offered optional wooden or metal handles with the former usually costing a little more. By 1900, making wooden handles had gone out of style. With few exceptions, any trivet or stand with a wooden handle generally predates 1920.

Inscriptions

Some trivets have markings on the back such as company names or stock numbers; a few trivets have inscriptions on the face.

Until the 1930's, a great variety of letterforms, styles and sizes were used. Large letters or numbers, serifed letters, and stylistic letterstyles may provide clues as to when a trivet was designed. Since the 1940's, any letters or numerals on the reverse of a trivet have been stamped in a standard Condensed Gothic capital. During World War II, the government required foundries to use a standardized marking for castings, and this accounts for the uniformity. A Condensed Gothic (without serifs) in a range of sizes became the standard alphabet used to identify castings.

Rimby trivets are initialed and dated using an incised, Openface Roman capital which was very popular in the 1840's. An older brass casting of *Grapes & Scrolls* is signed *Brenier* on the reverse. The letterforms are large,

Solid face and open face Romans, typically used around 1840.

Roman and Sharp Gothic letters used to keep track of castings and patterns, and for advertising. The manufacturer recommended Roman as being best for embossed, or raised, letters in advertising. Sharp Gothic was regarded as being most suitable for making depressed letters on dies.

A B C D E F G H

I J K L M N O P

Q R S T U V W

X Y Z &

$ 1 2 3 4 5

6 7 8 9 0

Condensed Gothic letters are now the standard typeface for marking iron castings.

A B C D E F G

H I J K L M N

O P Q R S T

U V W X Y Z

1 2 3 4 5 6

7 8 9 0 $

Light Egyptian letters were occasionally used between the late nineteenth century and World War II.

Solidface Roman capitals similar to those used by Rimby. This casting probably dates from the same general period as Rimby. Nineteenth century typefaces were more diverse and ornamental than those used in this century. Period styles of lettering, such as Art Nouveau, were likely to appear in a legend on the face of the trivet. If initials were part of the design, they generally reflected the styles of the day. Between 1870 and 1918, monograms, ligatures and initials were popular and the styles were characteristic of the period.

Raised or embossed lettering on the trivet reverse may be a clue to the age of the trivet. Wooden master patterns might have small lead letters attached to show the stock number or company name. More commonly, lettering or numerals were stamped into a thin metal strip that was attached to the wooden pattern with small brads. The strip and brads are clearly revealed in the casting, and this procedure suggests an older trivet or stand.

Marking the trivet or stand was somewhat different in the production of commercial sad stands. This is especially true in the period when sadiron manufacturers were highly competitive and most stands carried advertising. Foundries often had blank patterns that they could customize by changing brand or model names, slogans, or addresses.

Most of these tiny lead letters were supplied by one small firm in Hoosick Falls, New York. These letters were made from an alloy of lead and tin. The sides of the letters were given generous draft to allow them to leave the mold cleanly. The least satisfactory means for attaching these small letters was beeswax, but it was used for short production runs. On iron patterns, most letters were attached by soldering or sweating.

Sweating was done by carefully cleaning the area where letters were to be placed, and then tinning the area. The letters were placed in position and heated either with a soldering point or blowpipe. The heat melted the tinned surface adhering the letters as it cooled.

Occasionally some of the lead letters would drop off or become askew. It is not unusual to find three to seven castings of the same pattern with different lettering. If one of the variations carries a date, or company name, it is a key to the period when all the designs were produced.

There also were small brass letters with or without pins on the back. Brass letters with pins could be driven into wooden patterns; those without pins were soldered or sweated to metal patterns or glued to wooden patterns. Roman letters were judged to be best for advertising because tops of the letters were bolder. Sharp Gothic letters were regarded as best for marking patterns.

The Hopewell trivet, manufactured by Unicast in 1969 (pattern made in 1963), is a rare example of a modern reproduction using a raised panel and embossed letters on the reverse. For a few years, Virgina Metalcrafters used an embossed trade-mark, but they have changed to an incised version.

Old castings never identified the name of the trivet design on the reverse; only modern reproductions have adopted this practice.

After World War II, some manufacturers, including Griswold, began to market their stands with rubber caps on the feet to guard against marring counter tops or table surfaces. Somewhat later, manufacturers used plastic caps. In either instance, trivets with caps on the feet postdate World War II.

Other Sources for Dating

Little was published about trivets and stands, even during the period when they were being mass produced. Trivets were a relatively minor item in merchandizing and were scarcely advertised or noted. Trade catalogues from the nineteenth century seldom show more than two to six styles. Trade catalogues from the middle of the century only list trivets and, unfortunately, provide no illustrations. Often trivets were listed in a section following the illustrated pages under a heading "other products produced by."

1865 to 1920 is the major period in which trade catalogues were published. Many of the catalogues have been lost or have disintegrated. The cheap paper they were printed on was not completely deacidified so publications have turned brown, become brittle, and fallen apart. However, scattered around the country preserved in libraries, there are still a substantial number of catalogues available for study.

The Hagley and Winterthur libraries on the Dupont estates in Wilmington, Delaware, are exemplary. *A Guide to American Trade Catalogs 1744-1900* by Lawrence B. Romaine (published by R.R. Bowker Company, 1960) is an excellent guide to the location of institutions holding trade catalogues. Fortunately, many of the old trade catalogues have been transcribed to micro-film or micro-fische. In searching trade catalogue files, trivets are seldom found under that heading. Suggested headings under which trivets may be found are:

Foundries (brass and iron)	*Tinware*	*Laundry Supplies*
Hardware	*Stamping*	*Housewares*
Irons/ironing	*Utensils*	*Implements*
Novelties	*Stands*	*Stoves*
Mail Order Catalogues	*Kitchen*	*Wire Utensils*

The major companies manufacturing trivet reproductions since the 1930's and 1940's, namely Wilton, Virginia Metalcrafters and Wright, do not have complete production records regarding designs marketed between 1940 and 1985.

A number of museums, particularly those dealing with Americana, have trivets and stands as part of their collections. Museums with Early American Colonial displays are generally more interested in trivets and stands handcrafted by blacksmiths, but they may have some early cast-iron pieces. Museum staff members may have researched, or documented, the origin of their own trivets. Trivets are seldom the subject of an exhibit, but they may be included in a display such as a period kitchen or parlour.

A few years ago, I spent a very pleasant morning in shop-talk with a group of antique dealers in the Wexford General Store Antiques near Pittsburgh, Pennsylvania. We were discussing how to establish the age of a trivet through observation. We went through all the usual criteria of wear, dirt, corrosion, size, iron quality, etc., but we could not come up with any hard and fast criteria upon which we all could agree. The husband of one of the ladies present had been my chief source for trivets over a period of several years; and in my estimation, he always had the best trivets of any dealer in the area. I asked Mrs. Ott, "How does Hank pick the trivets he buys?" To paraphrase her reply, she said: "When Hank is going through a flea-market and sees an interesting trivet, he walks over and looks at it. He picks it up and examines it carefully, then he looks up at the sky and hefts the trivet several times. He then either puts the trivet back on the table or reaches for his pocketbook."

When everything else fails, intuition is the last and best resort.

Checklist of Clues for Dating a Trivet

This checklist precludes those designs which are signed, dated, patented or otherwise identified. These clues are based on physical properties that

PRICE LIST
and
ILLUSTRATED CATALOGUE
OF

HARDWARE

MANUFACTURED BY
THE

Reading Hardware Company,
READING, PA.
U.S.A.

W.M. M. GRISCOM.   MATTHAN HARBSTER.   W.M. HARBSTER.

PRINCIPAL OFFICE AT READING, PA.

WAREHOUSES.
NEW YORK CITY—81 Reade Street.   PHILADELPHIA—814 Commerce Street.

1885.

HALL & CARPENTER.

◁CATALOGUE▷
OF

TINSMITHS'

Tools and Machines

❖DEEP STAMPED WARE❖

COMMON STAMPED WARE, JAPANNED WARE
AND

MISCELLANEOUS GOODS.

PHILADELPHIA,
1866.

Title pages from two nineteenth-century trade catalogues.

can be observed. None of these conditions are absolutely definitive in themselves. There are too many variables connected with foundry practices to make an unconditional judgement regarding age.

1. ***Quality of iron or oxidization***. Old iron tended to be darker because of impurities and carbon. Old iron was usually made from ore and it had different properties than reduced scrap iron that is commonly used today. Trivets or stands which have naturally aged may be coated with a black powder, especially in the crevices. Any bright orange rust is of recent origin.

2. ***Cast-marks***. Sprue- or wedge-marks on the reverse of the trivet indicate that the piece was individually cast and probably predates the Civil War.

3. ***Gate-marks***. These are found on the platform rim. No attempt to remove the gate-marks other than to file the rough edges indicates the casting was made from a loose, or gated-pattern, and predates 1895.

4. ***Machine grinding***. Trivets may show evidence that gate-marks were removed with a grinding wheel. Deep, parallel grooves, which are slightly diagonal or vertical, indicate a casting made after 1895.

5. ***Fins***. Excess metal flashings are quite typical of loose or gated-patterns that preceded the use of matchplates. However, foundries making a limited number of castings might have used this older method because matchplate patterns were relatively expensive. With few exceptions, finning is most common on trivets before 1900.

6. ***Punched supports***. In a punched configuration there are three supports; they may differ in diameter, shape or length, and they may not be symmetrically placed. Often there will be a crumbling of the mold at the juncture of the support with the platform creating a rough cast of the leg or foot. This procedure was associated with flat-back casting and used for limited productions predating 1920.

7. ***Thin and delicate castings***. A trivet platform may be exceedingly thin, one eighth of an inch or less; or have delicate, lacy openwork, elaborate backcoping and a fine finish. These castings date from 1870 to 1918.

8. ***Attached legs***. Supports may be riveted or screwed into the platform. Legs may be ornamental or tooled. Most of these trivets will predate 1850.

9. ***Number of legs***. On those designs repeated by different manufacturers over a long period of time, versions with three legs will usually be older than those with four. However, some of the oldest designs were made with either three or four legs, i.e., Rimby's *Many Tulips* design.

10. ***Length of legs***. Trivets or stands with a platform height of one and one-half inches or more generally predate 1880; a platform height of one and one-quarter inches was common until circa 1920. There are modern reproductions of this height, mainly *Tulip* and *1829* made by Virginia Metalcrafters.

11. ***Shape and cross-section of the legs***. Legs or feet which are tapered, and somewhat smaller in diameter (as compared to reproductions) are associated with older castings. If the cross-sections are square or rectangular, T-shape, half-round or quarter-round, they are typical of castings from around 1865 to 1895.

12. *Size*. Of trivet designs which have been produced by many manufacturers over long periods of time, the larger sizes will be older. Longer legs generally go with larger platforms. Also, the large, handled trivets weighing two and three pounds are older, especially those with cast-marks.

In the case of designs which have been copied over a long period of time, the larger sizes with long legs probably predate 1920. Large trivets and stands with cast-marks on the reverse predate 1865.

13. *Styles*. Familiarity with period styles may provide a reasonable clue to the approximate time a design originated. Of equal importance is knowledge of styles by country and period. Most libraries have books on furniture styles and these can be useful references.

14. *Handles.* Many handcrafted trivets from the seventeenth and eighteenth centuries had wooden or glass handles and the practice was applied to cast trivets. The English used wooden handles on a number of designs in the nineteenth century as did a few American manufacturers. In many cases it was optional, and for slightly more money a customer could order the model with a wooden handle. It is doubtful that many trivets were made with wooden handles after the 1920's. Therefore, trivets or stands with wood handles generally are older. Glass handles were often used on elegant, handcrafted brass fireplace accessories, dating from the eighteenth and early nineteenth centuries.

15. *Inscriptions*. Gothic Condensed capitals are indicative of castings after 1940. Larger letterforms, serifed, or stylistic letters suggest older castings — between 1875 and 1920. Large, Open-Face Roman letters are typical of styles before 1865. Embossed letters, or a punched tape with brads showing where it was attached to a wooden pattern, are usually, but not always, an indication of an older casting.

16. *Finish*. Between 1880 and 1920, many manufacturers advertised their trivets and stands as being available in either brass or iron; or in a variety of finishes such as copper, nickel, brass, bronze, japanned, or painted. Many collectors finding trivets with the remains of a plated finish tend to dismiss them as being modern, when in truth they actually may be quite old.

17. *Bronze*. A number of trivets were cast in bronze between 1850 and 1900. It is doubtful that many bronze trivets were cast in this century.

18. *Wear*. The bottom of the feet, and especially the surface of the platform, may show wear suggestive of aging. On the older brass and bronze trivets, the longer legs may be bent and the platforms warped. Wear on the face of the platform may be more relevant than wear on the bottom of the feet.

19. *Design*. Designs which have been repeated over long periods of time may have variations. *Grapes & Scrolls* with a hanging hole is a recent casting. The older version of *Eagle & Heart* has a substantial gap between the top of the eagle's head and the laurel leaves. The newer castings have the eagle's head joined to the laurel leaves. It is important to study the older designs and compare them with reproductions as a means of identifying design variations.

To summarize, signatures, dates, patent markings, cast-marks, length and shape of legs, machine grinding, and size are perhaps the most reliable clues to dating the trivet.

Cross-Sections

A   B   C   D   E   F   G   H   I   J   K   L   M   N   O

Leg and Feet Shapes

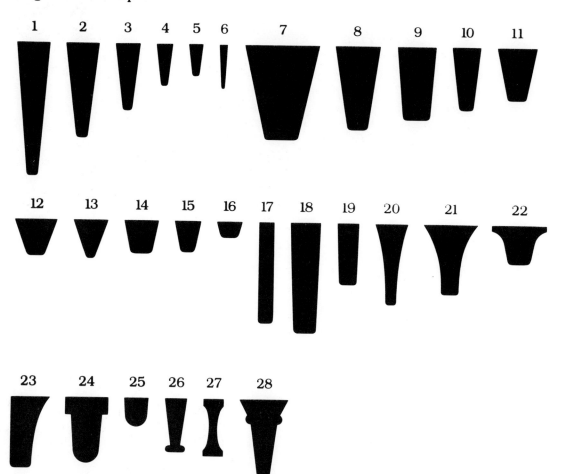

1   2   3   4   5   6   7   8   9   10   11

12   13   14   15   16   17   18   19   20   21   22

23   24   25   26   27   28

Cleat Shapes

C-1   C-2   C-3   C-4   C-5   C-6   C-7   C-8   C-9   C-10

Trivet feet and leg chart. This means for describing trivet supports is not precise, but it provides a reasonable approximation of shapes and cross-sections.

VII. CATALOGUE AND CATEGORY DESCRIPTIONS

Trivet designs can be divided into categories for purposes of classification. In this book classifications are made for easy reference and for organization of information. However, the distinctions that delineate trivet groupings may seem arbitrary. This is particularly true when applied to the criteria separating sad stands, kitchen trivets, and table stands. Trivets and stands from different categories were often used interchangeably, and many were designed to be used that way. Separating American and European designs was equally difficult and sometimes it was an arbitrary decision.

Measurements

In all instances length precedes width.

All measurements are in inches.

Measurements on trivets and stands are from the surface on which they sit to the top of the platform and do not include the rails, guides or posts. Linear measurements are given to only one sixteenth of an inch.

On all round stands (those without handles), the measurement is for the platform. Round stands with splayed supports do not include the support in the measurement, unless otherwise indicated. Trivets and stands from the same production run might vary as much as one-eighth inch in size or several ounces in weight.

Support Placement

F front **R** rear **S** sides, refers to placement and number of supports.

Catalogue Key

The letter prefix preceding the number indicates the collection; the number is the collection catalogue number, and the third alphabetical code indicates the category.

P	Paley Collection, Shelburne Museum, Shelburne, Vermont.
E	James Ellwood Collection, Scottsdale, Arizona.
M	Dale Collection, Metropolitan Museum of Art, New York City.
K	Rob Roy Kelly Collection, Tempe, Arizona.
D	Susan DeCordova Collection, Norwich, New York.
W	Wilton Manufacturing Company, Wrightsville, Pennsylvania.
CW	Carol Walker Collection, Waelder, Texas.

Category Codes:

HC	hand crafted	**MIS**	manufacturer's iron stand
KS	kitchen stand	**ST**	stove trivet
IR	iron rest	**PT**	plaque trivet
NEP	New England Pennsylvania	**M**	miniature trivet
MPS	multi-purpose stand	**ETS**	enameled table stand
TCT	tea, coffee, or table stand	**TS**	tile stand
DIS	decorative iron stand	**DBC**	decorative brass or copper

Scarcity Guide

VR very rare, **R** rare, **O** occasional, **C** common, **VC** very common.

Guide refers to castings pictured in the catalogue and not to the design.

It is difficult to know how rare some European trivets are since they may be scarce in America but abundant in Europe. Ratings are established on the basis of what may be found in this country.

*Blacksmith at work in the smithy around the turn of the century.
Photograph furnished by Shelburne Museum.*

Handwrought Trivets and Stands

This category can be more clearly defined because it includes only trivets and stands that were made by hand. Some hearth stands were cast in the nineteenth century, but the majority of hearth trivets were fabricated by blacksmiths. They were made as long as hearths were used in the preparation of food.

Blacksmiths were indispensible to the early settlements of this country. A community improved its chances for survival if it could boast a smithy. The blacksmith made nails, tools, implements, equipment and did repairs in addition to a multitude of other tasks and services. Along with development of the iron industry in America during the eighteenth century, there was an increase in the number of bloomery mills and forges that provided wrought iron for smiths.

A quantity of manufactured iron goods was imported into this country, especially from Bristol and London. Surviving manifests of imports from England to America reveal that trivets were not recorded as a regularly exported item. By the time of the Revolutionary War, large numbers of colonial forges and smithies were established, greatly reducing dependency on Europe for manufactured ironware. Little of the iron in this country was exported back to Europe; most of it was distributed within the colonies.

Many families emigrating to America brought ironware, including trivets. The trivets and decorative motifs served as models for American craftsmen. It is difficult to separate the early ironware that was imported from that which was made here unless it has a verifiable stamp.

In rural areas, blacksmiths were "jacks of all trades," making utensils and tools, shoeing horses and mules, sharpening edged-tools, and doing various wrought iron work as needed. Many farmers had an anvil and small forge in a farm shed or barn. On occasion, a farmer could make his own simple utensils; even though crude, they served the purpose.

Blacksmiths did not require a great deal of workspace; most worked out of relatively small buildings. The focus of the shop was the forge, which had a hood connected to the chimney, and an anvil nearby. A large leather bellows was aimed at the forge; there were adjacent workbenches and cooling tubs with an assortment of tools such as sledges, hammers, shears, drills, ball-peens, dies, pliers, tongs, etc. The floor was usually dirt or stone and cluttered with work to be done, finished work and scraps. More work, tools, or pieces for sale hung on the walls and rafters. For unknown reasons, most smithies tended to be poorly lighted. The interiors were covered with soot and coal dust and smelled smokey. No wonder they were called "black" smith shops!

Blacksmiths usually had one or two apprentices, as this was the traditional avenue for entering the profession. In the period around 1800, apprentices were expected to serve for about seven years. By the middle of the century, the apprentice system was less rigid and most apprentices served for two to four years. In America, a person could become an apprentice in two ways; one was voluntary, with parental consent; the other was compulsory, as bastards and orphans were required by law to apprentice in a trade. A youngster normally would perform his service between ten and sixteen years of age.

Each blacksmith specialized according to his own interests and abilities, but records show that most were capable of fashioning just about anything. Some concentrated on specific kinds of work and advertised themselves as sicklesmiths, scythesmiths, nailsmiths, stovesmiths, hingesmiths, coachsmiths, spoonsmiths, or other specialties. One group, called whitesmiths, worked in steel, doing fine work such as guns, locks, doctor and dental tools

Hand-forged trivet from the Rob Roy Kelly collection.

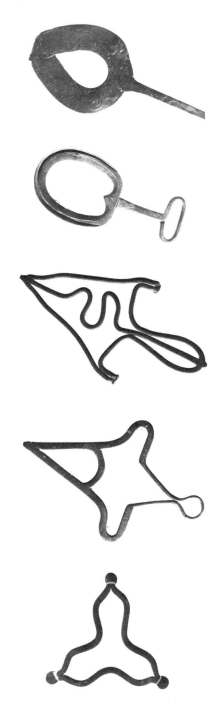

Hand-forged trivets from the Ellwood collection.

Kitchen hearth with many utensils used in preparation of food. Photograph furnished by Shelburne Museum.

Hand-forged trivets from the Ellwood collection.

and other utensils. This was precision work which required great skill and careful filing and polishing. There were some smiths who specialized in household ironmongery. They made skimmers, ladles, spatulas, tasters, crimpers, cutlery of all kinds, lamps, lanterns, skewers, pot hooks, trammels, dippers, dough scrapers, quilt clamps, hearth pans, pop-corn poppers, toasters, fireplace accessories and trivets.

Blacksmiths kept a supply of plate, hoop, rod and bar-iron on hand for their work. Most would have a small supply of brass and copper sheets and wire. For fine work, they preferred a Norwegian or Swedish iron; in the late nineteenth century, they began to use mild steel. Also, they bought wrought iron scrap for several cents a pound which they could rework into new products or use for repairs. Blacksmiths bent, twisted, hammered, riveted, chased, and forge-welded; the effects were often dramatic.

Most trivets were designed for specific functions. Restraint and simplicity, combined with sensitivity to proportion and shape, often resulted in works of surprising elegance. The open-work ornamentation of kitchen hearth trivets was usually accomplished through piercing the metal into open-work, contours and shapes, or combining metals such as copper and brass with iron. Surface decorations were punched or stamped, chiseled, filed, drawn, incised, or inlaid. Occasionally, brass or copper would be used with the iron, but in a minimal way such as rivets, or an added rim or plate. Brass and copper were more generously used in making parlour trivets.

Decorative motifs might include hearts, tulips, lilies, birds, fish or snakes. When blacksmiths used a snake design, it was usually a three-dimensional form rather than a flat surface decoration, since the form of the serpent lent itself to being shaped in iron. Serpents occasionally were used as decorative motifs on cast-iron trivets; this may have been a carry-over from smithing. Other decorative motifs used by blacksmiths were geometric designs based on triangles, squares, circles, bands, dots, crescents, stars and sunbursts. Blacksmiths sometimes decorated kitchenware with incised designs, particularly the flat handles of spatulas and ladles. Trivets were rarely decorated with incised designs. Hearts seem to be the most frequently used decorative element for trivets. Hearts were punched out as openwork; heart shapes were formed from metal, or interlocking hearts were made into a decorative lattice. The popularity of heart designs on handcrafted trivets carried over into cast trivets.

Kitchen hearths normally had a cross-bar and andirons. Hearth trivets were designed with high supports, usually four to fourteen inches long for holding vessels above the coals or flames. Trivets used for broiling frequently had either a square or round grill; some were constructed to rotate the grill similar to a "Lazy Susan." There were trivets for making toast, often with a bread rack which was made to swivel. Most kettle trivets were round, without handles, and there was considerable variance in the length of legs depending on whether the trivet was used for cooking or warming. Trivets without handles were moved around using a poker-like instrument with a hook on the end. If a trivet had a handle, it was generally a long one. Long handles on cooking trivets made it easier to move them about over hot coals in the fire. Some of these long-handled trivets were referred to as "spiders." All hearth stands were true trivets in that they had three supports.

In addition to hearth trivets, pans, kettles, grills and stands, blacksmiths made a variety of pressing iron rests and table stands. Even though the legs on iron rests were one or more inches in length, it is likely that most were used as rests rather than for heating irons over the coals. Many of these rests were constructed of hoop metal or rod; some were made of sheet iron and others of wrought iron. These stands had no guides or rails and could be used for pots or pans. Others had rails or guides and were used for irons. Table or counter stands tended to have shorter legs and were simple in construction. Many were formed by shaping an iron rod, hammering terminals and bending them down into feet.

As previously mentioned, there were sharp distinctions between trivets used in the kitchen and those used in the parlour. The former were utilitarian, functional and relatively simple in construction and design. The latter were elaborately decorated, stylish, and often incorporated several metals such as iron, brass or copper.

Parlour and Bedroom Fireplace Accessories

Until late in the nineteenth century, most bedrooms, at least the master bedroom, had fireplaces. Bedroom fireplace accessories were similar to those for the parlour. There was considerable variety and elegance to accessories for parlour and bedroom fireplaces. Fender and bracket trivets, "footmen," "winters," and "waiters" reflected styles such as Georgian, Regency or Stuart with baluster or cabriole legs and Chippendale fretwork in the platforms. Most fireplace accessories were made and marketed by metalsmiths and manufacturers skilled in brass work.

Fireplace accessories were fabricated by a variety of artisans to mirror furniture styles of the day. "Waiters," having four to six legs, resembled sidetables more than trivets or stands. Some waiters had a platform supported by a single shaft which sat on a tripod, or four-footed base, called a "winter" by Paley. Brass was extensively used and the cast platforms were decorated

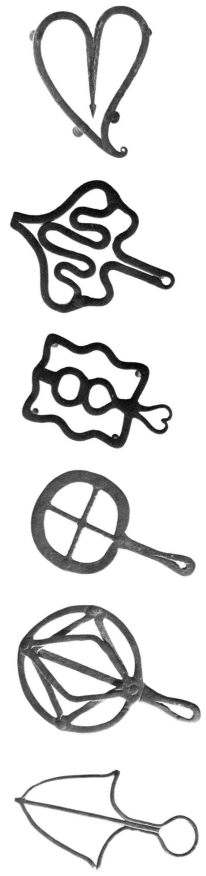

Hand-forged trivets from the Ellwood collection.

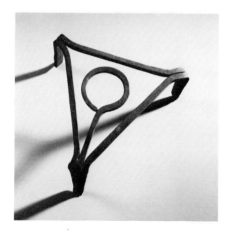

Hand-forged trivets from the Paley collection.

Parlour fireplace which is smaller than a kitchen hearth. Brass accessories are usually associated with parlour and bedroom fireplaces. Photograph furnished by Shelburne Museum.

by piercing and engraving. The platforms were separately cast and bolted or welded to the supports. Often the legs and sometimes the stretchers were made of iron. Designs were based on a variety of commonly used symbols such as the heart, flowers, birds, animals, foliage or geometric arabesque patterns. Many early fireplace stands, especially those made in England, had wooden handles. Platform shapes tended to be round, square or rectangular for waiters and footmen; fender trivets were often "U" or lyre shaped. Bracketed trivets were more varied in their contours. The larger pieces, such as waiters and winters, might have rims around the edge with hooks from which small tea kettles or pots could be hung to be kept warm.

Parlour fireplaces had grates, fenders and cross-bars. There were several trivet designs expressly made for these fireplaces. Fender trivets were made with two legs on the rear and a support at the front with two hooks so that the trivet could either stand on a flat surface or hang by the hooks from a grate or fender. Many fender trivets were constructed so that the platform could be slid closer or further from the fire to regulate the heat. Many of these fender trivets were exquisitely crafted of brass. They were imported from France and England during the seventeenth through the nineteenth centuries.

Fancy brass parlour trivets and stands from the Paley collection at Shelburne Museum.

Bracketed trivets were made with either three or four supports and had an attachment on the bottom of the platform which permitted fastening the trivet to the cross-bar and securing it firmly with a wing nut. Bracket trivets could also be used on tables or counters in the same way as conventional trivets. Bracketed trivets were similar to other cast trivets from the period, but none were made in traditional designs. Bracket trivets were more prevalent in Europe than in America. Most of them carry a Registered Number which indicates they were English in origin. Most bracket trivets were brass, bronze or iron, and the majority of them were cast. Other fireplace furnishings (waiters, a variety of fenders, footmen and fancy brass pieces) were handcrafted.

There were many three-legged round trivets designed for the parlour fireplace, and the majority were made in brass. They were more decorative and fragile than those made for the kitchen. The platforms were ornamented by piercing, and the legs were long and shaped with decorative terminals. Many of the motifs and symbols used to decorate these handcrafted parlour trivets and stands carried over into cast trivets of the nineteenth century.

Lower two pictures illustrate cross-bar trivets.

P-982-NEP-KS Iron (R)
12⁵/₁₆ x 7½ x 1³/₁₆   2 lbs
A-10   F 1   R 1   S 2
W.B.R. on handle reverse. One large gate-mark on rim. Commonly known as "Many Tulips." Wilton made a beautiful brass reproduction. Also it was reproduced by Harner. This design had either three or four legs.

P-300-NEP-KS Iron (VR)
8¼ x 5½ x 1⅝   1 lb 8 oz
A-20   F 1   R 2

E-372-NEP-KS Iron (VR)
7¾ x 5¼ x 1⅛   1 lb 1 oz
A-10   F 2   R 1

Early New England and Pennsylvania Trivets

Unlike other classifications in this book, which are defined by function, this category is based on period and geography. Kitchen stands and decorative iron rests in this grouping may or may not have been made in these regions, but the designs were closely associated with New England and Pennsylvania. Most of them were produced prior to the Civil War.

The earliest trivets produced in quantity that can be identified are those made by William Rimby, reputedly a blacksmith residing in Baltimore, Maryland. His trivets are initialed and dated between 1841 and 1843. Judging by the number of Rimby trivets found in the marketplace today, he must have been exceptionally productive. There is evidence that Rimby trivets were vigorously marketed in Pennsylvania and New England.

Only two Rimby designs are shown in this catalogue, but other sources show at least three others, and perhaps there were more. There is a heavy cast-iron trivet in the National Museum of American History collection which is dated 1829 (similar to P-996 on page 107), but it is unidentified as to source or maker.

Kitchen trivets and stands from this period are heavy castings, weighing a pound and a half to three pounds. The platforms usually are seven to eight inches in diameter with tapered legs an inch to two inches long. The handled kitchen stands are similar to many of the multi-purpose trivets, but they are distinctly larger and heavier. A few stands with handles are relatively small. These probably were used on tables to hold pots, small pans or hot plates.

The unhandled round stands of this era are unique because of their size, weight and length of legs. They are quite different from the tea, coffee and table stands. They should more appropriately be regarded as kitchen stands. At a later date, some of these round stands were made with handles.

Large decorative iron stands were used with box-irons; small ones with sad-irons. Weighing nearly a pound or more they were heavier than many made at a later date. Most of the trivets, stands and iron rests in this section have characteristic wedge- or sprue- marks on the reverse of the platform or handle. Legs tend to be long and tapered with a variety of cross-sections. Also, the castings generally are thicker than those produced after the Civil War.

A few trivets, stands or rests are included solely for their traditional designs. Even though they may have been cast at a later date, the designs are representative examples of the period. Although most trivet designs originated in Europe, Americans showed a distinct partiality to geometric, tulip, pineapple, swastika, pin-wheel and heart motifs in the designs they chose to reproduce. A few older trivets, whose age is suggested by size, weight and cast-marks are clearly English, German or French in origin. They most likely were brought into this country by immigrants, or possibly were imported as trade goods. They are easily identified by their extraordinary surface embellishment and fanciful shapes. Those European trivets which were uncommon, and rarely if ever reproduced in America, are illustrated in the Multi-Purpose Trivets section even though casting characteristics such as weight, size and cast-marks indicate they could be as old as trivets in this section.

P-34-NEP-KS Iron (VR)
11⅛ x 6⅞ x 1¾   2 lbs 2 oz
A-1 F 1 R 1 S 4
Filing on rim.

E-449-NEP-KS Iron (R)
10½ x 5⁵/₁₆ x 1¹⁵/₁₆   1 lb 11 oz
A-9 F 2 R 1

E-470-NEP-KS Iron (R)
13 x 8¹/₁₆ x 1¾   2 lbs
A-1 F 2 R 1
Old casting; Rimby design but not identified.

E-475-NEP-KS Iron (R)
12⅝ x 8¼ x 1⁷/₁₆   3 lbs 12 oz
A-10 F 1 R 1 S 1
Old casting; gate-mark on rim; careful filing.

E-720-NEP-KS Iron (R)
8½ x 5⅜ x 1   14 oz
A-3 F 2 R 1

E-130-NEP-KS Iron (VR)
6⅜ x 3½ x ¹⁵/₁₆   8½ oz
A-10 F 2 R 1 S 4
"TC" on face of handle.

M-21-NEP-KS Iron (VR)
9⅛ x 5¾ x 1¾   15¼ oz
B-18 F 2 R 1
Gate-marks on rim.

P-703-NEP-KS Iron (R)
11⅛ x 6¼ x 1⅞   2 lbs 1 oz
B-2 F 2 R 1
Large wedge-mark on reverse of platform.

E-559-NEP-KS Iron (R)
10½ x 5¹³/₁₆ x 1¹³/₁₆   1 lb 12 oz
B-1 R 1 S 2
Large sprue-mark on reverse of handle.

E-529-NEP-KS Iron (R)
10⅞ x 5⅞ x 1¹/₁₆ 1 lb 4 oz
K-10 F 2 R 1

E-138-NEP-KS Iron (VR)
6⁹/₁₆ x 3⅜ x 1 8½ oz
A-10 F 2 R 1
Sprue-mark on reverse of platform.

D-2-NEP-KS Iron (VR)
8⅜ x 5⅞ x 1¹/₁₆ 1 lb 4 oz
A-9 F 1 R 1 S 2
Old casting.

D-5-NEP-KS Iron (VR)
7¾ x 4⅝ x 1 12 oz
K-10 F 2 R 1
Right front leg is a riveted pin.

E-705-NEP-KS Iron (VR)
10¾ x 7 x 2³/₁₆ 1 lb 15 oz
B-1 F 2 R 1
Large sprue-mark at center of platform
reverse. One-eighth-inch rim around
entire platform.

E-707-NEP-KS Iron (VR)
12½ x 7⅜ x 1¹³/₁₆ 1 lb 13 oz
K-2 F 2 R 1
Old casting.

E-706-NEP-KS Iron (VR)
10 x 6⅜ x 1⅞ 1 lb 3 oz
K-1 F 2 R 1
Wedge-mark near center of platform
reverse.

E-904-NEP Iron (VR)
9 x 5 x 1¼ 1 lb. ½ oz
A-2 F 2 R 1
Large gate-mark on rim.

E-346-NEP-KS Iron (R)
6½ x 3⅝ x ¾ 10 oz
C-12 F 2 R 1
Wedge sprue-mark at the center of
platform reverse.

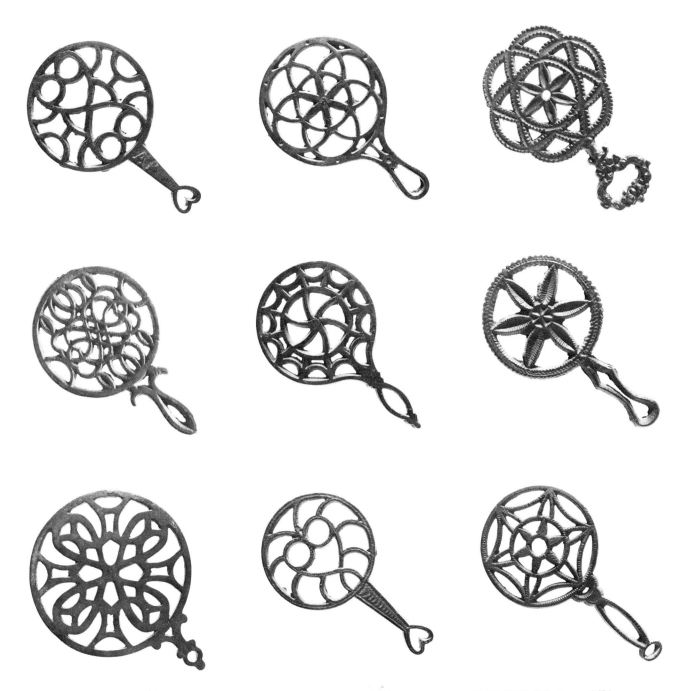

P-704-NEP-KS Iron (R)
10½ x 6½ x 1⅝   1 lb 11 oz
I-8 F 2 R 1
"AP" on face of handle. One leg broken;
two gate-marks on handle.

P-513-NEP-KS Iron (VR)
9⅞ x 6¼ x 1⁵/₁₆   1 lb 9 oz
A-9 F 2 R 1
Gate-mark on rim.

P-938-NEP-KS Iron (VR)
11½ x 8⅞ x 1¾   2 lbs 10 oz
A-1 F 1 R 1 S 2
Cast through rim.

P-1426-NEP-KS Iron (VR)
10⅜ x 6½ x 1⅛   1 lb 8 oz
A-10 F 2 R 1
Sprue-mark at center of platform reverse.

P-1341-NEP-KS Iron (VR)
10 x 5⅞ x 1⁵/₁₆   1 lb 13 oz
A-3 F 2 R 1
Two gate-marks on rim.

P-996-NEP-KS Iron (R)
10⅝ x 6³/₁₆ x 1¹⁵/₁₆   1 lb 13 oz
A-1 F 2 R 1
Pronounced gate-mark on rim. There is
another version of this design that is 11⅜
x 6½. On face of handle, "1829." Virginia
Metalcrafters has a reproduction of the
"1829" trivet.

P-301-NEP-KS Iron (VR)
9 x 5⅞ x 1¾   1 lb 11 oz
B-2 F 2 R 1
Gate-mark on rim; good quality casting.
Unusual handle does not fit platform
design.

P-1176-NEP-KS Iron (R)
9½ x 5¼ x 1⅛   1 lb 2 oz
A-15 F 1 R 2
Front leg riveted.

P-766-NEP-KS Iron (VR)
11¾ x 6⁷/₁₆ x __   1 lb 12 oz
B-14 F 2 R 1
Wedge-mark at center of platform reverse.
Legs cut down.

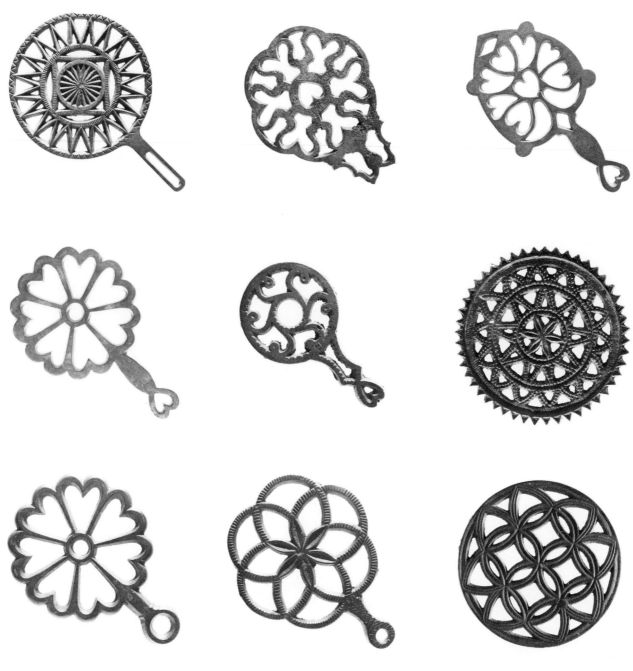

P-956-NEP-KS Iron (R)
12 x 8 x 1⁵/₁₆ 2 lbs 6 oz
A-20 F 1 R 2

E-376-NEP-KS Iron (R)
7⁵/₈ x 4⅞ x ⅞ 11 oz
A-11 F 2 R 1
Large gate-mark on handle.

P-75-NEP-KS Iron (R)
6⅞ x 5 x 1³/₁₆ 11¼ oz
A-20 F 2 R 1
Gate-mark on rim. Known as "Seven Hearts."

P-104-NEP-KS Iron (VR)
7½ x 5¾ x 1⅜ 1 lb 4 oz
A-2 F 2 R 1
Rough casting.

P-2026-NEP-KS Iron (VR)
6 x 3⁷/₁₆ x 1⅝ 9½ oz
B-2 F 2 R 1
Gate-mark on rim.

P-1177-NEP-KS Iron (R)
7¼ x 5⅝ x 1⅛ 13 oz
A-3 F 2 R 1
Two gate-marks on rim.

P-288-NEP-KS Iron (VR)
7⅝ x 4 x 1⁷/₁₆ 11 oz
B-2 F 2 R 2
Sprue-mark on back of handle. Beautiful old design was well-cast.

P-411-NEP-KS Iron (VR)
9 x 1¹⁵/₁₆ 3 lbs 1 oz
B-8 F 1 R 1 S 2
Large sprue cast-mark on reverse.

P-458-NEP-KS Iron (VR)
8¼ x 1¹¹/₁₆ 2 lbs 14 oz
A-2 F 1 R 1 S 2
One large gate-mark on rim. One leg broken and a new leg riveted.

M-8-NEP-KS Iron (VR)
10 x 8 x 1   2 lbs ½ oz
C-11 F 1 R 1 S 1
Large sprue-mark on revese; heavy old casting.

P-908-NEP-KS Iron (VR)
7⅛ x 1⅛   1 lb 9 oz
A-9 F 1 R 1 S 2
Large gate-mark on rim.

P-877-NEP-KS Iron (R)
6⁹/₁₆ x 1⅛   1 lb 8 oz
A-11 F 1 R 1 S 1
Gate-marks on rim; machine grinding.

P-402-NEP-KS Iron (R)
7 x 1¼   15 oz
A-20 F 1 R 1 S 1
Two gate-marks on rim.

P-398-NEP-KS Iron (VR)
5¾ x ¹³/₁₆   13 oz
N-10 F 1 R 1 S 1
Sprue-mark; heavily corroded on reverse.

P-90-NEP-KS Iron (VR)
6⅜ x 1⅜   1 lb 10 oz
A-2 F 1 R 1 S 1
Sprue-mark on reverse. Design also was made with a handle.

E-722-NEP-KS Iron (R)
7½ x 7 x 1⅜   1 lb 14 oz
A-2 F 1 R 1 S 1
Large sprue-mark at center of reverse.

P-139-NEP-KS Iron (VR)
7⅞ x 1³/₁₆   1 lb 12 oz
B-9 F 2 R 2
Gate-mark on rim. Unhandled version of "Twelve Hearts," originally shown by Rimby.

P-826-NEP-KS Iron (R)
7 x 1½   2 lbs 1½ oz
F-23 F 1 R 1 S 1
Sprue-mark on reverse.

P-1002-NEP-KS Iron (R)
6⅛ x 1¼ 1 lb 2½ oz
B-10 F 1 R 1 S 1
Gate-mark on rim.

P-830-NEP-KS Iron (VR)
6¾ x 1¼ 1 lb 9½ oz
B-10 F 1 R 1 S 1
Large gate-mark on rim.

P-1588-NEP-KS Iron (VR)
5¼ x 1³/₁₆ 1 lb 1 oz
B-9 F 1 R 1 S 1
Large wedge-mark on reverse.
Exceptional casting of rare design.

P-1322-NEP-KS Iron (R)
5¹⁵/₁₆ x 2¹³/₁₆ 2 lbs 2 oz
J-9 F 1 R 1 S 1
Gate-mark on rim; reverse draft.

P-31-NEP-KS Iron (VR)
8 x ⅞ 2 lbs 3 oz
B-15 F 2 R 2
Large sprue-mark at center of reverse.
Harner made a reproduction.

P-1589-NEP-KS/TS Iron (VR)
6¾ x ⅞ 1 lb 3 oz
A-15 F 1 R 1 S 1

M-19-NEP-IR Iron (VR)
7 x 3⁷/₁₆ x 1¼ 9¼ oz
A-8 F 1 R 2
Gate-marks at rear of platform.

P-1423-NEP-IR Iron (VR)
7¾ x 3½ x 1½ 15½ oz
B-20 F 1 R 2

P-1101-NEP-IR Iron (R)
9³/₁₆ x 4 x 1⁵/₁₆ 1 lb 6 oz
A-18 F 1 R 2
One-eighth-inch rails on front and sides.

P-1149-NEP-IR Iron (VR)
7¾ x 4 x ¾   12 oz
A-5 F 1 R 2
Sprue-mark at center of reverse.

P-899-NEP Iron (R)
8½ x 3¹³/₁₆ x 1⅛   14 oz
A-11 F 1 R 2
Two gate-marks on rim; filing; casting
break on rim.

P-1098-NEP-IR Iron (R)
7¼ x 4¼ x ¾   14 oz
A-14 F 1 R 2
Gate-mark on rim. One-eighth-inch rail
front and sides.

E-455-NEP-IR Iron (VR)
10 x 4⅜ x 1   1 lb 4 oz
A-3 F 1 R 2
One-quarter-inch rail around platform.
Gate-mark on rim.

E-89-NEP-IR Iron (R)
8 x 4½ x ¹³/₁₆   14 oz
A-14 F 1 R 2

E-84-NEP-IR Iron (R)
8¾ x 3½ x 1⁷/₁₆   13 oz
A-1 F 1 R 2
Sprue-mark on reverse.

E-415-NEP-IR Iron (R)
11⅛ x 4⅜ x 1⅛   1 lb 8 oz
C-10 F 1 R 2
Large wedge-mark on reverse.

E-104-NEP-IR Iron (O)
8 x 3½ x ¹³/₁₆   14 oz
B-15 F 1 R 2

E-336-NEP-IR Iron (O)
8½ x 3⁹/₁₆ x 1¼   12 oz
K-10 F 1 R 2
Another version of design cast in bronze.

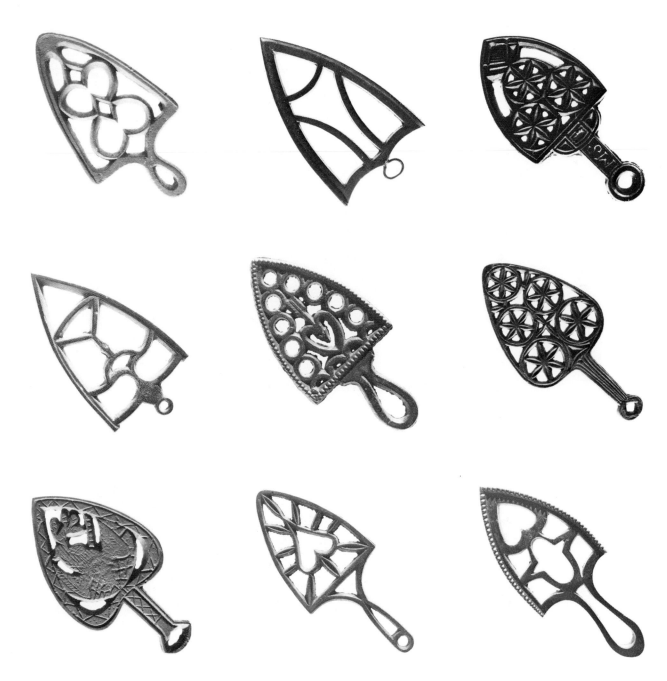

E-122-NEP-IR Iron (R)
7¾ x 4¼ x 1⅜   15½ oz
A-8 F 1 R 2
Sprue-mark on the reverse.

P-1549-NEP-IR (R)
8¼ x 4¼ x 1   1 lb 1½ oz
B-4 F 1 R 2
Wedge-mark on reverse. One-
sixteenth-inch rail on front and sides.

E-398-NEP-IR Iron (VR)
8 x 4⅜ x 1¹/₁₆   1 lb 2 oz
K-11 F 1 R 2
Sprue-mark on reverse; cut and filed.

P-302-NEP-IR Iron (VR)
8½ x 5 x ⅞   1 lb 3 oz
B-15 F 1 R 2
Large wedge-mark on reverse near rear of
platform. One-eighth-inch rail on front
and sides. Hanger is wire placed into
mold before pouring.

P-477-NEP-IR Iron (R)
9⅜ x 4½ x 1¼   1 lb 4 oz
A-3 F 1 R 2
One-eighth-inch beaded rail around
platform. Left rear leg is a riveted pin.

P-904-NEP-IR Iron (VR)
10½ x 4½ x 1¾   13¾ oz
A-2 F 1 R 2
Gate-marks on rim.

E-496-NEP-IR Iron (VR)
9½ x 4⅝ x 1¹¹/₁₆   1 lb 15 oz
A-8 F 1 R 2
Old casting.

E-460-NEP-IR Iron (VR)
9 x 4½ x 1¾   1 lb 1 oz
E-2 F 1 R 2
Front of trivet broken and repaired with
brass; front leg is a riveted post.

P-1154-NEP-IR Iron (R)
10⅝ x 4⁵/₁₆ x 1⅜   1 lb 9 oz
B-20 F 1 R 2
Large sprue-mark on reverse. One-eighth-
inch rail on front and sides. Fine old
casting.

Multi-Purpose Trivets and Stands

Multi-purpose trivets and stands fall into several groupings; kitchen stands, table stands, or iron rests. These trivets and stands either had no rails, posts, or cleats; or they had low rails measuring one-sixteenth inch or less. Kitchen and table stands usually had handles and four supports. Those shaped to the pressing iron were used as iron rests, but because of the flat platform surface, they also could be used as supports for pots or dishes. Most trivets made as iron rests were generic in design, decorative, handled and had three supports.

Multi-purpose stands were smaller than those produced at an earlier date, and many of the traditional models which previously had three legs were changed to four supports. Multi-purpose stands were associated with the period of the iron cooking range. It began circa 1870 and peaked near the end of the century. However, in rural areas wood/coal burning iron cook-stoves remained in use into the 1930's. Multi-purpose stands were generally used on kitchen tables or counters to protect surfaces. Sometimes they were used directly on the stove either to keep food warm or to prevent it from scorching.

Trivets and stands in this category were truly multi-purpose. They were used interchangeably for stove, counter or laundry; they held dishes, pans or pots; they were used for warming or cooking and sometimes as ice-box or meat rests.

A large number of the multi-purpose trivets and stands were traditional in design. In some cases, the designs were perpetuated for a hundred or more years with only slight variations in size, number of supports, weight or rather minor design modifications. It was mainly these old, traditional, multi-purpose stands which were reproduced in the revival period during the 1940's and 1950's.

It is difficult to precisely separate American from European castings as most designs produced in America initially came from England, France or Germany. Included in this category are a number of European trivets and it is doubtful that any of them were produced in America. Among these cast-iron stands there are several with wedge- or sprue-marks indicating they are quite old. Characteristic of "European" stands is an opulent, lavish, surface decoration which is uncharacteristic of American manufacturing. Americans favored simple designs having reasonably flat platform surfaces with conventional shapes.

Multi-purpose trivets and stands are perhaps the most diverse in size, shape and design of any trivet category.

P-768-MPS Iron (R)
8 x 5½ x ¾   7 oz
A-4 F 2 R 2
On face of handle, "Pat. May 17, 79." Two gate-marks on rim. Several reproductions with changes in weight and placement of supports.

E-515-MPS Iron (O)
7⅜ x 4¾ x ⅝   10 oz
A-14 F 2 R 1

K-112-MPS Iron (O)
7½ x 4⅞ x ¾   13½ oz
A-11 F 1 R 2

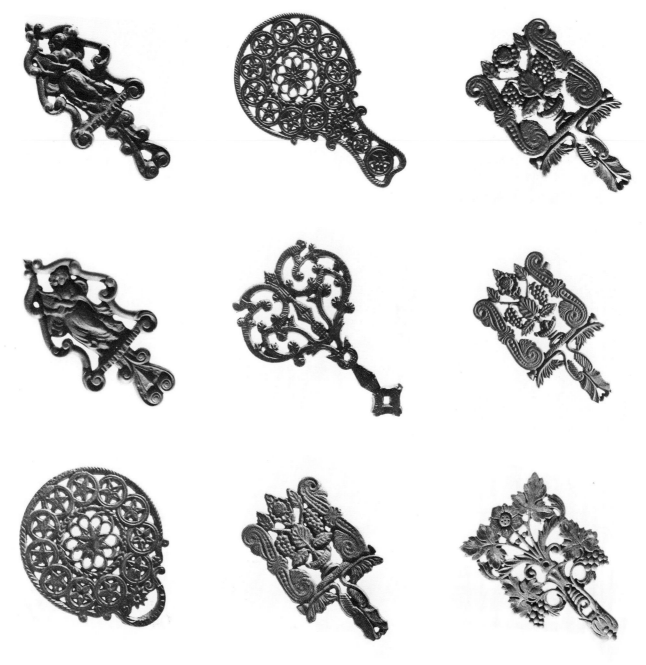

P-129-MPS Iron (O)
10 x 4¾ x 1⅝   2 lbs 2 oz
A-8 F 1 R 2
On face, "Jenny Lind." Two gate-marks
on rim. A popular trivet with collectors.

E-102-MPS Iron (R)
8¹⁄₁₆ x 4 ⅝ x 1³⁄₁₆   1 lb 8 oz.
A-10 F 1 R 2
On face, "Jenny Lind." Backcoping,
mostly in the figure.

P-1511-MPS Iron (R)
8⅛ x 6⅞ x 1⅜   2 lbs ¾ oz
B-2 F 2 R 2
On face of handle, "E.R. Manley." Sprue-
mark at center of reverse. Extensive
backcoping. Either the surface has
oxidized from heat or it is a poor casting.
Probably dates from the 1870's.
Sometimes called "Star & Braid."

P-1421-MPS Iron (VR)
11 x 6⅝ x 1⁷⁄₁₆   2 lbs 2½ oz
A-2 F 1 R 1 S 2
Three gate-marks on rim and handle.
Platform is the same as P-1511 but
smaller; backcoping is not as extensive.

P-30-MPS Iron (O)
9⅝ x 6⅜ x 1⅜   1 lb 9½ oz
A-9 F 2 R 1
Appears to be two gate-marks on rim and
probably machine grinding. Many versions
cast over a long period of time. Called
"Pineapple" or "Butterfly."

P-647-MPS Iron (R)
9 x 4⅞ x 1⁷⁄₁₆   1 lb 11½ oz
A-2 F 2 R 2
Cast through the rim but no obvious gate-

marks. Nickel finish eroded. Design
reproduced over a long time. Commonly
called "Grapes & Scrolls," sometimes just
"Grapes."

E-406-MPS Iron (R)
8⅝ x 5 x 1¼   1 lb 8½ oz
A-9 F 2 R 2
Posts on half-spherical bases

E-730-MPS Iron (R)
9¼ x 5 x 1¾   1 lb 4½ oz
A-1 F 2 R 2
Old casting.

E-459-MPS Iron (R)
8 x 5⅜ x ¹⁵⁄₁₆   1 lb 7 oz
A-9 F 2 R 2
On reverse, "The Forest City Foundries
Co. Cleveland Niagara Furnaces."

K-109-MPS Bronze (O)
8 x 6 x 1⅜ 1 lb 5 oz
E-18 F 2 R 2
Commonly called "Urn & Fern,"
sometimes "Mask." Titled "Doodler's
Dream" by Virginia Metalcrafters.
Numerous reproductions.

M-12-MPS Iron (VR)
8¾ x 5 x ⅝ 14 oz
A-15 F 2 R 2
Unusual interpretation of this design;
probably predates other designs.

E-418-MPS Iron (R)
8 x 6 x 1¾ 1 lb 2 oz
A-1 F 1 R 2
Gate-marks on rim.

E-488-MPS Iron (R)
7⅝ x 5¾ x 1¹/₁₆ 1 lb 4 oz
A-9 F 1 R 2
Large gate-mark on rim.

K-14-MPS Iron (R)
9 x 5¾ x 1⅜ 1 lb 4 oz
A-1 F 1 R 2
Gate-mark on rim. Commonly called
"Lincoln Drape," sometimes "Tassel &
Grain." Usually cast with four legs.
Numerous reproductions.

E-129-MPS Iron (R)
9¾ x 5⁵/₁₆ x 1¼ 1 lb 1 oz
A-1 F 2 R 2
Unusual handle for this design.

M-1-MPS Iron (VR)
9 x 5¾ x 1⅛ 1 lb 1 oz
A-3 F 1 R 2
Gate-mark on rim. Old casting. Very
unusual dimpled surface treatment of the
eagle. Many reproductions over a long
time. Commonly called "Eagle & Heart."

M-7-MPS Iron (VR)
7¼ x 3¾ x 1⅛ 10¼ oz
B-10 F 1 R 2
Gate-marks on rim. It appears that a
"Eagle & Heart" design with the rim
broken, or cut off, was used for the
pattern.

P-645-MPS Iron (R)
8½ x 5¼ x ¹³/₁₆ 14½ oz
K-C 6 F 2 R 2
On face, "McClary Mfg Co London Ont."
Eroded nickel finish.

K-28-MPS Brass (C)
6⅞ x 3⅞ x ½   7 oz
A-15 F 1 R 2
An obvious reproduction; eagle design is from the eighteenth century.

E-521-MPS Iron (R)
7⅜ x 4½ x ¹³/₁₆   10 oz
A-14 F 2 R 1
Gate-marks on rim; machine grinding.

M-9-MPS Iron (VR)
13¾ x 5 x 1   1 lb
A-9 F 2 R 2
On face, "United We Stand in America."
On reverse, "Uncle Sam." Illegible
company identification in script.

K-30-MPS Brass (C)
7 x 4¾ x ¾   9½ oz
A-11 F 2 R 1
Crude casting; appears to be recent but design is old.

E-512-MPS Iron (O)
7 x 4⅜ x ¾   12 oz
A-14 F 1 R 2

E-101-MPS Iron (VR)
7¼ x 7 x 1⁷/₁₆   15 oz
A-10 F 1 R 1 S 2
Gate-marks on handle and rim; filing. Old casting.

E-91-MPS Iron (R)
7 x 4⅜ x ⅝   8 oz
A-15 F 1 R 2
Shallow backcoping on handle; machine grinding.

E-68-MPS Iron (VR)
8⅛ x 5⅜ x 1⅛   9 oz
A-2 F 2 R 1
Gate-marks on rim.

M-11-MPS Brass (VR)
9 x 5½ x 1⅜   1 lb ¾ oz
K-18 F 2 R 2
The Ellwood Collection has the same design in Iron
8⅞ x 5⅜ x 1⅜   1 lb 2½ oz
D-2 F 1 R 2

E-483-MPS Iron (R)
9 x 5⅛ x 1⁹/₁₆ 1 lb 10 oz
D-8 F 2 R 2
Legs are curved; One-eighth-inch side rails.

E-414-MPS Iron (R)
9 x 5 x 1 1 lb 6 oz
A-11 F 2 R 2
Some backcoping; old casting.

E-345-MPS Iron (R)
8⁹/₁₆ x 4¾ x ¾ 8 oz
A-11 F 1 R 2
Nickel finish; filing on rim.

E-182-MPS Iron (VC)
8 x 5¾ x 1¹/₁₆ 2 lbs
A-11 F 2 R 2
On reverse, "Hopewell." Souvenir casting for Hopewell Village National Park. Based on a relic found during archaeological exploration of the Hopewell plantation. New pattern and castings by Unicast Company, Boyertown, Pennsylvania.

W-3-MPS Iron (O)
12 x 7½ x ⅞ 1 lb 15 oz
A-9 F 1 R 1 S 1
On reverse, "Wilton." A reproduction marketed in the late 1950's or early 1960's. Probably not many of this design were distributed.

E-473-MPS Iron (VR)
8½ x 4½ x ¾ 1 lb 4 oz
A-22 F 2 R 2
Large gate-mark on handle.

E-554-MPS Iron (R)
11⅝ x 5⅛ x 1¼ 1 lb 4 oz
A-2 F 2 R 2

E-520-MPS Iron (R)
10½ x 6⅝ x ¹⁵/₁₆ 1 lb 5 oz
A-8 F 1 R 2
Gate-marks on handle and rim.

E-802-MPS Iron (VR)
9¼ x 4³/₁₆ x 1⅛ 12½ oz
A-3 F 1 R 2
On face, "E P" "H M." Cast through rim.

E-514-MPS Iron (R)
8 1/16 x 4 5/8 x 7/8   1 lb 1 oz
A-11 F 2 R 1
On reverse, "S B Miller C."

M-3-MPS Iron (VR)
7 x 4 3/8 x 1 1/4   11 1/2 oz
A-2 F 2 R 1
Gate-marks on rim. Also cast in brass.

K-110-MPS Iron (O)
7 1/4 x 4 1/2 x 1/2   11 oz
A-13 F 2 R 2
On face, "John Adams." Gate-marks on rim; machine grinding. Perhaps marketed in the 1930's.

M-6-MPS Brass (VR)
3 7/8 x 3 1/2 x 1 5/8   9 3/4 oz
A-18 F 1 R 2
Reverse draft.

E-516-MPS Iron (VR)
7 3/8 x 4 3/4 x 3/4   10 oz
A-11 F 2 R 1
Gate-mark on rim; machine grinding.

E-517-MPS Iron (VR)
7 x 4 3/4 x 5/8   12 1/2 oz
A-14 F 2 R 1
Wood grain from pattern faintly visible on reverse.

E-486-MPS Iron (O)
9 7/8 x 4 7/8 x 1 5/8   1 lb 7 oz
A-2 F 1 R 2
Many variations of design; reproductions made over a long time. Commonly called "Peacock," or "Tree of Life Variant No. 2."

E-360-MPS Iron (O)
8 1/8 x 4 5/8 x 1 1/4   12 oz
A-8 F 1 R 2
Backcoping; machine grinding.

E-442-MPS Iron (R)
8 3/4 x 5 7/8 x 1 3/8   1 lb 2 oz
A-1 R 1 S 2
Unusual design; rimmed.

E-428-MPS Iron (VR)
8⅝ x 5¾ x ¹³/₁₆   1 lb
A-14 F 1 R 1 S 2
Gate-marks on rim; shallow backcoping.
Unusual and rare design. Note serpent
design handle.

M-10-MPS Iron (VR)
8¾ x 3¾ x ¾   8 ¼ oz
A-11 F 2 R 2 One on the handle.
Reverse draft; gate-marks on rim. Two
guide cleats on front of platform. There
are brass versions in The Metropolitan
Museum of Art collection.

K-119-MPS Iron (O)
8⅛ x 5⅜ x 1⅜   1 lb
A-2 F 2 R 1
Gate-mark on handle and rim. Many
reproductions of this design in a variety
of sizes, weight and heights. Commonly
called "Star," sometimes called either
"Western Star" or "Eastern Star."

E-804-MPS Iron (R)
7⅝ x 5 x 1⅛   9½ oz
A-3 F 2 R 1
On face, "Chalfant M.F.G. Co Philada No
5 Stand." Pronounced gate-marks on rim;
filing.

K-102-MPS Iron (O)
7¼ x 4⅞ x ¾   14 oz
A-11 F 2 R 1
Gate-marks on rim; machine grinding.

K-36-MPS Brass (R)
8⅛ x 3⅞ x ¹¹/₁₆   15 oz
A-19 F 2 R 2
Reverse shows imprint of a small tin strip
with the number 57 attached to the
wooden pattern with small brads. In the
Jane Daley collection at The Metropolitan
Museum of Art there is the same design,
cast in iron, but the number is 97.

P-1150-MPS Iron (O)
8⁹/₁₆ x 4¼ x ⅝   12 oz
A-15 F 2 R 2
Two filed gate-marks, one on the rim and
the other on the handle. This is an old
casting reproduced by many different
companies over a long period of time.
Frequently with a plated finish around
the turn of the century. Most often called
"Dumb Dutch."

P-758-MPS Iron (O)
8¾ x 5⅜ x ¹⁵/₁₆   1 lb 5 oz
B-15 F 2 R 2
Cast through the rim; careful filing on
edges. An old casting reproduced by many
companies over a long time in great
variety ranging from thin to heavy in
various sizes. Most often called "Tree of
Life."

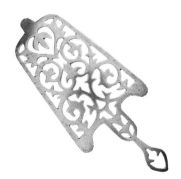
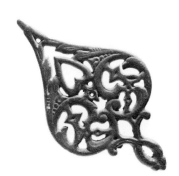

M-2-MPS Iron (R)
10 x 6⅜ x 1½   1 lb 11 oz
A-18 F 2 R 1
Many reproductions over a long time.
Commonly called "Hex." The Ellwood
collection has the same design;
9¾ x 6⅛ x 1⁵/₁₆   1 lb 10 oz
A-8 F 2 R1

E-526-MPS Iron (R)
11⅜ x 6¾ x 1⁵/₁₆   1 lb 6 oz
Post legs F 2 R 2
Gate-marks on handle rim.

P-627-MPS Iron (R)
7⅜ x 3½ x ¹⁵/₁₆   6½ oz
A-19 F 1 R 2

P-1700-MPS Iron (VR)
10⅝ x 5¹¹/₁₆ x 1   12 oz
A-10 F 2 R 2
Gate-mark on rim; interesting
reinforcement on the reverse. May be a
Scandinavian design.

K-56-MPS Iron (O)
6⅞ x 5½ x ¾   12 oz
Four turtle feet; F 2 R 2
On the reverse at the base of the tail,
"W". Gate-marks on the rim; filing.

P-868-MPS Iron (R)
8½ x 3¾ x 1¼   9 oz
A-3 F 1 R 2
Nickel finish.

P-829-MPS Iron (O)
8 x 4¾ x ⅞   11¼ oz
A-15 F 1 R 1 S 2
Wedge-mark near center of reverse. An
old casting reproduced by several
companies over a period of time. Most
often called "Snowflake." Sometimes cast
in brass. Numerous reproductions.

P-1798-MPS Brass (R)
7 x 5⁹/₁₆ x ¾   12½ oz
A-15 F 2 R 2
Reproduced in the 1950's by John Wright.

P-98-MPS Iron (R)
9¼ x 5¼ x ¾   14½ oz
O-15 F 1 R 2
Wilton produced a similar design.

E-356-MPS Iron (R)
7½ x 4⅝ x 1¹/₁₆   1 lb 4 oz
A-8 F 2 R 2
On reverse, "Made by Jerimiah Dwyer when serving as molders apprentice in 1852." (raised letters)

P-481-MPS Iron (VR)
8 x 4¾ x 1   1 lb 2½ oz
A-11 F 2 R 2

E-400-MPS Iron (VR)
7¾ x 4⅝ x 1¾   1 lb 7 oz
A-19 F 2 R 2
Nickel finish.

P-91-MPS Iron (R)
8¼ x 4⅝ x ½   14½ oz
A-16 F 2 R 1
Harner made a reproduction.

P-1851-MPS Iron (VR)
8½ x 5⅞ x 1¼   1 lb 3½ oz
A-20 F 2 R 1

K-75-MPS Brass (R)
9⅛ x 5⅜ x ⁹/₁₆   7 oz
A-11 F 1 R 2
Clear file marks; an old casting.

P-127-MPS Iron (VR)
8⅛ x 5 x ⅞   10 oz
L-C 7 F 1 R 1 S 2
Incised scrolling on face of handle.

K-150-MPS Tin (VR)
10½ x 6⅛ x 1   11 oz
No supports; one-inch rim with perforations for heat to escape.

P-460-MPS Iron (O)
7½ x 5⅝ x 1   8½ oz
A-2 F 2 R 1
Gate-marks on rim. Pattern backcoped. This design was made with several different handles.

CW-4-MPS Iron (VR)
7¾ x 4½ x 1⅜   13 oz
K-2 F 1 R 2

P-1510-MPS Iron (R)
8½ x 4⅜ x 1½   14¾ oz
A-20 F 1 R 2
Gate-mark on rim.

P-775-MPS Iron (R)
8½ x 4³/₁₆ x ¾   15½ oz
A-11 F 1 R 2
Filed gate-marks on rim. Superb Casting;
exceptionally sharp detail.

P-801-MPS Brass (R)
9½ x 4⅜ x 1⁵/₁₆   1 lb 6½ oz
D-19 F 1 R 2
Portrait of George Washington. Reputedly
this brass version was cast in 1876 as a
souvenir of the Philadelphia Centennial
Exposition. The reverse suggests that the
original pattern was sculpted in wax or
clay.

E-920-MPS Iron (0)
8¼ x 4¼ x 1¼   1 lb 3½ oz
A-8 F 2 R 2
Gate-marks on rim; machine grinding.
Some versions of this design have handle
at opposite end; some versions have
supports formed by extension of rim

P-84-MPS Iron (0)
5¼ x 4 x ¾   10 oz
No supports; sits on rim. On face, "Pat.
May 14. 81 by Wm. H. Thayer." Cast in
brass as well as iron. Multi-use kitchen
tool; advertised as suitable for lifting hot
pans, pots or shallow plates, as a stove-lid
lifter, as a carrying hook or meat
tenderizer; and as a flat iron stand.

CW-1-MPS Iron (VR)
7¼ x 4⁵/₁₆ x ⅝   9 oz
A-10 F 32 R 2
On face, "Tenderizer F-15 Pat. Pending."
Thirty-two feet in front were for
tenderizing meat; also could be used as an
iron rest, crown bottle opener, nail puller,
hammer or screw driver.

P-774-MPS Iron (VR)
9⅛ x 4½ x 1¼   15 oz
A-28 F 2 R 1

K-33-MPS Iron (VC)
10⅜ x 6⅝ x 1⅛   1 lb 11 oz
A-18 F 1 R 1 S 2
This modern reproduction was made by
Virginia Metalcrafters. It was frequently
produced in the 1950's and 1960's. The
unhandled version was the older design
(see E-722-NEP). Most often called
"Tulip."

W-1-MPS Iron (C)
12 x 7⅜ x ⅞ 1 lb ½ oz.
A-9 F 2 R 1
On reverse, "Wilton." An unusual design produced by Wilton Products in the 1950's. Few were marketed.

P-1469-MPS Iron (0)
8¼ x 3½ x ⅞ 10½ oz.
A-9 F 2 R 2
Machine grinding; backcoped. Three-sixteenths-inch railing around entire platform.

P-1319-MPS Iron (0)
5¾ x 4 x 1⅛ 13¼ oz.
H-C 8 F 2 R 2
Two gate-marks on rim; filing. Three-sixteenths-inch rail around entire platform.

P-1479-MPS Iron (VR)
10¼ x 4¾ x 1⅜ 14½ oz.
A-10 F 1 R 2
Excellent casting, file marks on rim.

P-1544-MPS Iron (0)
7¾ x 4½ x ⅞ 12½ oz.
A-11 F 1 R 2
Unusual handle for this design.

E-106-MPS Iron (R)
9½ x 4¾ x -- 1 lb
Legs cut off. F 1 R 2

P-984-MPS Iron/wood (R)
8¾ x 4¼ x ⅞ 11 oz.
Front M-C 1 Rear M-C 6
On face, "1880." Horseshoe backcoped.

P-464-MPS Iron (0)
7½ x 4⅛ x ¾ 10 oz.
Front M-C 1, Rear M-C 6
On face, "1881." Gate-mark on rim.

E-341-MPS Iron/wood (R)
9 x 4¼ x ⅞ 9½ oz.
Front M-C 1 Rear M-C 7
On face, "1883."

P-1845-MPS Iron (O)
7⁵/₁₆ x 4⅛ x ¾ 11 oz
Front M-C 1   Rear M-C 6
On face, "1884." Gate-mark on rim. Same
design was made with a wooden handle.

P-1846-MPS Iron (O)
7½ x 4⅛ x ¾ 10½ oz
Front M-C 1   Rear M-C 6
On face, "1885." Two gate-marks on rim.

P-1275-MPS Iron and wood (R)
9⅜ x 4⁵/₁₆ x ¾ 10½ oz
Front M-C 1   Rear M-C 6
On face, "1886." Large gate-mark on front
cleat.

P-993-MPS Iron (O)
7½ x 4⅛ x ¾ 10½ oz
Front M-C 1   Rear M-C 6
On face, "1887."

P-1261-MPS Iron (O)
7³/₁₆ x 3¹⁵/₁₆ x ¾ 10¾ oz
Front M-C 1   Rear M-C 6
On face, "1888." Nickel finish eroded.

P-991-MPS Iron (O)
7 x 3⅞ x ¾ 9½ oz
Front M-C 1   Rear M-C 6
On face, "1889."

P-387-MPS Iron (O)
7½ x 4⅛ x ¾ 11 oz
Front M-C 1   Rear M-C 6
On face, "1890."

P-438-MPS Iron (O)
7½ x 4⅛ x ¾ 10½ oz
Front M-C 1, Rear M-C 6
On face, "1894."

P-1147-MPS Iron (R)
7⅜ x 4¼ x ⅞ 1 lb 1 oz
A-10 F 2 R 2
On face, "Good Luck For Us All." Gate-
mark on rim.

M-13-MPS Iron (VR)
7⅞ x 4 x 1½   12½ oz
A-1 F 2 R 2
On face, "Good Luck For Us All." Stops on front and rear of platform.

E-379-MPS Iron (O)
7 x 3⅞ x ⅝   7 oz
Front M-C 1 Rear H-C 8
Two gate-marks on rim.

E-380-MPS Iron (C)
5⅛ x 3⅝ x 7/16   5 oz
Front M-C 1 Rear M-C 2
On face, "Good Luck Pat'd 1885." Gate-mark on front platform rim.

E-441-MPS Brass (R)
6⅛ x 4⅞ x 1¼   1 lb
M-9 F 2 R 2
On face, "Good Luck." Backcoping.

E-261-MPS Iron (O)
3¾ x 3⅝ x ⅜   6 oz
Cleats F 1 R 2
On face, Patent Appld. For Union Web. Gloucester Mass." On reverse, "Good Luck."

E-393-MPS Iron (R)
5⅛ x 4⅜   12 oz
No supports. On face, "Luck." There are three one-sixteenth-inch cleats on face. Can be turned over and used as a stand.

E-337-MPS Iron (R)
5½ x 4¾   14 oz
No supports. Backcoped; cleats on face.

E-388-MPS Iron (R)
5 x 4½ x ⅞   12½ oz
A-11 F 1 R 2
Figure backcoped; three-eighth-inch cleats on face. May be President Garfield.

E-426-MPS Iron (R)
5 x 4⅜ x ¾   11 oz
A-5 F 1 R 2
Figure backcoped; one-eighth-inch cleats on face. May be President Cleveland.

P-1548-MPS Iron (R)
5 x 4⅜ x 1¼ 14½ oz
A-3 F 2 R 2
On face, "Garfield." Gate-mark on rim
and figure is backcoped.

P-642-MPS Iron (O)
7¼ x 4 x ¹¹⁄₁₆ 6½ oz
Front M-C 1, Rear M-C 6
Gate-mark on front cleat.

P-761-MPS Iron (C)
7¼ x 4⅛ x ¾ 11 oz
Front M-C 1, Rear M-C 6
On face, "Good Luck." Gate-mark on rim;
machine grinding.

P-189-MPS Iron (C)
6¾ x 3¾ x ⅝ 5¾ oz
Front M-C 2, Rear M-C 6
Painted black over a nickel finish.

P-1841-MPS Iron (VR)
6½ x 5⁵⁄₁₆ x 1⅛ 1 lb 3½ oz
A-11 F 2 R 2
On face, "Buy Holt's Stoves, N. 2nd. St."
Backcoped leaving a three-eighth-inch rail
on the underside.

P-1099-MPS Iron (VR)
6½ x 5⁵⁄₁₆ x 1³⁄₁₆ 1 lb 2½ oz
A-8 F 2 R 2
On face, "S.A. Sundam 550 Hudson St.
Stove Store." Originally nickel finish.

K-44-MPS Iron (O)
8¾ x 4⅝ x ⅝ 12 oz
Front C-1 Rear H-C 7
On face, "Good Luck to All Who Use This
Stand." On reverse, "Pat App'ld For."
Nickel finish eroded.

E-384-MPS Iron (R)
7⅝ x 4½ x ⅝ 8½ oz
Front M-C 1 Rear H-C 8
On face, "Stevenson Bros. Hardware Co.
Bloomington Ill."

P-792-MPS Brass (O)
4⅜ x 4³⁄₁₆ x ⅞ 6 oz
A-10 F 2 R 2

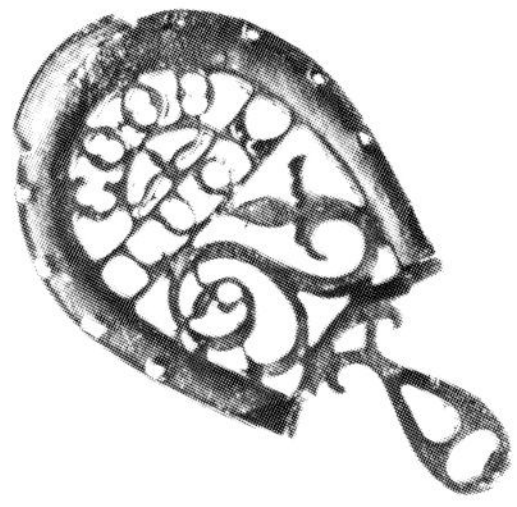

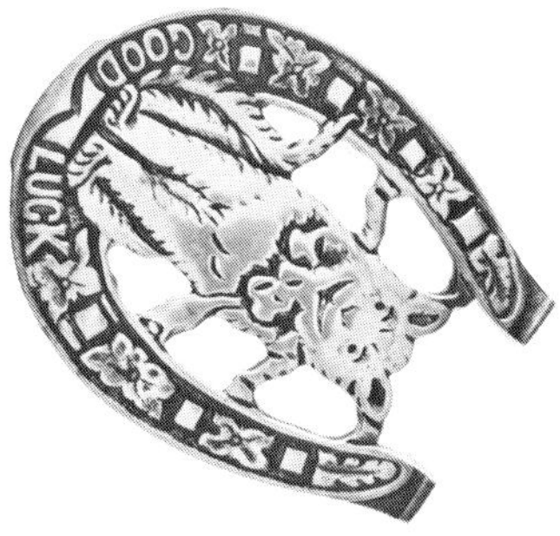

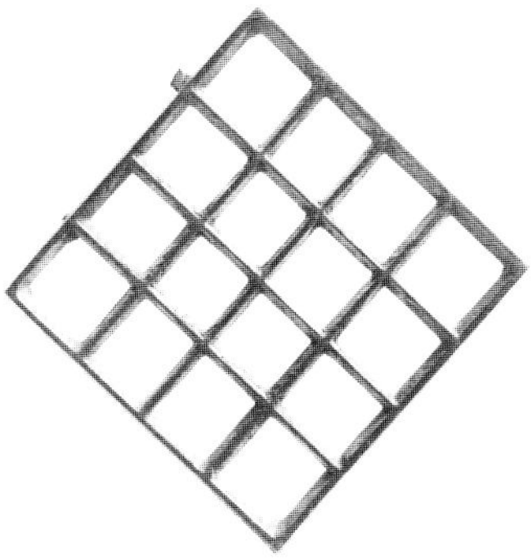

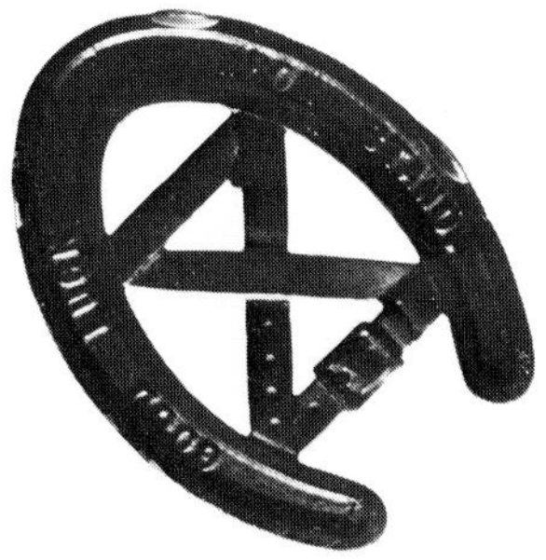

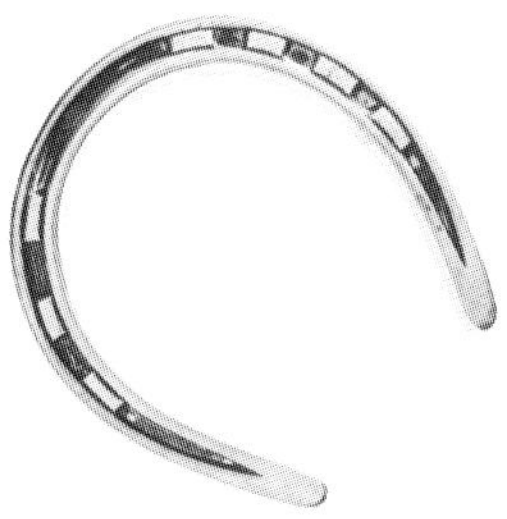

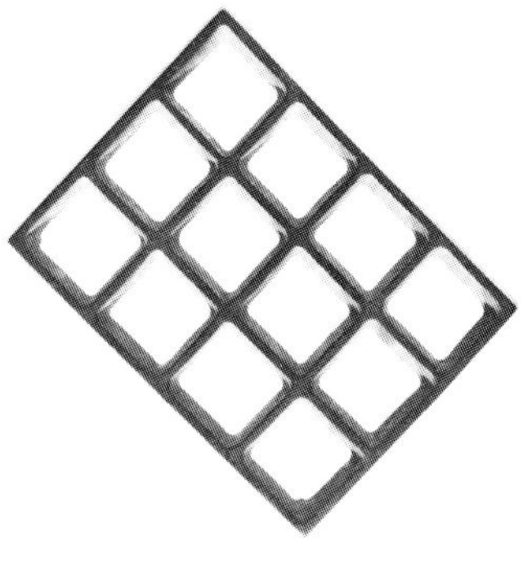

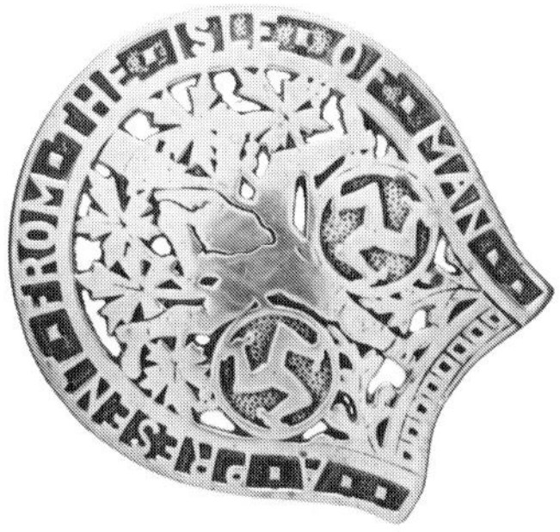

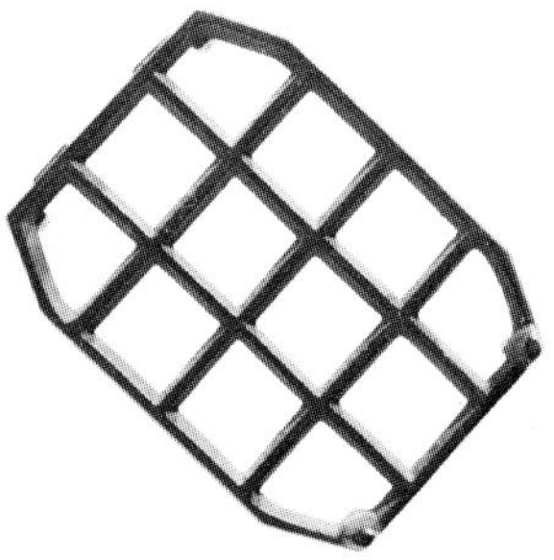

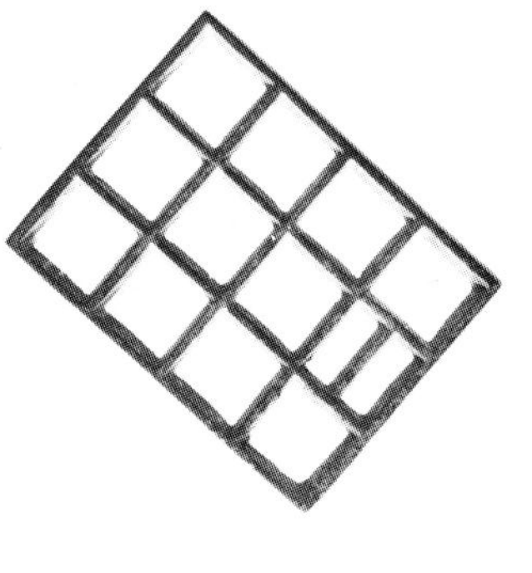

E-421-MPS Iron (O)
$7\frac{1}{4}$ x $4\frac{1}{4}$ x $\frac{13}{16}$ 10 oz
Front M-C-1 Rear H-C 8
On face, "Good Luck." Rough casting; gate-marks on rim are filed.

E-374-MPS Iron (R)
$5\frac{3}{4}$ x $4\frac{1}{4}$ x $\frac{3}{4}$ 14 oz
Two heavy bisected cleats
F 1 R 2 S 4
On face, "Good Luck Iron Stand." On the reverse, "Bradley Co's Patent Frankford, Phila. PA." Two one-quarter-inch guide cleats on each rail. Large gate-marks on rim.

P-1557-MPS Brass (R)
$5\frac{7}{8}$ x $5\frac{3}{8}$ x $\frac{7}{8}$ 1 lb
A-11 F 2 R 1
On face, " A Present From Isle of Man." On reverse, "S.W.D. Rd. 209667". Quarter-inch rim around bottom of platform.

P-977-MPS Brass (R)
$6\frac{9}{16}$ x $5\frac{1}{16}$ x $1\frac{1}{4}$ 1 lb $\frac{1}{2}$ oz
J-C 6 F 2 R 2
On face, "Good Luck."

P-791-MPS Brass (O)
$4\frac{1}{4}$ x $3\frac{7}{8}$ x $\frac{15}{16}$ 4 oz
A-19 F 2 R 2
Extensive backcoping.

P-810-MPS Iron (C)
$4\frac{3}{8}$ x $3\frac{5}{16}$ x $1\frac{3}{16}$ $5\frac{1}{4}$ oz
D-3 F 2 R 2
Gate-marks at one end; guide posts for pressing iron on one end.

P-415-MPS Iron (C)
$4\frac{7}{8}$ x 1 $8\frac{1}{2}$ oz
D-3 F 2 R 2
Two cross-bars are also the gates; gate-marks obvious.

P-39-MPS Iron (C)
$4\frac{7}{16}$ x $3\frac{3}{8}$ x 1 7 oz
D-3 F 2 R 2
Machine grinding.

P-83-MPS Iron (C)
$4\frac{3}{8}$ x $3\frac{1}{4}$ x $\frac{15}{16}$ $5\frac{1}{4}$ oz
D-4 F 2 R 2
Note provision for stove lid lifter.

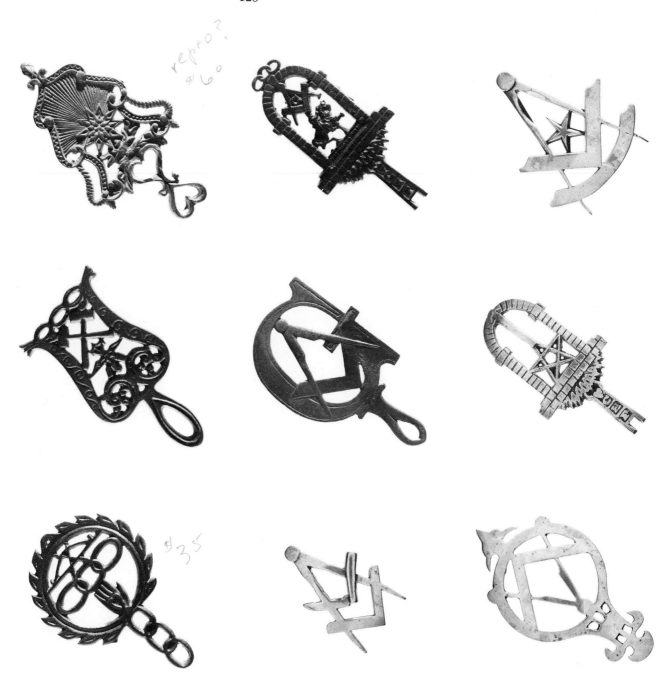

P-89-MPS Brass (O)
9⅜ x 5⅛ x 1⅞   1 lb 6 oz
A-2 F 1 R 2
Order of Cincinnatus but also called
"Sunburst" or "Christmas Tree." Cast in
iron, brass and bronze. Reproduced over a
long time; variations in size and length of
legs.

E-553-MPS Iron (R)
8 x 4½ x 1¼   1 lb 2 oz
K-8 F 2 R 2
May be a sprue-mark on reverse; filing on
rim.

P-407-MPS Iron (O)
8¼ x 5½ x 1½   15 oz
A-2 F 1 R 2
Odd Fellows Lodge. Cast in iron, brass
and bronze. Reproduced many times.
Sometimes called "Heart in Hand." Filing
on the edges; an old casting.

P-1816-MPS Iron (O)
8¾ x 4⅜ x 1¹/₁₆   14 oz
A-11 F 1 R 2
Masonic Lodge. On face, "King William
1645 (?) O. N. F." Frequently cast in
brass, occasionally in bronze. Two gate-
marks on rim.

P-1578-MPS Iron (R)
9 x 5¼ x 1¼   15½ oz
A-2 F 2 R 2
Masonic emblem.

P-581-MPS Brass (R)
4½ x 2⅝ x 1   4 oz
A-19 F 1 R 2
Masonic Emblem.

P-871-MPS Brass (R)
6⅝ x 5 x 1   13 oz
A-9 F 1 R 2
Masonic emblem. Design was produced in
several sizes.

P-564-MPS Brass (O)
7⅞ x 4 x 1⅛   15 oz
A-11 F 1 R 2
Masonic. On face, "C.H.F."

P-1651-MPS Brass (R)
7⅝ x 4⅛ x 1⅛   9½ oz
A-9 F 2 R 1
Masonic emblem.

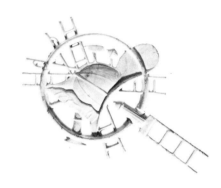

P-35-MPS Brass (R)
8½ x 4¼ x 1 14½ oz
A-10 F 1 R 2

E-20-MPS Iron (R)
7¾ x 5¼ x 1³⁄₁₆ 1 lb
A-11 F 2 R 1
Gate-mark on rim; machine grinding.
Masonic emblem.

K-7-TCT Iron (R)
6⅛ x ¹⁵⁄₁₆ 1 lb 4 oz
A-11 F 1 R 1 S 1
On face, "DUV," (daughters of Union
Veterans.) Gate-marks on rim; machine
grinding. Exceptionally fine casting.

P-1401-MPS Brass (VR)
9⅞ x 4⅞ x 1½ 1 lb 1 oz
A-19 F 1 R 2
Firefighting.

E-530-MPS Iron (O)
11⅜ x 7¾ x ¾ 1 lb 9 oz
A-14 F 2 R 2
On the reverse, "UC JM 302."
Firefighting.

E-334-MPS Iron (VR)
8⅞ x 4⅛ 12 oz
Legs have been cut. F 1 R 2
Tools of a molder (iron casting). Some
backcoping.

E-135-MPS Iron (VR)
8⅝ x 4 x 1 12 oz
A-19 F 1 R 2
Tools of a blacksmith.

P-1832-MPS Iron (R)
7¼ x 3⁷⁄₁₆ x ⅝ 5 oz
A-5 F 1 R 2
On face, "Britain's Might Iron Stands."
On reverse, "Reg. No. 352236." Military.
Large gate-marks on rim; backcoping.

P-1665-MPS Iron (R)
9 x 6¼ x 1½ 1 lb 14½ oz
A-8 F 2 R 2
Nautical. Large gate-mark on rim;
backcoping.

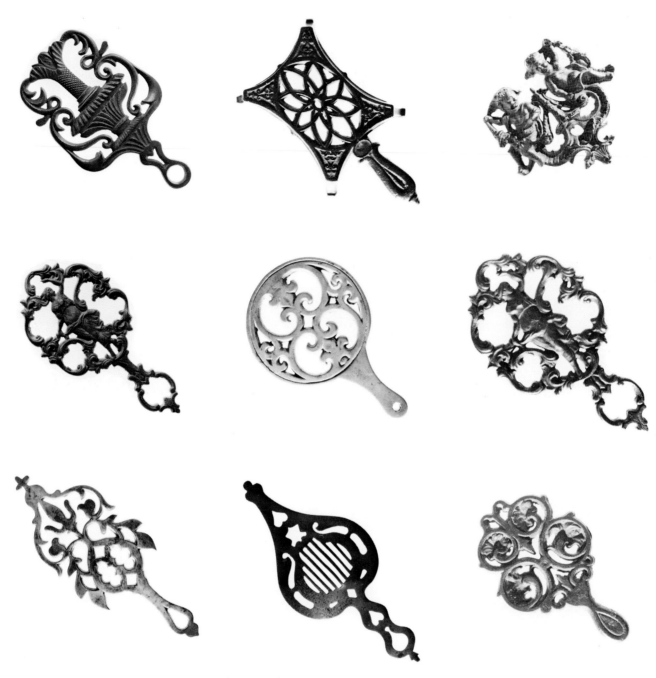

There are a number of trivets in the Paley Collection which appear to have originated in Europe. The designs are distinctly different from those found in this country. In some instances they carry a foreign imprint on the reverse or a registered number indicating British origin.

M-16-MPS Brass (VR)
8¾ x 5⅛ x 1½   1 lb ¼ oz
A-1 F 1 R 2

M-20-MPS Brass (VR)
9⅞ x 5 x 1   1 lb
A-10 F 2 R 2

E-523-MPS Brass (R)
10¾ x 4 x 1⅜   15½ oz
A-18 F 1 R 2

E-533-MPS Iron (VR)
8⅞ x 5½ x 2   1 lb 7½ oz
Splayed feet F 2 R 2
Large sprue-mark on reverse.

E-447-MPS Brass (R)
8⅝ x 5⅝ x 1½   1 lb 12½ oz
K-8 F 1 S 2

E-507-MPS Brass (R)
11⅛ x 4¾ x 1³/₁₆   14 oz
A-18 F 1 R 2

E-708-MPS Iron (VR)
6¾ x 7⅜ x 1½   1 lb 12 oz
K-11 F 2 R 1
Extensive backcoping; fine casting. Very irregular platform surface because of modeling.

E-371-MPS Iron (R)
8¾ x 4⅞ x ¹⁵/₁₆   14 oz
A-11 F 2 R 2
Extreme backcoping.

E-416-MPS Iron (VR)
8⅜ x 5⅛ x 1⅜   1 lb 14 oz
A-7 F 2 R 1 S 2
Old casting; gate-mark on rim.

E-555-MPS Iron (R)
8½ x 4⅞ x 1⁷/₁₆   1 lb 7 oz
Riveted supports.   F 1   R 2
Round head posts riveted to a cast
platform. Backcoped. See *Pressing Irons
and Trivets,* Berney p. 137.

P-1027-MPS Iron (VR)
10¼ x 5 x 1³/₁₆   1 lb 8 oz
Front M-C 4, Rear A-13   F 2   R 2
On face, "Jubilee 1887." Bracket device on
reverse. Large gate-mark on handle.

P-1955-MPS Iron (VR)
10 x 6⁹/₁₆ x 1⅛   1 lb 7½ oz
A-9   F 2   R 2
On reverse, "Rd. No. 33143." Bracket and
bracket device on reverse.

P-1883-MPS Iron (VR)
10 x 4⅞ x 1⁵/₁₆   1 lb 5 oz
20-C 6   F 2   R 1
On reverse, illegible Register number.
Stock number 14. Bracket device has been
cut off.

P-92-MPS Iron (VR)
10⅜ x 5¼ x ⅝   1 lb 9 oz
A-25   F 2   R 1
Gate-mark on rim. Handle probably a
premade ornamental piece, as the handle
is cast in the round and the platform is
flat on the reverse.

P-1514-MPS Iron (VR)
10 x 5¹/₁₆ x 1¼   1 lb 4 oz
Front J-C 6, Rear A-4   F 2   R 1
On reverse, "Rd. No. 588469," and bracket
device. Two gate-marks on rim.

P-1360-MPS Iron (R)
9 x 5⅝ x 1¼   2 lbs 6¾ oz
A-10   F 2   R 2

P-181-MPS Iron (VR)
11½ x 8 x 1⅜   1 lb 10¾ oz
A-20   F 1   R 2
Large gate-mark on rim.

P-930-MPS Iron (VR)
9 x 5⅜ x 1³/₁₆   14 oz
A-10   F 2   R 1
On reverse, "Rd. No. 617458 2470." Gate-
mark on rim; machine grinding.

P-1127-MPS Iron (VR)
9½ x 6 x 1³/₁₆   13 oz
A-3 F 2 R 2
On reverse, "Rd. No. 96845," and bracket device. Gate-mark on rim.

P-202-MPS Iron (VR)
8¹⁵/₁₆ x 5⁵/₁₆ x ¾   1 lb 4½ oz
A-14 F 2 R 2
Wedge-mark on reverse where handle meets the platform.

P-1678-MPS Iron (VR)
8⅜ x 5⅜ x 1¹/₁₆   13 oz
A-3 F 2 R 2
On reverse, "Rd. No. 27270." Gate-marks on rim. Trivet orignally had a japanned finish.

P-1329-MPS Iron (VR)
9¾ x 5¾ x 1¼   1 lb
A-3 F 2 R 2
On reverse, "Rd. No. 24900." Seven gate-marks on left rim.

P-787-MPS Iron (VR)
9¹¹/₁₆ x 4⅛ x 1¼   1 lb 5¾ oz
J-C 6 F 2 R 2
On reverse, "Rd. No. 36610 No. 21," and bracket device. Gate-mark on rim.

P-1108-MPS Iron (R)
7¾ x 5⅛ x 1½   1 lb 4½ oz
A-10 F 2 R 1
Very deep surface relief. It would be difficult to set objects on the surface. Gate-mark on rim filed smooth.

P-1425-MPS Iron (VR)
8 x 5½ x 1¼   15½ oz
B-10 F 2 R 1
Gate-mark on rim filed smooth. Legs probably drilled and fitted onto a wire guide in making the pattern.

P-366-MPS Iron (VR)
8¾ x 5⅜ x 1⅜   1 lb 3 oz
A-10 F 1 R 2
Two initials on reverse; one is "W", the other is unclear. Shallow backcoping; two gate-marks on rim.

P-1844-MPS Iron (VR)
8½ x 4½ x 1⁷/₁₆   14½ oz
B-20 F 1 R 2
Two gate-marks on rim. Curious bent handle. Excellent casting.

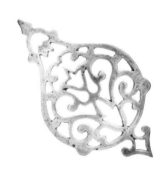

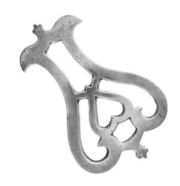

P-1583-MPS Iron (VR)
10 ⅞ x 7⅛ x 1¹¹/₁₆   1 lb 14 oz
A-17 F 2 R 1
Legs are riveted to platform. Sprue-mark on reverse.

P-76-MPS Iron (R)
7⅜ x 4¼ x 1³/₁₆   10 oz
A-3 F 2 R 1
Shallow backcoping on reverse of handle. Unfiled gate-mark on rim.

P-394-MPS Brass (VR)
9 x 5½ x 1⅛   1 lb 2½ oz
A-9 F 2 R 1
Quarter-inch rim around bottom of platform.

P-627-MPS Brass (R)
7¾ x 4½ x 1   10½ oz
A-9 F 1 R 2
Similar design Iron (not shown)
7 x 3¾ x 1⅜   9 oz
J-8 F 1 R 2
On face, "Carron," (Scottish foundry). On reverse, "2." Reverse draft.

P-1424-MPS Brass (R)
8¾ x 4⅜ x 1¾   1 lb 10½ oz
A-20 F 1 R 2

P-594-MPS Brass (R)
6½ x 4¼ x 1¼   12¾ oz
A-10 F 1 R 2

P-1392-MPS Brass/glass (VR)
7½ x 4¼ x ¹⁵/₁₆   7½ oz
Ornamental splayed cleats   F 2 R 2
Milk glass insert.

P-292-MPS Brass (R)
7⁹/₁₆ x 4¼ x 1¼   8¾ oz
A-19 F 1 R 2

P-353-MPS Brass (O)
9¾ x 5⅛ x 1⅛   1 lb 4 oz
Ornamental splayed cleats   F 2 R 2
On reverse, "Carron," (Scottish foundry). This design often cast in iron and several sizes. Old design.

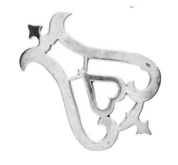

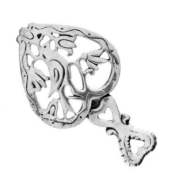

P-529-MPS Brass (R)
8¾ x 4⁹/₁₆ x 1   1 lb 5 oz
Splayed ornamental cleats   F 2   R 2
Variation of P-353.

P-332-MPS Brass (R)
7⅞ x 4 x 1¼   6½ oz
A-19   F 1   R 2

P-695-MPS Brass (R)
7⅞ x 4⅜ x 1   8¾ oz
A-19   F 2   R 1

P-1663-MPS Brass (R)
6¼ x 3⁹/₁₆ x ¹¹/₁₆   7 oz
D-14   F 1   R 2

P-869-MPS Brass (R)
7 x 4⅝ x ¾   8¼ oz
A-11   F 1   R 2

P-214-MPS Brass (R)
9 x 3⅞ x 1⅜   12 oz
A-19   F 1   R 2

P-857-MPS Brass/wood (R)
9¼ x 3¹³/₁₆ x 1   12½ oz
A-3   F 1   R 2
Handle screwed into platform.

P-1614-MPS Brass (VR)
7⅞ x 4¼ x 1⅛   14 oz
A-21   F 2   R 1
Figure backcoped.

P-1128-MPS Brass (R)
6⅝ x 3¹³/₁₆ x ½   4½ oz
A-15   F 1   R 2
Extensive backcoping.

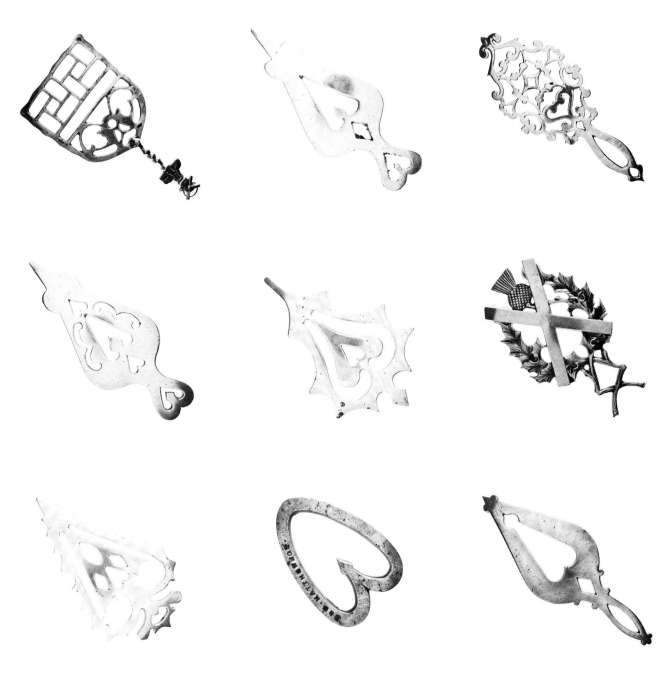

P-254-MPS Brass (VR)
10¼ x 5¼ x ¾   9¾ oz
A-15 F 2 R 1
Handle made separately and screwed into
platform. Hanging wire on handle.

P-1429-MPS Brass (R)
10½ x 4¼ x 1⅛   1 lb ½ oz
A-10 F 1 R 2

P-701-MPS Brass (R)
6¾ x 3¹³/₁₆ x 1   8 oz
A-3 F 1 R 2

P-540-MPS Brass (R)
10 x 4 x 1⅜   15½ oz
A-24 F 1 R 2

P-1595-MPS Brass (R)
7 x 4½ x 1   8 oz
A-19 F 1 R 2

P-1019-MPS Brass (R)
5½ x 3⅞ x 1¹³/₁₆   9½ oz
A-19 F 1 R 2
On face, "Mrs. Matthewson."
Letters stamped into brass.

P-1836-MPS Brass (R)
10⅛ x 4 x 1¼   11 oz
A-10 F 1 R 2

P-1818-MPS Brass (R)
7⅜ x 4⅜ x 1¼   12½ oz
Short posts and bell shaped cups form the
supports. F 2 R 2
Extensive backcoping.

P-217-MPS Brass (R)
11¼ x 4⅛ x 1⅛   1 lb
A-15 F 1 R 2

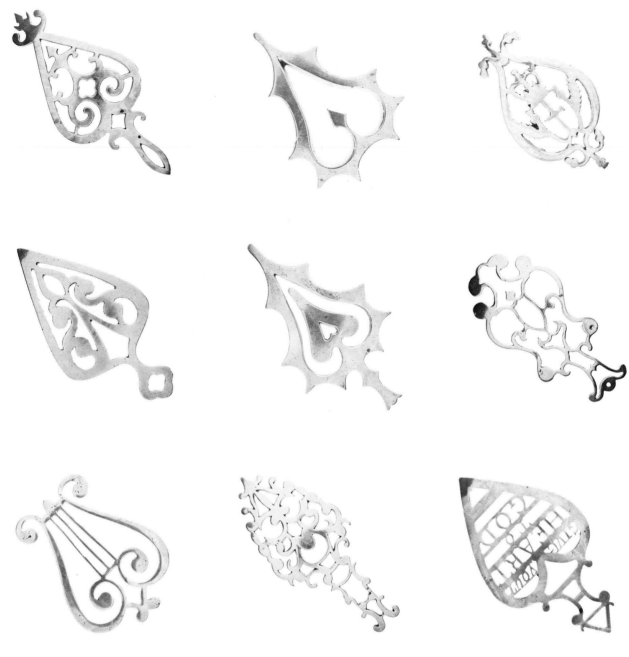

P-431-MPS Brass (O)
11 x 5 x ¾   11½ oz
A-9 F 1 R 2

P-586-MPS Brass (O)
7½ x 3⅞ x 1¼   13 oz
A-18 F 1 R 2

P-155-MPS Brass (R)
5⅜ x 4¹/₁₆ x ¹¹/₁₆ 4¾ oz
A-19 F 1 R 2

P-664-MPS Brass (R)
6⅛ x 4⅜ x ¹⁵/₁₆ 8½ oz
A-14 F 1 R 2

P-1053-MPS Brass (R)
7¾ x 4¼ x 1   8 oz
A-17 F 1 R 2

P-389-MPS Brass (R)
9⅞ x 4⅜ x 1⅛   11½ oz
A-19 F 1 R 2

P-CCC-MPS Brass (R)
6⅜ x 3⅜ x 1³/₁₆ 7½ oz
A-18 F 1 R 2

P-1231-MPS Brass (VR)
9⅜ x 4¹¹/₁₆ x 1⁵/₁₆ 12 oz
A-19 F 2 R 2

P-863-MPS Brass (R)
9½ x 5³/₁₆ x ⅞   10 oz
A-11 F 1 R 2
On face, "Give Your Heart To God."

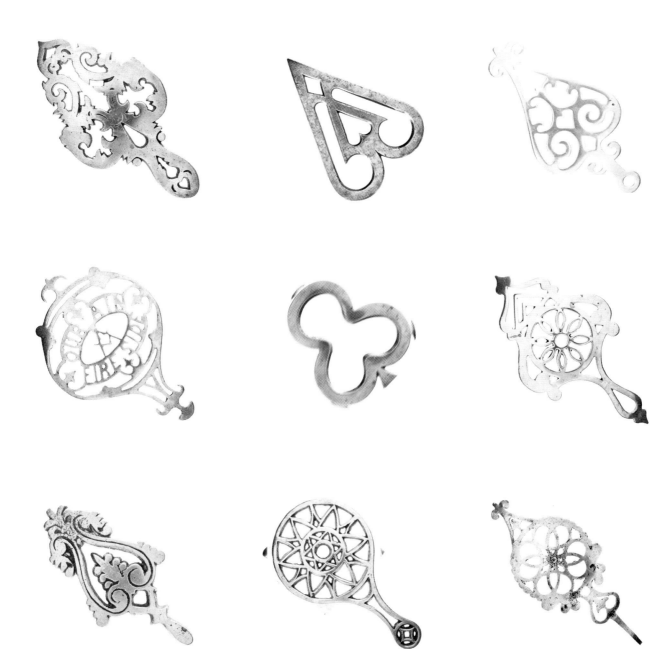

P-1106-MPS Bronze (VR)
8¼ x 4¼ x 1¼ 13 oz
N-11 F 1 R 2

P-954-MPS Brass (R)
7⅜ x 4¾ x 1⅜ 9½ oz
A-18 F 2 R 1
On face, "Our Ain Fire Side."

P-1288-MPS Brass (VR)
6¾ x 3⅜ x 1¼ 13 oz
A-9 F 1 R 2

P-1550-MPS Brass (R)
5⅝ x 4⅛ x ⅞ 6¾ oz
A-3 F 1 R 2

P-793-MPS Brass (O)
4¹⁵⁄₁₆ x 4⅛ x ¹¹⁄₁₆ 3¾ oz
Rim extended into cleats. F 1 R 2
On reverse, "Rd. 62449."

P-653-MPS Brass (R)
8 x 4⅝ x ¾ 1 lb
Splayed cleats F 2 R 2
Eleven-sixteenths-inch sloped and
scalloped rail on bottom of platform. Less
rim on handle.

P-436-MPS Brass (R)
7 x 3⅜ x 1¼ 8 oz
D-H F 1 R 2

P-59-MPS Brass (R)
9½ x 5 x 1⅛ 14 oz
J-C 6 F 1 R 2

P-1165-MPS Brass (VR)
9⅝ x 4 x 1 11½ oz
A-19 F 1 R 2
Length measurement includes tang for a
missing handle.

P-215-MPS Brass (VR)
8⅜ x 4 x 1   9 oz
A-9 F 1 R 2

P-50-MPS Brass (R)
9½ x 3⅞ x 1⅝   9 oz
A-18 F 1 R 2

P-1819-MPS Brass (VR)
6⅜ x 3½ x ¾   4 oz
A-4 F 2 R 1

P-333-MPS Brass (R)
8¼ x 4⅛ x ¾   12 oz
A-21 F 1 R 2

P-551-MPS Brass (R)
9¼ x 5 x 1⅞   15½ oz
A-1 F 1 R 2

P-778-MPS Brass (O)
8⅝ x 5⅛ x 1¹/₁₆   13 oz
Front M-C 4 Rear A-19 F 2 R 2
On face, "60 years of H.M. Reign." On
reverse, "Reg'd." One-eighth-inch rim
around bottom of platform. Extensive
backcoping.

P-167-MPS Brass (O)
6¼ x 3⁷/₁₆ x 1   8¼ oz
A-19 F 1 R 2

P-1126-MPS Brass (R)
7¼ x 4½ x ¹³/₁₆   7 oz
A-4 F 1 R 2
On face, "Africa's Hero Lord Roberts."
Extensive backcoping.

P-556-MPS Brass (R)
9 x 6⁵/₁₆ x ⅞   1 lb 3½ oz
Front K-C 6 Rear A-9 F 2 R 2
On face, "The Cup; Peace & Plenty That
Cheers." On reverse, "Greenlees, Glasgow,"
(somewhat illegible).

A marvelous Victorian cookstove.

Stove and Cereal Trivets

With the advent of the cast-iron kitchen range, a number of stands were expressly designed for use on cook stoves. Some were used to prepare cereals, gravies, sauces or foods which easily scorched. Also, these stands helped to lower heat to simmer or warm foods. The stands usually had short feet, a half-inch or less, and most had an opening to insert a stove-lid lifter. Hankenson called these stands "cereal trivets." Cereal trivets were often distributed as premiums, notably by The Quaker Oats Company. Premium stands frequently had advertising, directions for use, or patent numbers on the face or reverse.

A few stands were fashioned to be used over the opening when a stove lid was removed and extreme heat was required. Stands designed for this purpose had much longer legs than cereal trivets. There are some grid stands with provision for a stove-lid lifter. This strongly suggests they too were used on kitchen stoves. It is reasonable to assume that other trivets could also have been used on the stove top to keep food warm, or to prevent scorching.

Griswold Housewares Company marketed a number of stove stands; cereal stands were usually identified as trivets on the reverse. Griswold also made cast-iron steaming racks that fit into the bottom of Griswold kettles. These steaming racks were often confused by collectors with cereal trivets.

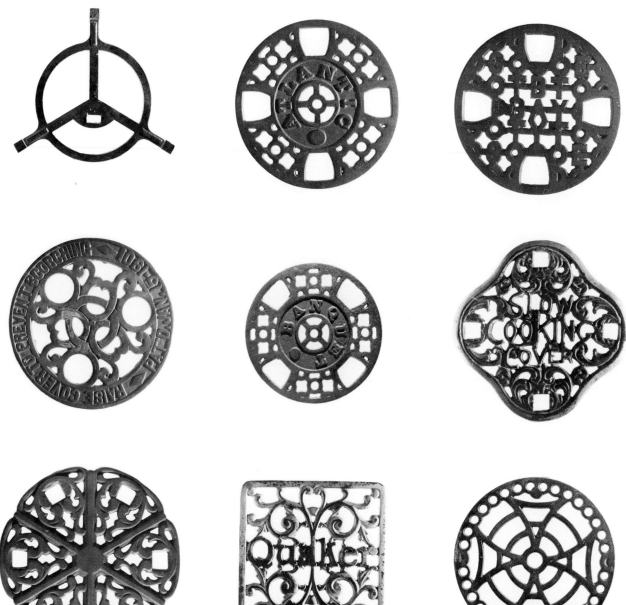
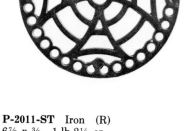

P-1320-ST Iron (O)
7 x 1   9 oz
F 1   R 1   S 1
Supports are extensions of the rim
splayed and bent into legs and feet. For
use over an open fire with the stove-lid
removed. Provision for stove-lid lifter.

P-1391-ST Iron/ Enameled finish (O)
6¼ x ½   10¾ oz
F-15   F 1   R 1   S 1
On face, "Raise Cover to Prevent Scorching. Pat'd. Jan 15, 1901." Provision for
stove-lid lifter.

P-1191-ST Iron (R)
7⅝ x ½   1 lb 13 oz
M-C 1   F 1   R 1   S 1
On reverse, "Simmering Cover. W & P
Mfg. Co." Provision for stove-lid lifter.
Large sprue-mark on reverse.

P-1327-ST Iron (R)
8¾ x ⅜   1 lb 1 oz
Supported by rim. On face, "Atlantic."
Provision for stove-lid lifter.

E-702-ST Iron (R)
6¾ x ⅜   1 lb 2 oz
Segmented rim. On face, "Banquet." Provision for stove-lid lifter.

P-1365-ST Iron (R)
6¾ x ⁷⁄₁₆   1 lb
Corner cleats. F 2   R 2
On face, "Quaker." On reverse, "Simmering Cover T.I.W. 733." Nickel finish
eroded; backcoped.

P-2011-ST Iron (R)
6⅞ x ⅜   1 lb 2½ oz
Supported by rim. On face, letterforms
but the message is not clear. Provision for
stove-lid lifter. Large wedge-mark on reverse.

P-986-ST Iron (O)
7 x ⁹⁄₁₆   1 lb 15½ oz
Corner cleats. F 2   R 2
On face, "Slow Cooking Cover." Provision
for stove-lid lifter. Wedge-mark; nickel
finish eroded.

P-1518-ST Iron ((C)
6⅞ x ½   13¾ oz
A-14   F 2   R 2
Two gate-marks on rim; machine grinding.

P-1257-ST Iron (R)
6¾ x ⁵/₁₆ 11 oz
F 1 R 1 S 2
Feet are bent down sections of rim; rim
openings fit a stove-lid lifter.

P-685-ST Iron (C)
7 x ⁵/₁₆ 15 oz
A-11 F 1 R 1 S 1
On reverse, "The Griswold Mfg Co. Erie,
PA USA Trivet 7."

P-1814-ST Iron (R)
7⅝ x 6¾ x 1 1 lb ½ oz
G-C 9 F 1 R 1 S 1
On face, "Buck's Stove & Range Co. St
Louis." On reverse, "171." Provision for
stove-lid lifter.

E-184-ST Iron (O)
6⁹/₁₆ x ⅜ 1 lb 4 oz
One-quarter-inch cleats. F 2 R 2
On face, "Turn This Cover To Raise It
and Prevent Cereals From Burning." On
reverse, "A-20-68."

P-1585-ST Iron (O)
5⅝ x ⅝ 11¼ oz
A-17 F 2 R 2
On face, "Irving Ranges. Rosemont Heat-
ers. John Getz's Sons, Sales Agents, York,
Pa." Nickel finish.

E-179-ST Iron (O)
6¾ x ⅜ 1 lb 2 oz
Four one-eighth-inch cleats. F 2 R 2
On face, "Raise register and Cereals Never
Burn." On reverse, model number and
other information illegible.

Tea, Coffee and Table Stands

Table stands represent a category quite different from kitchen stands and iron rests. Table stands were produced by a variety of manufacturing methods in a wide range of materials. This book focuses on those cast in iron or brass, but other examples are included. The principal functions of these stands were to hold pots, serve food or protect furniture surfaces. Most table stands tended to be lighter-weight and more delicately ornate than trivets made for the kitchen. Undoubtedly these small decorative table stands occasionally served as iron rests.

Most platforms were scarcely more than a quarter- to a half-inch high. Many designs were based on English Regency styles with three to six small ornamental paw feet or ornate supports. These small footed stands probably date back to the latter part of the eighteenth century. They certainly are among the oldest stands found and reproduced in this country. Platforms often featured arabesque based on floral or geometric designs. On the older castings, platforms were concave. Most were cast in iron initially, but later, many designs were also cast in brass.

During the late nineteenth century, manufacturers marketed table stands in the style of old Regency designs, but monograms, ligatures, and advertising were incorporated. Most table stands were round without handles. A few were oval-shaped to hold platters. Platter stands were handled or unhandled and often were mounted on casters or ornamental ball feet. Some were adjustable in size with the platform in two pieces mounted on runners. The size of the platform could be set by sliding the platform sections back and forth.

There were a number of elegant table stands made of silver, or silver-plated, which were used for social dining occasions. Some had delicate metal frames and etched glass or china insets. Many of these had etched metal surfaces, or elaborate, stamped openwork.

Also, cast-iron was used for table stand frames with tile insets. These could be handled or unhandled. Around the turn of the century, many tiles carried advertising messages, and stands were used as premiums. The Ellwood collection has a curious round cast-iron stand with a square tile inset. The Tea Tiles shown in another section of this book actually are of this type, but they are larger and much more elaborate. Enameled Stands can be classified as table stands, but their size, finish and design sets them apart from others in this section.

Quite a few table and kitchen stands were made of wire, stamped metal, and wood. Twisted wire utensils are characteristic of the late Victorian era. A variety of kitchen and iron rests, baskets, cooking spoons, pillow fluffers, egg cookers and other household items were ingeniously contrived from wire. Wrapping, coiling, crimping, using different weights of wire in combination with metal clips, tubes or metal strips resulted in lightweight but sturdy utensils. Wire stands had some special functions. They were used as cooling stands for pastries or bread, as meat rests, and in ice boxes to raise food above moist or wet shelves. A number of wire stands served as steaming racks at the bottom of kettles. Houseware companies regularly marketed wire stands from the 1870's through the 1930's.

Another group of stands made for the kitchen or as iron rests were stamped tin or light-weight steel. Decoration was often done by piercing and shaping the metal. Stamped designs were done with machinery and dies. A steel die was used to punch out the shape including supports and pierced decoration. Supports were extensions of the rim bent down to form feet. Other times a male and female die were used to shape the metal into decorative rims or embossed designs. Stamped metal designs were made of tin, occa-

P-1579-TCT Iron (R)
5¼ x ⅜ 7¼ oz
Four paw feet. On face, "R H Co." Gate-mark on rim. Beautiful casting.

P-1581-TCT Iron (R)
5½ x ⁷⁄₁₆ 8 oz
Four paw feet. Two gate-marks on rim.

sionally brass or brass-plated metal, and light-weight steel. Many stamped tin stands were surprisingly handsome pieces. Stamped steel stands tended to be more functional but less decorative.

Some wooden stands were covered with brass or copper sheeting. The metal was decorated with criblé patterns made with a punch and hammer. There seems to be no limit to the variety of materials and designs for table stands. Brass table stands were either imported from the Orient, or reproduced in Oriental styles by Europeans and Americans. Many Oriental trivets and stands are still being imported into this country.

P-177-TCT Iron (O)
5 x ⅜   7 oz
Six paw feet. One gate-mark on rim.

P-137-TCT Iron (R)
5⁵⁄₁₆ x ⅜   8 oz
Six paw feet. ?edge-mark on reverse.

P-602-TCT Iron (R)
4⅞ x ⁷⁄₁₆   5 oz
Four paw feet. Gate-mark on rim.

P-86-TCT Iron (R)
4⅞ x ⁷⁄₁₆   5¼ oz
Four paw feet. Sprue-mark on reverse.

P-85-TCT Iron (O)
5⅜ x ½   8¾ oz
Three paw feet. Wedge-mark on reverse.

P-1364-TCT Iron (R)
5 x ⁵⁄₁₆   7¼ oz
Six paw feet. Gate-mark on rim.

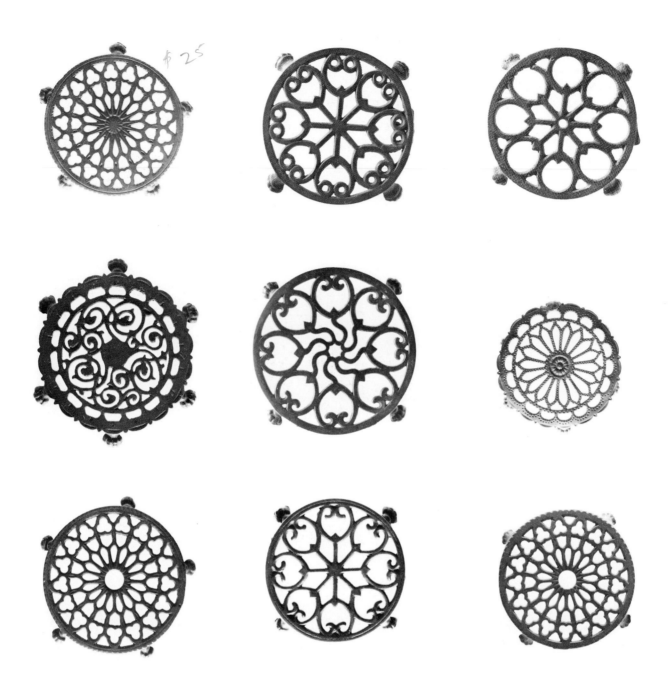

P-102-TCT Iron (O)
5 x ½   7 oz
5 paw feet.

P-180-TCT Iron (O)
5⅜ x ½   8¾ oz
6 paw feet. Wedge-mark on reverse.

P-103-TCT Iron (C)
5 x 9/16   7 oz
5 paw feet. Gate-mark on rim.

P-1182-TCT Iron (O)
5¼ x ½   8½ oz
Four paw feet. Large gate-mark on rim.
Also cast in brass.

P-403-TCT Iron (R)
5⅝ x ⅝   7¼ oz
Four paw feet. Two gate-marks on rim.

E-362-TCT Iron (O)
5 5/16 x ⅝   7 oz.
Paw feet. F 2   R 2

P-1817-TCT Iron (O)
5⅛ x ⅝   7½ oz
Four paw feet. Large gate-mark on rim.
Badly corroded; old casting.

E-723-TCT Brass (R)
5¼ x 15/16   9 oz.
Six paw feet. F 2   R 2   S 2
Paw feet are vertically extended; height
and surface dimpling are uncommon. One
support damaged and reattached.

P-29-TCT Iron (C)
4⅞ x 9/16   5¾ oz.
Four paw feet. Two gate-marks on rim.

 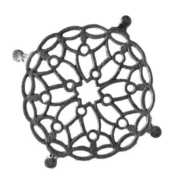 

P-28-TCT Iron (O)
4⅞ x ¾   6½ oz.
Four paw feet. Nickel finish eroded.
Sometimes cast in brass.

P-168-TCT Iron (O)
5 x ½   6½ oz
Four paw feet. Two gate-marks on rim.

P-1411-TCT Iron (O)
5¼ x ½   7½ oz
Four paw feet. Two gate-marks on rim.
Also cast in brass.

P-817-TCT Iron (O)
4⅞ x ⅝   6 oz
Four paw feet. Two gate-marks on rim.

P-105-TCT Iron (O)
5⅛ x ¾   7½ oz.
Four paw feet. Two gate-marks on rim.

P-269-TCT Iron (O)
5 x ½   4 oz.
Four paw feet. On face, "L."

E-390-TCT Iron (R)
5¼ x 9/16   13 oz
Paw feet. F 2 R 2 S 2
Cast through rim. Wilton made reproductions of this design.

E-90-TCT Iron (R)
5⅝ x ½   11 oz
Paw feet. F 2 R 2 S 2
Wedge-mark on reverse.

E-24-TCT Iron (R)
6¼ x ⅜   12 oz.
F 2 R 2
Extensions of rim similar to paw feet.
Gate-marks on rim; machine grinding.

E-378-TCT Iron (R)
7¾ x 5⅛ x ⁹⁄₁₆   13 oz
Paw feet. F 1   R 2
Unusual handled, paw-footed stand. Gate-mark on rim. The Metropolitan Museum of Art has the same design but slightly larger; 8⅜ x 5⅜ x ½.

E-186-TCT Iron/tile (R)
7¼ x ½   1 lb 3½ oz
Six Paw feet. F 2   R 2   S 2
Feet were drilled so stand could be secured to table or counter top.

K-11-TCT Iron (O)
7 x ⅝   1 lb 2 oz
Five Paw feet. F 1   R 2   S 2
On reverse, "Griswold Trivet 1739 1."

P-397-TCT Iron (C)
4⅜ x ⁷⁄₁₆   9¼ oz
N-15   F 2   R 2
" Ober, Chagrin Falls, Ohio."

P-874-TCT Iron (R)
4⅝ x ¾   9 oz
D-15   F 2   R 2
Monogram "OMCo" (Ober Mfg. Co.)

P-278-TCT Iron (C)
4¾ x ¾   9½ oz
F-15   F 2   R 2
Monogram "OMCo." Nickel finish eroded.

P-179-TCT Iron (C)
4¼ x ⁷⁄₁₆   9¼ oz
N-15   F 2   R 2
Made by Ober.

P-572-TCT Iron (O)
4½ x ¾   8½ oz
D-15   F 2   R 2
"Ober Chagrin Falls O."

P-1921-TCT Iron (R)
3⅛ x ⅝   3½ oz
D-5   F 2   R 2
"OMCo." Nickel finish.

P-136-TCT   Iron   (VR)
4¼ x ⅝   9 oz
N-14   F 2   R 2
On reverse, "Ober Mfg Co Chagrin Falls
O." Nickel finish.

K-42-TCT   Iron   (R)
5⅜ x ¾   9 oz
A-11   F 2   R 2
On reverse, "Ober."

E-367-TCT   Iron   (VR)
6¹/₁₆ x ¹³/₁₆   11 oz
A-11   F 2   R 2
On reverse, "Ober." Originally nickel finish; painted black.

K-9-TCT   Iron   (O)
6⅛ x ¹³/₁₆   14 oz.
Supports formed by extensions of rim.
F 2   R 2
On reverse, "CC." Five-sixteenths-inch rim
around bottom of platform. Gate-mark on
rim; machine grinding.

E-518-TCT   Iron   (R)
4¾ x ¾   9 oz.
A-11   F 2   R 2
On the face, "No. 1," with illegible
inscription.

E-46-TCT   Iron   (R)
5⅛ x ⅝   10 oz.
Cast ball feet.   F 1   R 1   S 1
Concave platform; unusual design.

E-77-TCT   Iron   (R)
7½ x ½   14 oz.
F-C 8   F 2   R 2   S 4

P-1517-TCT   Iron   (VR)
8¼ x ⅞   1 lb 5½ oz
A-22   F 2   R 1
On face, monogram "ANC & Co." Gates
removed by machine grinding.

P-1515-TCT   Iron   (R)
7¾ x 1³/₁₆   1 lb 7 oz
A-25   F 1   R 2
Gate-mark on rim; machine grinding.

P-199-TCT Iron (R)
9½ x 1⅛ 1 lb 4 oz
A-3 F 1 R 1 S 2
Gate-marks on inside of center ring.

P-1516-TCT Iron (R)
8¾ x 1⅜ 1 lb 13½ oz
A-8 F 1 R 1 S 1

P-1321-TCT Iron (R)
8½ x 1⁷/₁₆ 1 lb 1 oz
A-2 F 2 R 2
Reverse draft.

E-183-TCT Iron (O)
7⅜ x ⅜ 12½ oz
A-16 F 1 R 1 S 1

E-907-TCT Iron (R)
7 x 1⅛ 1 lb 5½ oz
Three splayed cleats extend from rim.
F 1 R 1 S 1
On face, "Pat. April 6 1882 A. W___G__
__ROTH," partially illegible.

P-1701-TCT Iron (R)
7⅝ x ⅝ 14 oz
D-4 F 1 R 2 S 2

E-527-TCT Iron (R)
7⅞ x 1¹/₁₆ 1 lb
Three one-inch ball feet. F 1 R 1 S 1
On reverse, triangular trademark partially
obliterated.

P-1630-TCT Iron (R)
8½ x 1⅛ 1 lb 14½ oz
Six ornamental cleats extend from underside of one-quarter-inch rim. Nickel finish
badly corroded.

P-945-TCT Iron (R)
8¾ x ⁹/₁₆ 1 lb 4½ oz
M-C 2 F 1 R 1 S 4
On reverse, "9J." Shallow backcoping.

P-430-TCT Iron (R)
8 x ⅜   1 lb 1 oz
A-16 F 2 R 2 plus an additional four feet at center of platform reverse.

E-52-TCT Iron (R)
6½ x ¹¹⁄₁₆   1 lb 7 oz
B-14 F 2 R 2

E-803-TCT Iron (R)
6½ x 1½   1 lb 2½ oz
A-18 F 1 R 1 S 1
Two gate-marks on rim.

P-1181-TCT Iron (VR)
9⅜ x ½   1 lb ¾ oz
G-15 F 2 R 2 S 2
Two gate-marks on inside center ring.

K-80-TCT Iron (O)
4½ x ¾   5 oz
A-3 F 1 R 1 S 1
Platform cast from a hand-forged stand; blacksmith's overlap weld on ring is evident in the casting.

E-59-TCT Iron (O)
5 ⅝ x 2¹⁄₁₆   1 lb 3½ oz
Ornamental splayed extensions of rim.
F 1 R 1 S 1
Probably cast in England.

E-60-TCT Iron (O)
5¹¹⁄₁₆ x 2¼   1 lb 3½ oz
F 1 R 1 S 1
Supports are splayed extensions of rim. Another version is three and three-eighths inches high with three-inch pre-made ornamental legs screwed into the platform.

P-1862-TCT Iron (O)
5⅛ x ¾   10¼ oz
Three splayed cleats. Filed gate-mark on rim.

P-377-TCT Iron (O)
5 x ¾   7¼ oz
Four splayed cleats rolled at ends.

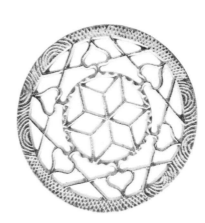

P-320-TCT Iron (R)
5¹/₁₆ x ¹¹/₁₆   9 oz
Four splayed cleats. Two gate-marks on rim.

P-349-TCT Iron (R)
5⅜ x ¹¹/₁₆   10¾ oz
Four splayed cleats. On reverse, "Pat Apd For Sundry Mfg Co." Two sprue-marks on reverse. P-320 and P-349 probably made by same manufacturer.

E-61-TCT Iron (R)
6 x 1½   13 oz
A-2 F 1 R 1 S 1
Nickel finish; decorative incised platform.

E-467-TCT Iron (O)
4⅞ x ¹³/₁₆   6 oz
F 1 R 1 S 1
Supports are coiled and bent iron strapping riveted to platform.

E-160-TCT Iron (R)
6⅞ x ½   14 oz
A-15 Fifteen feet.

E-709-TCT Iron (R)
6⅛ x ½   12½ oz
A-16 F 1 R 1 S 1
Reverse draft.

E-97-TCT Iron (R)
5⅞ x 2⅝   12 oz
K-8 F 1 R 1 S 1
Gate-mark on rim; hearth stand.

E-58-TCT Iron (R)
6 x 2⅝   12 oz
G-9 F 1 R 1 S 1
On reverse, "2885 14."

E-361-TCT Iron (R)
6½ x 1⁷/₁₆   1 lb 5 oz
A 2 F2 R 2
Nickel finish.

  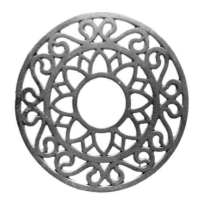

  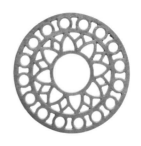

  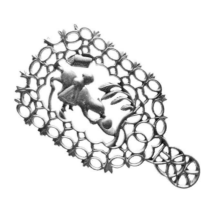

E-105-TCT Iron (VR)
7⅞ x 1½   1 lb 12 oz
A-2 F 1 R 1 S 1
Large sprue-mark on reverse; fine old casting.

P-146-TCT Iron (O)
4¹⁵⁄₁₆ x ⅜   6 oz
Four splayed cleats. Large gate-mark on rim.

P-514-TCT Iron (O)
5¼ x ⅝   8½ oz
A-14 F 2 R 2
Gate-marks on rim; filing. Four quarter-inch guide cleats on top of platform.

P-738-TCT Iron (R)
5⅜ x ⅝   11¼ oz
A-15 F 2 R 2
Four quarter-inch guide cleats on top of platform.

P-2012A-TCT Iron (O)
4¹⁵⁄₁₆ x ½   7½ oz
M-C 2 F 2 R 2
Two gate-marks on rim.

P-2012B-TCT Iron (O)
4¹⁵⁄₁₆ x ½   9¼ oz
M-C 2 F 2 R 2
Gate-marks removed by machine grinding.

P-727-TCT Iron (O)
6⅝ x ⅝   12½ oz
A-15 F 2 R 2
Large gate-mark on rim. Nickel finish eroded.

E-901-TCT Iron (R)
5⅞ x ⅝   1 lb ½ oz
A-10 F 2 R 2
Advertised by Reading Saddle & Manufacturing Company, c. 1919.

P-1227-TCT Iron (VR)
11⅜ x 6⅜ x 1¼   1 lb 13 oz
A-10 F 2 R 2
Photograph is of a Virginia Metalcrafters reproduction, but all measurements were taken from a slightly damaged original. No backcoping on the original; backcoping and Virginia Metalcrafter's Betty Lamp symbol on the reproduction. Design dates from World War I era.

P-1088-TCT Iron (C)
9⅝ x 7¾ x ½   15 oz
A-15 F 2 R 2 Middle 1
Recent casting, probably 1950's or later.

P-1148-TCT Iron (R)
8⅜ x 4½ x ⅝   9 oz
C-7 F 1 R 1 S 2
Nickel finish; size suggests use as an iron rest.

P-1453-TCT Tin (R)
10⅛ x 7⅝
Supports formed by extensions of rim bent down into feet.

P-1471-TCT Iron (R)
7⅛ x 4½ x ⅝   9 oz
M-C 4 F 1 R 1 S 2
Nickel finish; size suggests use as an iron rest.

E-383-TCT Iron (R)
7¼ x 4¼ x ½   9 oz
D-15 F 1 R 1 S 2
Size suggests use as an iron rest.

P-444-TCT Iron (VR)
9½ x 1⅛   2 lbs 7¼ oz
A-11 F 1 R 1 S 1
On face, "M. Millet A Blere (?) Fonderie," somewhat illegible. Sprue-mark on reverse.

P-463-TCT Iron (R)
7¼ x ⅞   1 lb 7½ oz
A-14 F 1 R 1 S 1
Wedge-mark on reverse.

P-1735-TCT Iron (R)
8¼ x 1³/₁₆   2 lb 4 oz
Splayed ornamental cleats. F 1 R 1 S 1
On face, "H & S," "J.S. Hess & Son Middelfart." On reverse, "F."

P-1771-TCT Iron (VR)
9¾ x 1¹¹/₁₆   2 lbs 6½ oz
F 2 R 2
Five-sixteenths-inch rim which extends into cleats on bottom of platform. Also has posts and casters. Nickel finish.

P-1497-TCT Iron (R)
5⅛ x ⅞   1 lb 2½ oz
H-C 2 F 2 R 2
Machine grinding on rim.

P-1702-TCT Iron (VR)
5⅝ x 1   13 oz
A-4 F 1 R 1 S 1
On reverse, "No. 35 Rd. 640747."
Gate-mark on rim.

P-1770-TCT Iron (R)
7⅜ x ⁹/₁₆   1 lb 15 oz
A-14 F 2 R 2
On reverse, "2 D 2." Nickel finish eroded.

P-1478-TCT Iron (R)
6⅜ x ½   8¾ oz
A-15 F 2 R 2 S 2

P-1850-TCT Iron (VR)
5¾ x 1   1 lb 2½ oz
G-C 6 F 1 R 1 S 1
On face, "Deo Regi Fratribus Honor Fidelitas Benevolentia. Concord, Beauty, Truth, Wisdom, Peace, Strength."

P-1444-TCT Iron (R)
5¾ x 1¼   1 lb 4 oz
Four ornamental splayed cleats.

P-1352-TCT Iron (O)
4¾ x ⅝   5 oz
Four ornamental splayed feet. Two gate-marks on rim.

P-1963-TCT Brass (VR)
7⅜ x ⅞   1 lb 2 oz
A-11 F 1 R 1 S 1

P-1519-TCT Brass (VR)
8¼ x ⁹/₁₆   1 lb 2 oz
G-14 F 1 R 1 S 1

P-1446-TCT Brass (VR)
5⅞ x ¾ 1 lb 8 oz
Extensions from bottom rim form cleats.
F 1 R 1 S 1
On face, "Forget Me Not." On reverse, "Registered."

P-561-TCT Brass (VR)
6⅜ x ⅞ 13¼ oz
Extensions from bottom rim form cleats.
F 1 R 1 S 1
On face, "Our Ain Fire Side." Same design made with a handle.

P-1778-TCT Brass (R)
6¼ x 1 1 lb 5½ oz
A-9 F 2 R 2
On face, "A Present from the Isle of Man."

P-1490-TCT Brass (VR)
5¾ x ⅞ 12½ oz
F 1 R 1 S 1
Extensions of bottom rim form cleats.

P-1445-TCT Brass (R)
6¼ x 1¼ 1 lb 1 oz
A-10 F 2 R 2
Bracket device on reverse has been cut off.

P-1491-TCT Brass (R)
5⅜ x ¹³/₁₆ 6¼ oz
F 1 R 1 S 1
Pre-made supports screwed into cast platform.

P-526-TCT Brass (VR)
4⅝ x 1¼ 9 oz
F 1 R 1 S 1
Extensions of bottom rim form cleats. Cleats are pierced.

P-952-TCT Brass (O)
4¼ x 4³/₁₆ x ¹¹/₁₆ 5½ oz
A-15 F 1 R 2
On face, "Edward And Alexandra Crowned June 1902."

P-1090-TCT Brass (R)
5⅞ x 1¹¹/₁₆ 10 oz
F 1 R 1 S 1
Pre-made supports screwed into cast platform.

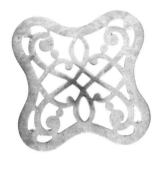
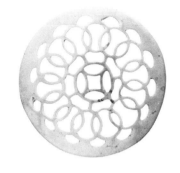

P-1492-TCT Brass (R)
4¾ x 1   10 oz
F 2   R 2
Pre-made supports screwed into cast platform.

P-730-TCT Brass (VR)
5⅛ x ⅝   8½ oz
F 2   R 2
Pre-made supports screwed into cast platform.

P-1362-TCT Brass (O)
10⅛ x 6½ x ⅝   3¼ oz
A-19 F 1   R 1   S 4
On reverse, "Made in Italy."

P-1797-TCT Brass (R)
5¼ x ¾   8¾ oz
A-14 F 1   R 1   S 1

P-1926-TCT Brass (VR)
5⅝ x 3⅞ x ⅜   6 oz
A-16 F 2   R 2

P-1545-TCT Brass (VR)
4⅞ x 4¹³/₁₆ x ⅜   5½ oz
F 1   R 2   S 2
One cleat at front, two in rear, one A-5 support on each side. Appears to be nickeled brass.

P-1807-TCT Brass (R)
6¹¹/₁₆ x 1⅛   1 lb 15½ oz
Corner cleats. H-C 8   F 2   R 2

P-1296-TCT Stamped Brass (R)
5 x ⁹/₁₆   3½ oz
F 2   R 2
Extensions of rim form cleats.

P-1503-TCT Stamped Brass (R)
7½ x ½   8½ oz
F 2   R 2
Supports are pre-made ball feet.

156

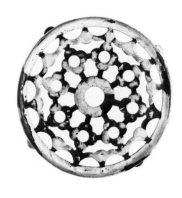

P-925-TCT Hammered Brass (R)
6³/₁₆ x ⅝   3½ oz
A-11 F 2 R 2
Supports are rolled brass cones braised to bottom of platform.

P-455-TCT Stamped Brass (R)
9 x 1¼   13¾ oz
F 2 R 2 Casters.

P-662-TCT Stamped Brass (R)
5⅝ x 1   4 oz
F 1 R 1 S 1
Quarter-inch scalloped rim with supports braised to bottom of platform.

P-1895-TCT Tin (R)
5⅛ inches diameter.
F 2 R 2
Supports formed by extensions of rim bent down into feet.

P-1559-TCT Tin/Enameled (R)
7 inches diameter.
F 2 R 2
Supports formed by extensions of rim bent down into feet.

P-212-TCT Tin (R)
6 inches diameter.
F 2 R 2
Supports formed by extensions of rim bent down into feet. Painted.

P-210-TCT Stamped metal (C)
5 x ½
F 2 R 2
Supports formed by bending down stamped feet.

P-1814-TCT Tin (R)
7 x 1   4¼ oz
F 2 R 2
Supports formed by extensions of rim bent down into feet.

P-845-TCT Tin (R)
9½ x 1½   8½ oz
F 1 R 1 S 1
Three cast-iron paw feet riveted to concave platform.

 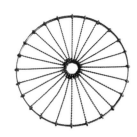 

P-1865-TCT Tin (R)
5¾ inches diameter.
F 1 R 1 S 1
Supports formed by extensions of rim bent down into feet. Painted. There is a stamped brass version of this design.

P-1638-TCT Tin (R)
6⅝ x 3⅛   13½ oz
F 2 R 2
Supports formed by stamped legs bent down into feet. Painted.

P-1384-TCT Tin (R)
8⅛ inches diameter.
F 2 R 2
Supports formed by extensions of rim bent down into feet. Painted.

P-1055-TCT Tin (R)
9 inches diameter. 7¼ oz
F 2 R 2
Supports formed by extensions of rim bent down into cleats.

P-1449-TCT Tin (R)
8¾ inches diameter. 9 oz
Supports formed by extensions of rim bent down into cleats.

P-382-TCT/KS Wire (C)
6 inches diameter.
Quarter-inch metal rim.

P-878-TCT/KS Wire (R)
5⅞ inches diameter.
Crimped quarter-inch metal rim; metal cylinders hold wire at center.

P-290-TCT/KS Wire (O)
5¾ inches diameter.
Twisted wire.

P-582-TCT/KS Wire (O)
6 inches diameter.

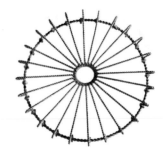

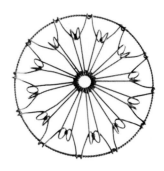

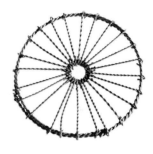
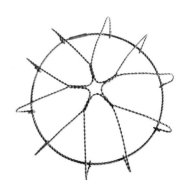

P-1854-TCT/KS Wire (R)
5⁵/₁₆ inches diameter.
Coiled wire over a heavier wire frame;
metal clips.

P-764-TCT/KS Wire (O)
6 inches diameter.
Wire wrapped around metal washer at
center.

P-1004-TCT/KS Wire (C)
5¾ inches diameter.
Rim formed by two strands of twisted
wire.

P-289-TCT/KS Wire (C)
5⅞ inches diameter.

P-920-TCT/KS Wire (O)
6 inches diameter.

P-1006-TCT/KS Wire (O)
6⅞ inches diameter.
Two weights of twisted wire.

P-1499-TCT/KS Wire (O)
6⅞ inches diameter.
Twisted wire.

P-702-TCT/KS Wire (R)
7⅞ inches diameter.
Outer rim twisted wire; spokes are decorative crimped wire; loop extensions form
supports.

P-348-TCT/KS Wire (C)
6¼ inches diameter.
Coiled spring wire.

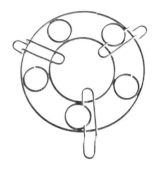  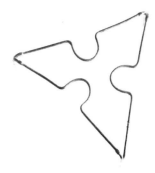

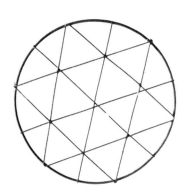 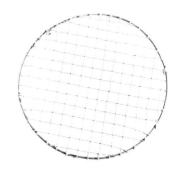 

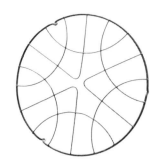  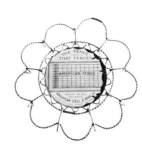

P-1855-TCT/KS Wire (C)
5¼ inches diameter.
May be steaming rack.

P-836-TCT/KS Wire (O)
9 inches diameter.

P-963-TCT/KS Wire (O)
8 inches diameter.
Wire soldered to rim.

P-747-TCT/KS Wire (R)
7 inches diameter.
Supports formed by metal clips each
holding four wires.

P-955-TCT/KS Wire (O)
8 inches diameter.
Two weights of wire; inner wires wrapped
around rim wire. A meat rest.

P-714-TCT/KS Wire (O)
8½ inches excluding supports.

P-1734-TCT/KS Wire (R)
5½ x 4¾
An interpretation of iron rod design
favored by blacksmiths.

P-1058-TCT/KS Wire (R)
9½ inches diameter.
Undoubtedly handcrafted.

P-1207-TCT/KS Wire/Tin (R)
6½ inches diameter.
On face, "Plain and Ornamental Wire;
The fence that fences; American fence
made in all weights; American Steel and
Wire Co. Chicago, New York, Denver, San
Francisco."

Enameled Table Stands

(See pages 161 to 163.)

Paley selected a number of enameled, cast-iron table stands for his collection. Twenty-seven of them are illustrated in this section. While they probably were made in France and originally were quite elegant, most are heavy, cast-iron table stands having concave platforms with enamel coatings that have crackled or chipped with age and use. A number of them have large wedge-marks confirming they are quite old. It is possible that enameled stands are more plentiful in Europe, but they are rarely found in this country.

Tile Stands

(See pages 164 to 166.)

This category includes stands of wood, wire or cast-iron with china or ceramic tile insets. The more elaborate versions were called "tea tiles," with large insets and elaborate wooden frames. Some even had music boxes or a bell on the bottom to summon the maid. They were used in the dining room or parlour when tea was served. The smaller, utilitarian tile stands were used in the kitchen or on the dining table to hold hot serving dishes.

Six-inch tile stands with twisted wire frames began to appear in houseware catalogues about 1865 and were advertised as late as the 1920's. Many of the tiles in these stands were produced by Mintons China Works, England.

There were numerous stands having cast-iron frames, handles, and tile insets produced in the late nineteenth and early twentieth centuries. Often they carried advertising or decorative motifs on the face. Unfortunately, no examples of these tile stands are illustrated.

Enameled Table Stands

P-494-ETS Iron/enamel (R)
7¾ x 1   1 lb 6 oz
Rim extended to form supports.
F 1   R 1   S 1
Provision for casters.

P-721-ETS Iron/enamel (R)
8⅝ x 1   1 lb 5¾ oz
Rim extended to form three supports.
F 1   R 1   S 1

P-1069-ETS Iron/enamel (R)
7¾ x ¾   1 lb 2½ oz
Rim extended to form eight supports.
F 2   R 2   S 4
Large wedge-mark.

P-1690-ETS Iron/enamel (R)
7⅞ x ¾   1 lb ½ oz
Rim extended to form four supports.
F 2   R 2

P-1566-ETS Iron/enamel (R)
7½ x 1   1 lb 4½ oz
Rim extended to form five supports.
F 2   R 1   S 2
Large wedge-mark.

P-1761-ETS Iron/ceramic (R)
8⅛ x 1⅛   2 lbs 9½ oz
Rim extended to form three supports.
F 1   R 1   S 1
Large wedge-mark.

P-1214-ETS Iron/enamel (R)
9½ x 1⅛   2 lbs 3¾ oz
Rim extended to form six supports.
F 1   R 1   S 4

P-493-ETS Iron/enamel (R)
7¾ x ¾   1 lb 2¾ oz
Rim extended to form five supports.
F 1   R 2   S 2
Large wedge-mark.

P-1211-ETS Iron/enamel (R)
8¾ x ¾   1 lb 6½ oz
Rim extended to form three supports.
F 1   R 1   S 1
Large wedge-mark.

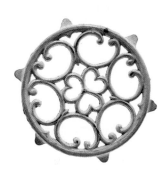

P-491-ETS Iron/enamel (R)
7¾ x ⅞   1 lb 2½ oz
Rim extended to form six supports.
F 2   R 2   S 2

P-1213-ETS Iron/enamel (R)
8⅛ x 1   1 lb 7½ oz
Rim extended to form three supports.
F 1   R 1   S 1

P-1924-ETS Iron/enamel (R)
9⅛ x 6¼ x ¾   1 lb 5¾ oz
A 10   F 2   R 2
Bottom of platform is not enameled.

P-1212-ETS Iron/enamel (R)
8⅜ x ⅞   1 lb 3½ oz
Rim extended to form three supports.
F 1   R 1   S 1

P-1525-ETS Iron/enamel (R)
7¼ x ⅞   1 lb 10¾ oz
Rim extended to form four supports.
F 2   R 2
On the reverse, "Model L Depose."

P-1034-ETS Iron/enamel (R)
7⅛ x 1   1 lb 1 oz
Rim extended to form three supports.
F 1   R 1   S 1

P-504-ETS Iron/enamel (R)
7½ x 1   1 lb 5 oz
Rim extended to form three supports.
F 1   R 1   S 1
Large wedge-mark

P-1767-ETS Iron/enamel (R)
7⅞ x ⅞   1 lb 7 oz
Rim extended to form three supports.
F 1   R 1   S 1
On the reverse, "PW-90-7 Modell
Depose."

P-492-ETS Iron/enamel (R)
7⅛ x ¾   1 lb
Rim extended to form six supports.
F 2   R 2   S 2

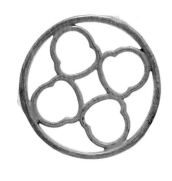
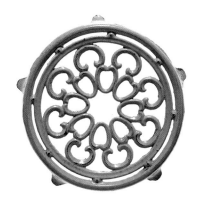

P-1035-ETS Iron/enamel (R)
8¾ x 1⅛   1 lb 5½ oz
Rim extended to form supports.
Provision for casters.
F 2   R 2

P-839-ETS Iron/enamel (R)
8¾ x 1⅜   2 lbs 1¾ oz
Rim extended to form six supports.
F 2   R 2   S 2
On the reverse, "Lemaire No. 1 Godin."
Casters that swivel.

P-1632-ETS Iron/ceramic (R)
9 x 7⅜ x ⅞   2 lbs 2¾ oz
Rim extended to form three supports.
F 1   R 1   S 1
On the reverse, "Mle Depose PW."
Dull finish.

P-1068-ETS Iron/enamel (R)
7½ x 1   1 lb ½ oz
Rim extended to form three supports.
F 1   R 1   S 1

P-1636-ETS Iron/enamel (R)
7⅝ x 1   14½ oz
Rim extended to form three supports.
F 1   R 1   S 1

P-1806-ETS Iron/ceramic (R)
7⅞ x ¹³/₁₆   2 lbs
Rim extended to form three supports.
F 1   R 1   S 1
Large wedge-mark.

P-1637-ETS Iron/enamel (R)
7⅝ x 1¹/₁₆   1 lb 1½ oz
Rim extended to form five supports.
F 1   R 2   S 2

P-505-ETS Iron/enamel (R)
9 x 1   1 lb 9 oz
Rim extended to form five supports.
F 1   R 2   S 2

P-1561-ETS Iron/enamel (R)
13⅜ x 9⅜ x 1¾   3 lbs 4½ oz
Rim extended to form four supports.
F 2   R 2
On reverse, "2."

Tile Stands

P-1884-TS Tile/wire (O)
6 inches. Wire stand.
On face, "High Fork, Derbyshire."
On reverse, "Mintons China Works
Stoke on Trent."

P-1367-TS Tile/wire (O)
6 inches. Wire stand.
On reverse, "Mintons China Works
Stoke on Trent."

P-1720-TS Tile/wire (R)
5⅞ inches. Wire stand.
On reverse, "137."

P-1132-TS Tile/wire (R)
6 inches. Wire stand.
On reverse, "Mintons China Works
Stoke on Trent."

P-2015-TS Tile (R)
6 inches. Metal frame.
On reverse, "Mintons China Works
Stoke on Trent."

P-538-TS Tile/wire (R)
5¾ inches. Wire stand.

P-872-TS Tile/brass (R)
6 inches. Brass frame.

P-1299-TS Tile/britannia (R)
6 inches. Ornate britannia frame.
On reverse, "Mintons Collins & Co.
Patent Tile Works Stoke
on the Trent."

P-1586-TS Tile/wire (R)
5⅞ inches. Wire stand.
On reverse, "2."

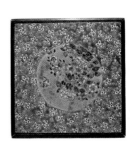

P-1025-TS Tile/wire (R)
6 inches. Wire stand.
On face, "The Seasons."

P-916-TS Tile/wire (R)
6 inches. Wire stand.

P-1186-TS Tile/wire (R)
6 inches. Wire stand.
On reverse, "Mintons Tile Works
Stoke on Trent."

P-1946-TS Tile (R)
6⅛ inches. Ceramic feet.
Identified in "Pictorial Pot-lid Book" by
Harold George Clarke, as glazed color
picture on Staffordshire pottery,
c. 1840-1860.

P-1089-TS Tile (R)
5⅞ inches. Nickeled iron
frame. On reverse, "T.A.S. Rd.
No. 34889."

P-777-TS Tile/britannia (R)
8 inches. Britannia frame.
On reverse, "Mintons China Works
Stoke on Trent.

P-1947-TS Tile (R)
8 inches. Ceramic feet.

P-718-TS Tile/wood (R)
8 inches. Wood frame.
Has a bell on bottom to summon maid.
Metal cover for the spring box is
engraved "Lepose A.H."

P-1809-TS Tile/wood (R)
9⅞ inches. Wood frame.

P-1037-TS Tile/wood (VR)
8³/₁₆ inches. Wood frame.
Music box inside; paper label
imprinted "two airs;
1. La Jumbe en bois
2. Yaguil Amous Polka."

P-1385-TS Tile (R)
7⅞ inches. Wood frame.

P-618-TS Tile/wire (R)
6 inches. Wire frame.
On reverse, "Mintons China Works
Stoke on Trent."

P-700-TS Tile/wire (R)
6 inches. Wire frame.
On reverse, "Mintons China Works
Stoke on Trent."

P-1718-TS Tile (R)
7¼ inches. Nickeled metal frame.
On reverse, "1788 W. 20."

P-1130-TS Tile/wire (R)
5½ inches. Wire frame.
On reverse, "Made in Germany."

P-1375-TS Tile/copper (R)
6 inches. Copper frame.
On reverse, "Rd No 574963."

P-1135-TS Tile (R)
4¼ inches. Plated metal frame.
On reverse, "Trent." Corner brace
inscribed "James W. Tufts, Boston, Qua-
druple Plate Warrented 30, 1905."

P-1290-TS Tile (R)
6½ inches. Plated metal frame.
On face, "Cupar Cross and Townhall."

Iron Rests and Stands

The development of iron rests between the eighteenth and twentieth centuries reflects continuous changing of styles and technologies. Beginning in the eighteenth century, long-legged, handcrafted brass and copper stands were made for box irons; the designs depended on contour with simple open-work and polished surfaces.

In the nineteenth century, box irons were replaced by sadirons, and stands became smaller. Enormous numbers of iron and brass castings were mass-produced. Designs became more elaborate, detailed and varied; some surfaces were lavishly encrusted with ornamentation. Supports were shorter, and rims, guides, and posts were commonplace. Many iron rests from this period were made, both decorative and generic, to be sold separate from irons and also may be best described as "decorative and generic" in use.

In the latter part of the nineteenth and into the twentieth century, generic styles began to disappear in favor of manufacturer's stands designed to be sold in conjunction with irons. Elaborate decoration gave way to trademarks, business names, addresses, and advertising slogans. Few of the commercial stands were cast in brass.

After World War I, the design emphasis for iron rests shifted to cost-effective and functional considerations. Aluminum, steel and stamped metal were often substituted for cast-iron. Many of the iron rests produced in this period by contrast seem extremely plain and uninteresting.

Throughout the evolution of iron rests, there were always two grades of stands. Utilitarian stands were economically cast or handcrafted in iron, while the more stylish versions were fashioned in brass.

Other stands were specifically made for commerical use in tailoring shops and laundries. These large stands weighing two to five pounds, with few exceptions, were utilitarian in appearance.

Decorative Stands Made of Brass or Copper Plate

(See pages 169 to 176.)

Once pressing irons incorporated heat with pressure, a stand was needed to hold the hot iron when not in use. They were called rests, holders, stands or trivets. Most had three supports, one at the front and two at the rear. Shapes usually were spade, heart, or triangle.

Charcoal and box irons came into general use during the seventeenth century. Charcoal irons were pointed metal boxes frequently made of brass with handles and hinged lids. Hot charcoal was placed into the box on a small grill that had short feet. (These grills often are confused by collectors with iron rests.) In the box iron, a heated iron lug was inserted. It was customary to have several lugs heating while one was in use. Box irons were large and often weighed as much as five pounds. The stands used for box irons were larger than those used with sadirons. The fancy brass box irons were prized possessions prominantly displayed in the home.

There are a large number of old brass and copper iron rests that were handcrafted. Seventy-two examples from the Paley Collection are illustrated in this section; less than half of the total he collected. Most of them probably date from the eighteenth and nineteenth centuries.

The handcrafted stands appear to have been made for box-irons as they are somewhat larger than those later made for sadirons. The plates were either cut or cast with a perfectly smooth, polished surface; the edges were filed, and ornate tooled legs were attached to the platform by either screw-

"Common Tailor's Iron."

"Common Sad Iron."

"Chinese Common Sad Iron."

"New England Pressing Iron."

Illustrations from a turn-of-the-century catalogue of the Colebrookdale Iron Company.

Box iron.

Sadiron with a curious heat shield.

Sadiron.

Fuel iron. Photographs by Craig Smith.

ing or riveting. The tooled legs were pre-made and could have been purchased from hardware merchants or brass manufacturers. Some legs simply were adapted brass or copper bolts and screws. Most of these rests were two to three inches high; the majority having no guides so they could be used for pots or dishes as well as for irons. Also, there are some which obviously are table stands.

The early designs relied on shape and proportion; some were pierced in restrained open-work patterns; and others were elaborately scrolled, foliated, or etched. The different skills of the craftsmen are apparent. A few of these early brass and copper stands have pleasing, rustic, primitive qualities suggesting they may have been made in the home. A few show names, dates or short sayings engraved on the plate.

Unusual examples in this collection are the solid copper trivets. While manufacturers cast trivets in bronze and made copper-plated iron trivets, trivets of solid copper are rare.

P-565-DBC-HC Brass (VR)
7¼ x 5⅛ x 1¼   10½ oz
Three screwed in pre-made legs.
F 2 R 1
Cut and pierced platform.

P-576-DBC-HC Brass (VR)
9½ x 4½ x 1   8½ oz
Three screwed in posts.
F 1 R 2
Cut and pierced platform.

P-1893-DBC-HC Brass (VR)
12¾ x 4⅜ x 1   9 oz
Three screwed in pre-made legs.
F 1 R 2
Cut and pierced platform.

P-1555-DBC-HC Copper (VR)
5½ x ⅜   13½ oz
Three ball feet braised to the plate.
F 1 R 1 S 1
Cut and pierced platform.

P-604-DBC-HC Brass (VR)
10⅛ x 4⁵/₁₆ x ¾   9 oz
Front, one pre-made brass support; rear,
two riveted iron posts.

P-1891-DBC-HC Brass (VR)
9½ x 5⅜ x 1⅜   1 lb
Three screwed in pre-made legs.
F 1 R 2
Cut and engraved platform.

P-1645-DBC-HC Brass (VR)
4⅝ x 4⅝ x ⅝
Three screwed in copper bolts.
F 1 R 2
Cut and pierced platform.

P-1911-DBC-HC Brass (VR)
8⅝ x 4 x ⅞″   7¾ oz
Three riveted posts.
F 1 R 2
Cut and pierced platform.

P-672-DBC-HC Brass (VR)
5¾ x 5¹¹/₁₆ x 1¹¹/₁₆″   1 lb 7 oz
Three riveted posts.
F 1 R 2
Cut and pierced platform.

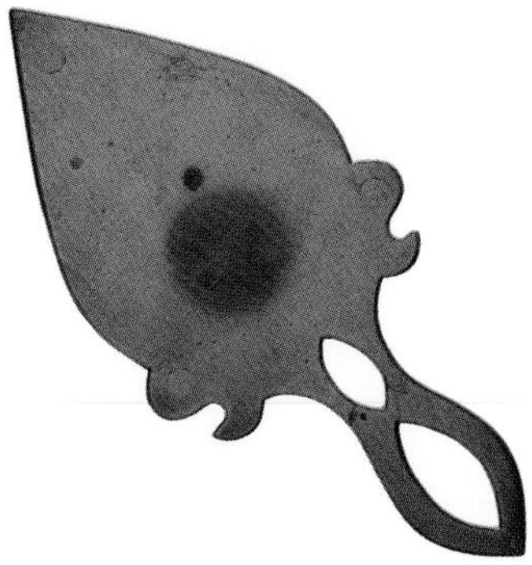

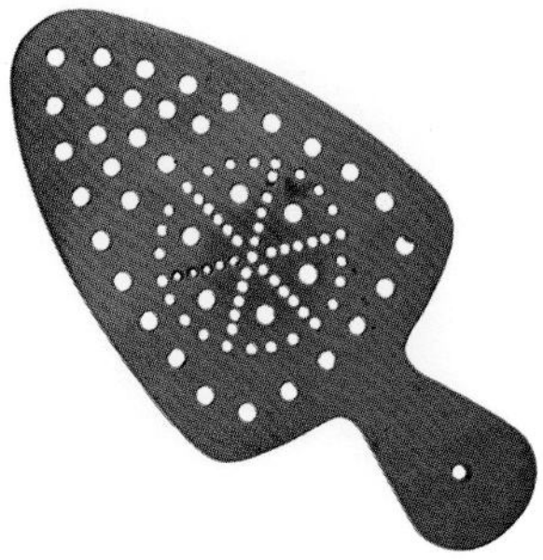

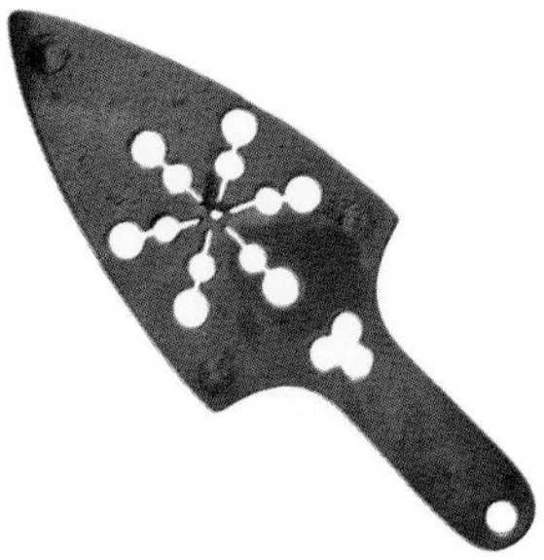

P-375-DBC-HC Brass (VR)
11¼ x 4¾ x ⅞ 11 oz
Three screwed in brass screws.
F 1 R 2
Cut and pierced platform.

P-1745-DBC-HC Brass (VR)
5⅞ x 4⅛ x ½″ 5 oz
Four screwed in brass bolts.
F1 R 1 S 2
Cut and pierced platform.

P-861-DBC-HC Brass (VR)
8⅝ x 4¾ x 1¼″ 1 lb 4 oz
Three screwed in pre-made legs.
F 1 R 2
Cut and pierced platform.
One-quarter-inch rail front and sides.

P-670-DBC-HC Brass (VR)
9¾ x 4⅜ x 11/16 12¼ oz
Three screwed in pre-made feet.
F 1 R 2
Cut and pierced platform.

P-334-DBC-HC Brass (VR)
8 x 4½ x ½ 12½ oz
Three screwed in posts.
F 1 R 2

P-343-DBC-HC Brass/iron (VR)
8⅞ x 3¼ x 1⅝ 11¾ oz
Three riveted iron posts.
F 1 R 2
Cut and pierced platform.

P-25-DBC-HC Brass (VR)
9⅛ x 5¼ x 1¼ 12 oz
Three screwed in pre-made legs.
F 1 R 2
Cast platform.

P-934-DBC-HC Brass (VR)
9¾ x 4½ x 1¾ 9½ oz
Three riveted posts.
F 1 R 2
Cut and pierced platform.

P-1042-DBC-HC Brass (VR)
10⅜ x 4¼ x 15/16 9½ oz
Three screwed in pre-made legs.
F 1 R 2
Cut and pierced platform.

P-1971-DBC-HC Brass (VR)
6½ x 5⅝ x 1⅛   10¾ oz
Three riveted posts.
F 1   R 2
Cut and pierced platform.

P-854-DBC-HC Brass (VR)
9⁵/₁₆ x 4¾ x 1¼   12½ oz
Three screwed in pre-made legs.
F 1   R 2
Cut and pierced platform.

P-713-DBC-HC Brass (VR)
11 x 5½ x 1⁵/₁₆   1 lb 1 oz
Three riveted copper posts.
F 1   R 2
Cut and pierced platform.

P-1388-DBC-HC Brass (VR)
9¾ x 4⅜ x ¾   12 oz
Three screwed in pre-made legs.
F 1   R 2
Cut and pierced platform.

P-1775-DBC-HC Copper (VR)
10 x 4⁵/₁₆ x 2¼   1 lb 1½ oz
Three riveted pre-made legs.
F 1   R 2
Cut and pierced platform.

P-683-DBC-HC Brass (VR)
8⅜ x 4¼ x ½   11 oz
Three riveted posts.
F 1   R 2
Cast plate platform.

P-1310-DBC-HC Brass (VR)
9½ x 4¼ x ¾   11¼ oz
Three riveted pre-made feet.
F 1   R 2
Cut and pierced platform.

P-1097-DBC-HC Brass (VR)
8⅞ x 5⅛ x 1   12 oz
Three screwed in pre-made feet.
F 1   R 2
Cut and pierced platform.

P-1309-DBC-HC Brass (VR)
6 x 4⅛ x 1¼   12½ oz
Three screwed in posts.
F 1   R 2
Cast platform.

P-479-DBC-HC Brass (VR)
10½ x 4⅝ x ¾   1 lb 3 oz
Three riveted brass bolts.
F 1 R 2
Cut and pierced platform.

P-78-DBC-HC Brass (VR)
10 x 4¼ x 1   12 oz
Three riveted posts.
F 1 R 2
Cut and pierced platform.

P-1119-DBC-HC Brass (VR)
4⅜ x 2⅝ x 2¼   8¾ oz
Four screwed in posts.
F 2 R 2
Cut and pierced platform.

P-1269-DBC-HC Brass (VR)
7½ x 4⅜ x ⅝   7 oz
Three screwed in pre-made feet.
F 1 R 2
Cut and pierced platform.

P-976-DBC-HC Brass (VR)
8½ x 4⁹/₁₆ x 1³/₁₆   8 oz
Three screwed in pre-made legs.
F 1 R 2
Cut and pierced platform.

P-1043-DBC-HC Brass (VR)
10½ x 4 x 1½   11½ oz
Three riveted posts.
F 1 R 2
Cut and pierced platform.

P-1912-DBC-HC Brass (VR)
9⅞ x 4¼ x ⅝   10¾ oz
Three riveted pre-made feet.
F 1 R 2
Cut and pierced platform.

P-790-DBC-HC Brass (VR)
9 x 5 x 1   1 lb 1 oz
Three riveted posts.
F 1 R 2
Cut and pierced platform.

P-1558-DBC-HC Brass (VR)
8 x 5⅜ x 1   10 oz
Three riveted posts.
F 1 R 2
Cut and pierced platform.

P-280-DBC-HC Brass (VR)
8⅜ x 3¾ x 1¹/₁₆   6 oz
Three screwed in pre-made legs.
F 1 R 2
Cut and pierced platform.

P-637-DBC-HC Brass (VR)
7⁹/₁₆ x 4⅜ x ½   1 lb 1 oz
Three screwed in round head bolts.
F 1 R 2
Cut and drilled platform.

P-1965-DBC-HC Brass (VR)
10⅛ x 4⅜ x 1⁷/₁₆   15½ oz
Three riveted copper posts.
F 1 R 2
Cut and pierced platform.

P-1864-DBC-HC Brass (VR)
7¼ x 4⅛ x 1   11½ oz
Three riveted posts.
F 1 R 2
Cut and drilled; light chasing around
edge and in center of platform.

P-1439-DBC-HC Copper (VR)
9 x 4½ x 1⅝   14½ oz
Three riveted posts.
F 1 R 2
Inscription, "Emrys George."
Cut and pierced platform.

P-1206-DBC-HC Brass (VR)
9 ¹³/₁₆ x 5 x 1   1½ oz
Three riveted iron posts.
F 2 R 1
Cut and pierced platform.

P-1050-DBC-HC Brass (VR)
8¾ x 5¼ x 1¾   15½ oz
Three riveted pre-made legs.
F 1 R 2
Cut and pierced platform with decora-
tive chasing.

P-1888-DBC-HC Brass (VR)
10¾ x 4½ x 1⅝   1 lb 3 oz
Three screwed in pre-made legs.
F 1 R 2
Cut and engraved platform.

P-330-DBC-HC Brass (VR)
10⅛ x 4¾ x 1⅝   12½ oz
Three screwed in pre-made legs.
F 1 R 2
Cut and pierced platform.

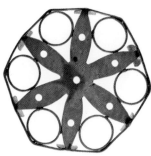

P-425-DBC-HC Brass (VR)
11⅜ x 5¼ x 1⅞ 1 lb
Three bent cleats riveted to platform.
F 1 R 2
Cut and pierced platform.

P-446-DBC-HC Brass (VR)
7¾ x 1⁵/₁₆ 13¼ oz
Rim extended to form six round
supports.
F 1 R 1 S 4
Cut and pierced platform.

P-121-DBC-HC Brass (VR)
9⅛ x 5¾ x 1¹³/₁₆ 13½ oz
Four screwed in and riveted
pre-made legs.
F 1 R 1 S 2
Cut and pierced platform with etched
design.

P-373-DBC-HC Brass (VR)
9⅝ x 4¼ x 1⁵/₁₆ 11½ oz
Three riveted posts.
F 1 R 2
Cut and pierced platform.

P-665-DBC-HC Brass (VR)
8 x 3¹³/₁₆ x 1¼ 13 oz
Three riveted posts.
F 1 R 2
Cut and pierced platform.

P-633-DBC-HC Brass (VR)
9⅜ x 4⅛ x 1³/₁₆ 10¼ oz
Three riveted posts.
F 1 R 2
Cut and pierced platform.

P-1600-DBC-HC Brass (VR)
9⅞ x 5 x 1⅛ 13½ oz
Three screwed in pre-made legs.
F 1 R 2
Cut and pierced platform.

P-374-DBC-HC Brass (VR)
9⅝ x 4¹³/₁₆ x 1¼ 10¾ oz
Three screwed in and filed
pre-made legs.
F 1 R 2
Cut and pierced platform.

P-131-DBC-HC Brass (VR)
8¾ x 4⅞ x 1⅞ 12¼ oz
Three screwed in and filed
pre-made legs.
F 1 R 2
Cut and pierced platform.

P-1577-DBC-HC Brass (VR)
7¼ x 5¾ x 2½   11½ oz
Three hand forged and riveted iron legs.
On face, "EE" and "1879."
F 1 R 2
Cut and pierced.

P-391-DBC-HC Brass (VR)
8 x 5¼ x 1⅜   1 lb 2 oz
Three riveted pre-made legs.
F 1 R 2
Cut and pierced platform. Measurement
does not include tang; wood
handle is missing.

P-1377-DBC-HC Brass (VR)
8¹¹/₁₆ x 4⅜ x 1½   12 oz
Three riveted posts.
F 1 R 2
Cut and pierced platform.

P-1430-DBC-HC Brass (VR)
9½ x 5¾ x 1¾   1 lb 4 oz
Three riveted posts.
F 1 R 2
Cut and pierced platform.

P-1556-DBC-HC Brass (VR)
9⅝ x 4½ x ¾   10 ½ oz
Wire rim bent down to form three
supports.
F 1 R 2
Cut and pierced platform.

P-1823-DBC-HC Brass (VR)
10 x 5¼ x 1¹/₁₆   1 lb
Three screwed in pre-made feet.
F 1 R 2
Cut and pierced platform.

P-1432-DBC-HC Brass (VR)
8¾ x 4⁵/₁₆ x 1½   11 oz
Three riveted copper posts.
F 1 R 2
Cut and pierced. Feet are copper
posts pounded flat at one end and
bent into feet.

P-1903-DBC-HC Brass (VR)
10 x 5⅞ x 1   11¼ oz
Three riveted pre-made legs.
F 1 R 2
Cut and pierced platform.

P-1916-DBC-HC Brass (VR)
10⅛ x 4⅞ x 1   1 lb
Three posts.
F 1 R 2
Cut and pierced platform.

P-866-DBC-HC Brass (VR)
10½ x 5⅜ x 1⅛   1 lb 2½ oz
Three screwed in iron posts.
F 1   R 2
Cast platform.

P-1225-DBC-HC Brass (VR)
6⅞ x 5½ x 1⅛   11½ oz
Three riveted copper posts.
F 1   R 2
Cut and pierced platform.

P-1892-DBC-HC Brass (VR)
13 x 4¾ x 1⅛   13¼ oz
Three screwed in pre-made legs.
F 1   R 2
Cut and pierced platform.

P-1964-DBC-HC Brass (VR)
11¼ x 5⅜ x ¹⁵/₁₆   1 lb
Rim extended to form three supports.
F 1   R 2
Cut and pierced platform.

P-1110-DBC-HC Brass (VR)
8¼ x 3¾ x 1   10 oz
Supports formed by extensions of
scalloped rail riveted to platform.
F 1   R 2

P-1857-DBC-HC Brass/iron (VR)
8¼ x 4 x 1⅛   12 oz
Three pre-made legs.
F 1   R 2
Unusual cast-iron trivet with brass
sheeting hammered around iron.

P-1447-DBC-HC Brass (VR)
8¼ x 4½ x 1   1 lb 5 oz
Three riveted pre-made legs.
F 1   R 2
Cut and pierced; rails at the front and
riveted guides on the sides of platform.

P-1462-DBC-HC Brass (VR)
10 x 4⅜ x 2   1 lb 6 oz
Three riveted copper rivets.
F 1   R 2
Cast platform.

P-677-DBC-HC Copper (VR)
6½ x 5¼ x 1¼   1 lb
Four riveted posts.
F 2   R 2
Cut and pierced platform.

Decorative Iron Stands

Sadirons came into general use in the eighteenth century. They were smaller than box irons and made of solid iron. With the first sadirons, the entire iron was heated so it was necessary to have more than one. Later, sadirons were designed with detachable handles and several interchangeable lugs were heated while one was in use.

Stands served as rests for hot irons when it was necessary to sit them down during ironing. Decorative iron stands are mostly associated with sadirons, but they also were used with charcoal, fuel and electric irons. A number of decorative stands were made for specialty irons, such as the cathedral stand for the tailor's goose.

Since many of the decorative stands had no rails, guides or cleats, they also served as stands for serving dishes and coffee or tea pots. Some decorative stands could be classified in the multi-purpose category of trivets, but they are grouped with iron stands because their shapes conform so closely to irons of the period.

In the eighteenth century, iron furnaces produced most sadirons. After the middle of the nineteenth century, independent foundries and manufacturers made sadirons in enormous quantities. During the Civil War and post-war periods, America was probably the foremost center for sadiron production. American sadirons were exported to Europe and around the world.

While some manufacturers furnished a stand with each iron they sold, there were still many decorative iron rests being marketed separately. Trade catalogues show that generic ornamental stands were sold until the 1930's, even though commercial stands with advertising were more common.

Remarks about "European" design in the multi-purpose trivet section apply to decorative iron stands as well. Many cast-iron and brass stands shown in this section, which appear to be distinctly European in decoration, most likely were not made in this country. Also, there are a large number of plate-finish cast brass stands with exaggerated contours in a style more typical of European than American design. American design is most apparent in the production of commercial stands sold in conjunction with irons.

Decorative iron stands were made in traditional styles to fit a variety of irons. Most had handles and conformed to established heart, shield, cathedral and triangular shapes. A great many generic decorative stands were cast in brass and some in bronze.

See decorative iron stands shown in the New England Pennsylvania category. These are some of the oldest castings of decorative iron stands. A few decorative iron stands are also illustrated in the multi-purpose trivet section.

P-384-DIS Iron (R)
9½ x 4⅛ x 1⅛   13¾ oz
B-10   F 1   R 2
On reverse, "Muel."
Filed gate-marks on rear of platform.

E-900-DIS Iron (VR)
10½ x 4¾ x 1¼   1 lb 7 oz
A-20   F 1   R 2
On reverse, "E.S." in Fat Face Roman, indicating it is an old trivet. One-eighth-inch top rail around platform.

P-785-DIS Iron (R)
8⅞ x 4¼ x 1⅛   1 lb 1 oz
A-11   F 1   R 2
Front leg slanted forward; one back leg angled. Legs were probably punched into mold.

E-480-DIS Iron (R)
10¾ x 5¾ x 1¼   2 lbs 2 oz
A-8 F 1 R 2
On reverse, "F. Dtula." One-eighth-inch
top rail around platform. Old casting.

E-509-DIS Iron (R)
8½ x 4¼ x 1¹³/₁₆   1 lb 9 oz
Post in front; A-8 legs at rear.
F 1 R 2
One-half-inch top rails front and sides of
platform.

E-452-DIS Iron (O)
9¾ x 4½ x 1⅝   1 lb 6 oz
A-8 F 1 R 2
One-eighth-inch top rail around platform.

E-56-DIS Iron (R)
10⅛ x 4¼ x 1½   1 lb 2 oz
A-1 F 1 R 2
Shallow top rail around platform. Old
casting.

E-440-DIS Brass (O)
9 x 3¾ x 1   15½ oz
Splayed ornamental cleats.
F 1 R 2
One-quarter-inch scalloped rail around
bottom of platform. Sprue-mark on
reverse.

E-451-DIS Brass/wood (R)
8½ x 4 x 1½   12 oz
Supports are posts with cone-shaped
terminals.
F 1 R 2
Nine-sixteenths-inch top side rails on
platform. Hanging ring on wooden handle.

E-26-DIS Iron (O)
7½ x 3¹¹/₁₆ x ¹³/₁₆   1 lb
A-12 F 1 R 2
Gate-mark on rim; machine grinding.

E-80-DIS Iron (O)
8⅜ x 3⅝ x ¹¹/₁₆   12 oz
A-11 F 1 R 2
One-sixteenth-inch top rail around
platform. Gate-marks on handle and rim.

E-76-DIS Iron (R)
9 x 3⅞ x ¹⁵/₁₆   1 lb 1 oz
A-11 F 1 R 2
On face, "DE."
One-quarter-inch top rails front and sides
of platform. Two large gate-marks on rim.
Old casting.

E-73-DIS Iron (VR)
9¾ x 4½ x ⅝   1 lb 2 oz
A-14 F 1 R 2
Three-sixteenths-inch scalloped top rails
front and sides of platform. Old casting.

E-11-DIS Iron (O)
6⅞ x 2½ x 1¼   8 oz
A-2 F 1 R 2
One-eighth-inch top rail around platform.

E-83-DIS Iron (R)
9⅝ x 4⅜ x 1⅛   1 lb 1 oz
A-10 F 1 R 2
Gate-mark on rim; filing. Old casting.

E-476-DIS Bronze (R)
9¼ x 4¼ x ¹³/₁₆   1 lb 2 oz
A-9 F 1 R 2

M-15-DIS Iron (R)
8⅝ x 4 x ⅞   1 lb ½ oz
A-21 F 1 R 2

M-17-DIS Iron (R)
9¾ x 4⅜ x 1½   1 lb ½ oz
A-9 F 1 R 2

M-14-DIS Iron (R)
8¾ x 4⅝ x 1¾   1 lb ½ oz
A-18 F 1 R 2

M-18-DIS Brass (VR)
9 x 3¾ x 1¼   1 lb
A-18 F 1 R 2
Painted black with gilded bands on the
bee design.

P-156-DIS Iron (VR)
7 x 3¾ x ⅝   7 oz
A-15 F 1 R 2
Shallow backcoping on reverse of bird and
floral elements.

P-796-DIS Iron (R)
8⅞ x 4½ x ¹⁵/₁₆ 1 lb 1 oz
A-10 F 1 R 2
Gilded finish.

E-800-DIS Iron (VR)
8½ x 4 x 1⅝ 1 lb ½ oz
A-18 F 1 R 2
Masonic emblem. Unusual handle;
backcoping.

E-801-DIS Iron (VR)
10½ x 4¼ x 1¼ 1 lb ½ oz
A-9 F 1 R 2
Backcoping; filing. Unusual design based
on German Romanesque figure.

E-382-DIS Iron (O)
5¾ x 3½ x ¾ 4 oz
A-5 F 1 R 2
On reverse, illegible Register number;
backcoping.

E-536-DIS Soapstone (VR)
6¼ x 4 x 1¾ 2 lbs 3½ oz
Heavy posts.
F 1 R 2
On face, "LL." On reverse, "Ch. Else
1885." Originally painted and gilded.

P-1852-DIS Iron (VR)
10 x 4⅞ x ⅞ 1 lb ½ oz
A-15 F 1 R 2
Gate-marks removed by machine grinding.

P-1078-DIS Iron (VR)
11 x 4⅝ x 1¼ 1 lb 3½ oz
B-9 F 1 R 2

P-1104-DIS Iron (R)
7¼ x 3⅛ x ⅝ 5¼ oz
A-4 F 1 R 2
Two gate-marks on rim; backcoping.

P-AAA-DIS Iron (R)
9½ x 4¼ x 1¼ 15 oz
A-8 F 1 R 2

P-1084-DIS Iron (R)
9¼ x 4 x 1⅛   12½ oz
A-10 F 1 R 2
Illegible letters on reverse. Three gate-marks on rim; extensive backcoping.

P-2004-DIS Iron (R)
8⅜ x 3⅝ x 1   8½ oz
I-9 F 1 R 2
Badly corroded.

P-1457-DIS Iron (VR)
9½ x 4⅜ x 1¼   1 lb 9½ oz
A-9 F 1 R 2
Deep relief design on face of platform with one-quarter-inch rails front and sides of platform.

P-1569-DIS Iron (R)
11 x 4½ x 1⅝   1 lb 7½ oz
A-8 F 1 R 2
On reverse, "W 2." Shallow top rails front and sides of platform. Backcoping on reverse of rail and handle. Piece broken off from bottom of right rail.

P-1356-DIS Iron (R)
11⅝ x4⅜ x 1⅛   1 lb 12 oz
A-11 F 1 R 2
Large gate-mark on rim; filing.

P-1192-DIS Iron (R)
11⅝ x 4¾ x 1⅝   1 lb 12 oz
A-8 F 1 R 2
One-eighth-inch top rail around platform. Front leg longer than rear supports.

P-1454-DIS Iron (VR)
10⅛ x 4³⁄₁₆ x 1¼   1 lb 8 oz
A-9 F 1 R 2
On reverse, "FP."
Large gate-mark on rim. One-quarter-inch top rails front and sides of platform.

P-1520-DIS Iron (VR)
10⅛ x 4⅞ x 1   1 lb 5½ oz
A-24 F 1 R 2
One large gate-mark on rim. One-eighth-inch top rail around platform. Casting reveals legs were riveted to pattern.

P-731-DIS Iron (VR)
9⅛ x 4⅜ x 1½   1 lb 1 oz
A-9 F 1 R 2
Gate-mark on one-eighth-inch top rail around platform. Shallow backcoping on handle.

P-1079-DIS Iron (R)
9¹¹/₁₆ x 4⁹/₁₆ x 1⅝   1 lb 4 oz
A-1 F 1 R 2
One-eighth-inch rail around platform.
Backcoping on handle.

P-441-DIS Iron (VR)
9⅝ x 3⅞ x 1⅜   1 lb 1 oz
A-10 F 1 R 2
On reverse, "PW." Three-sixteenths-inch
top rails front and sides of platform.
Reinforcement and backcoping on reverse.
Nickel finish eroded.

P-1215-DIS Iron (VR)
10¼ x 4½ x 1⁹/₁₆   1 lb 5½ oz
A-8 F 1 R 2
One-quarter-inch sloping top rails front
and sides of platform. Backcoping on
reverse of rail.

P-1386-DIS Iron (VR)
8½ x 3⅝ x 1⅛   15 oz
A-9 F 1 R 2
On reverse, "HC."
Three-sixteenths-inch top rails front and
sides of platform. Broken right rail.

P-1331-DIS Iron (VR)
10¼ x 4¼ x 1¼   1 lb 2½ oz
A-3 F 1 R 2
Two gate-marks; one on rim and another
on handle. One-eighth-inch top rail
around platform.

P-256-DIS Iron (R)
9⅞ x 4¾ x ⅞   1 lb 8 oz
Splayed ornamental cleats.
F 1 R 2
One-quarter-inch top rails front and sides
of platform.

P-580-DIS Iron (O)
9¼ x 4¼ x 1¼   15 oz
A-16 F 1 R 2
On reverse, "A. Kenrick & Sons No. 8 Rd.
15023." Long gate-mark on rim. One-
quarter-inch scalloped bottom rail on
platform reverse. A five-eighths-inch
guide post on each side toward front of
platform.

P-1534-DIS Iron (O)
10⅝ x 4½ x 1¼   1 lb 1½ oz
A-28 F 1 R 2
On reverse, "A. Kendrick & Sons, No. 9,
15022." Two guide posts on top near front
of platform. Bottom rail is scalloped.

P-523-DIS Iron (O)
8⅜ x 3⅝ x ⅝   11 oz
A-15 F 1 R 2
One-sixteenth-inch top rail around
platform.

P-73-DIS Iron (C)
8½ x 3⅞ x 1⅛   10½ oz
A-8 F 1 R 2
One-eighth-inch top rail around platform;
backcoping.

P-54-DIS Brass (VR)
8⅝ x 4⅛ x 1½   11 oz
A-17 F 1 R 2
Shallow top rails front and sides of
platform.

P-953-DIS Brass (VR)
8⅛ x 4 x 1⅛   11 oz
A-10 F 1 R 2
One-sixteenth-inch top rail around
platform.

P-760-DIS Brass (R)
9⅝ x 3⅞ x 1   1 lb 8 oz
A-11 F 1 R 2
One-quarter-inch top rails front and sides
of platform.

P-924-DIS Brass (VR)
7 x 4⅛ x ⅞   13 oz
A-15 F 1 R 2
One-sixteenth-inch rail around platform.

P-171-DIS Brass (R)
9⅞ x 4⅝ x 1¾   1 lb 2 oz
A-18 F 1 R 2

E-921-DIS Iron (R)
10⅞ x 4½ x 1¼   1 lb 10 oz
A-8 F 1 R 2
Old casting.

P-405-DIS Iron (VR)
8⅛ x 4⁷/₁₆ x 1¼   13½ oz
A-3 F 1 R 2
Sprue-mark on reverse.

E-387-DIS Iron (R)
8⅛ x 4½ x 1¹/₁₆   15 oz
C-4 F 2 R 2
Two one-eighth-inch top guide cleats on
side rails of platform. Note similarity of
peacock design to others in multi-purpose
stands.

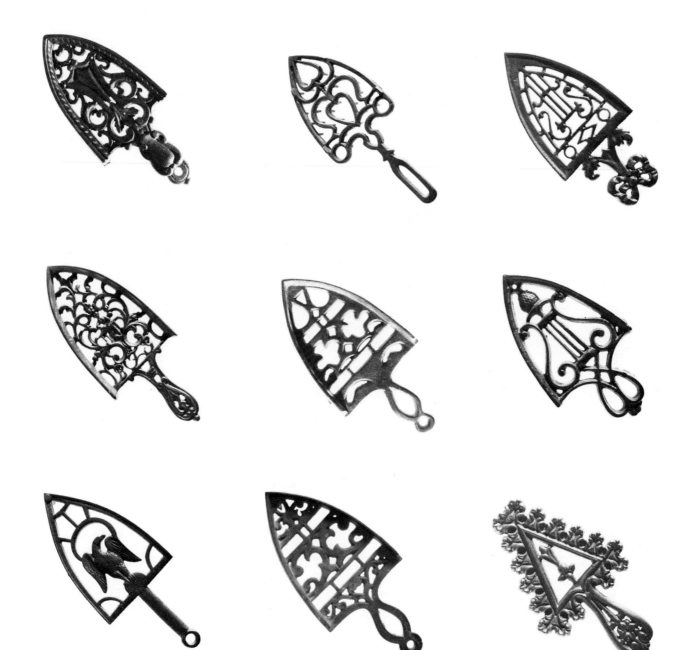

P-719 Iron (VR)
11 x 5 x 1¼   1 lb 8½ oz
A-11 F 1 R 2
One-half-inch top rails front and sides of
platform. Extensive backcoping.

P-1530-DIS Iron (VR)
11½ x 4⅞ x 1   1 lb 2 oz
A-11 F 1 R 2
Three-eighths-inch top rails front and
sides of platform. Backcoping on reverse
of rails.

P-601-DIS Iron (VR)
10¼ x 4⁷/₁₆ x 1⅜   1 lb 2½ oz
A-3 F 1 R 2
Two gate-marks on rim. Front leg riveted;
trivet apparently was so designed.   One-
sixteenth-inch top rails front and sides of
platform.

P-947-DIS Iron (VR)
11¾ x 4¾ x 1⅛   1 lb 10 oz
Approximately 55 thin supports of which
about 15 are broken. Purpose for multiple
supports is unclear. Two gate-marks on
rim.   Two cleat guides on each side rail.

P-1224-DIS Iron (VR)
9¾ x 4⅞ x 1½   1 lb 10 oz
A-9 F 1 R 2
Two gate-marks on rim. One-half-inch top
rails front and sides of platform.

E-902-DIS Iron (R)
9⅛ x 4½ x 1¼   1 lb 4½ oz
A-10 F 1 R 2
One-half-inch top rails front and sides of
platform.

P-286-DIS Iron (VR)
8½ x 4⅛ x ⅞   13¾ oz
E-10 F 1 R 2
One-sixteenth-inch top rails front and
sides of platform. Also cast in brass.

P-270-DIS Iron (O)
7½ x 4³/₁₆ x 1½   1 lb
A-2 F 1 R 2
One-eighth-inch top rails front and sides
of platform. Obviously an old casting.

P-1783-DIS Iron (VR)
8⅝ x 5⅜ x 1¹/₁₆   1 lb 5 oz
A-11 F 1 R 2
Sprue-mark on reverse. Platform is
reinforced; backcoping on handle.

E-347-DIS   Iron   (R)
8⅜ x 4¼ x 1¼   1 lb 1 oz
A-9   F 1   R 2
One-eighth-inch top rails front and sides
of platform.

E-64-DIS   Iron   (O)
7⅛ x 3⅞ x 1   9 oz
A-8   F 1   R 2
On reverse, "3." One-sixteenth-inch top
rail around platform.

E-54-DIS   Iron   (O)
7⅞ x 3½ x ⅞   7 oz
A-19   F 1   R 2
Backcoping on reverse of handle.

P-673-DIS   Iron   (R)
8¾ x 5 x ½   7½ oz
A-5   F 1   R 2
Nickel finish eroded.

E-429-DIS   Iron   (O)
7½ x 3¼ x ⅜   4 oz
A-15   F 1   R 2
On face, "25." Gate-marks on rim; filing.

P-579-DIS   Iron   (VR)
7⅜ x 4⅜ x 1⅜   13½ oz
A-10   F 1   R 2

P-414B-DIS   Iron   (C)
8¼ x 4⅛ x 1¼   13 oz
N-9   F 1   R 2
Two gate-marks on rim; filing. Extensive
backcoping.

P-1990-DIS   Iron   (VR)
8⅛ x 4½ x 2   1 lb 6 oz
A-2   F 1   R 2
One gate-mark on rim. One-sixteenth-inch
top side rails on platform.

P-1272-DIS   Iron   (O)
9 x 3⅞ x 1¾   15½ oz
A-17   F 1   R 2
On reverse, "Salter." One-sixteenth-inch
top rail around platform. Shallow
backcoping.

P-1886-DIS Iron (R)
9¼ x 3¾ x 1   10½ oz
A-4 F 1 R 2
One large gate-mark on handle.

P-287-DIS Iron (R)
9½ x 4¼ x ¾   9½ oz
J-C 3 F 1 R 2
One-quarter-inch rail around bottom of platform is extended to form supports.

P-312-DIS Iron (VR)
11 x 5⅛ x ¾   1 lb 3 oz
Rim extended into splayed supports.
F 1 R 2
One-eighth-inch top side rails on platform. Nickel finish eroded.

E-354-DIS Iron (O)
11⅜ x 3⅝ x 1⁵⁄₁₆   1 lb
N-C 9 F 1 R 2
Nickel finish.

E-402-DIS Iron (R)
12¼ x 3⅝ x 1¼   1 lb 5½ oz
A-9 F 1 R 2 S 2
On face, "Vacuum Oil Company Use Petroleum Sunflower." Nickel finish.

E-404-DIS Iron (O)
11¾ x 3⅞ x 1¼   1 lb 4 oz
D-10 F 1 R 2
On reverse, "Muster Geschutzt." Five-sixteenths-inch top rail around platform. Nickel finish.

E-414-DIS Iron (O)
13½ x 3¾ x 1⁵⁄₁₆   1 lb 10½ oz
D-10 F 1 R 2
On reverse, "Muster Geschutzt." Three-eighths-inch top rail around platform. Nickel finish.

P-1436-DIS Iron (O)
9⅝ x 2¾ x 1¼   14½ oz
A-3 F 1 R 2
Illegible letters on reverse of sun. Legend believed to be same as E-414. Two gate-marks on rim and handle. Three-sixteenths-inch top rail around platform.

P-1412-DIS Iron (R)
11¾ x 3¾ x 1¼   1 lb 9½ oz
N-24 F 1 R 2
On reverse, illegible imprint and same circular panel as P-1436. Gate-marks on

rim. One-quarter-inch top rail around platform. Modeling and backcoping on reverse.

E-373-DIS Iron (R)
12⅝ x 4 x 1⁹⁄₁₆   1 lb 8 oz
Front L-9 Rear H-9 F 2 R 2
Three-sixteenths-inch top rail around platform.

E-392-DIS Iron (R)
11¼ x 4 x 1   1 lb
A-9 F 1 R 2
One-eighth-inch top rails front and sides of platform. Gate-marks on rim; machine grinding.

P-184-DIS Iron (R)
12⅝ x 5 x ¾   1 lb 9 oz
N-C 8 F 1 R 2
Large gate-mark on rim at rear. Shallow top rail around platform.

P-1146-DIS Iron (R)
13⅛ x 4⅜ x 1¼   2 lbs ½ oz
A-9 F 1 R 2
On the reverse, "3."
Gate-marks on rim. Shallow top rail around platform.

P-783-DIS Iron (R)
10½ x 3⅝ x 1   13 oz
A-24 F 1 R 2
On reverse, "439." Small Star of David where handle joins platform. Shallow top rails front and sides of platform.

P-1543-DIS Iron (R)
12 x 4⅛ x 1   1 lb 5½ oz
A-10 F 1 R 2
Large gate-mark on rear of platform. Shallow one-eighth-inch top rail around platform.

P-784-DIS Iron (R)
10¾ x 3⅞ x ⅞   14 oz
A-21 F 1 R 2
One-eighth-inch top rail around platform. Nickel finish eroded.

P-1997-DIS Iron (O)
7 x 2⅜ x ¾   4 oz
D-4 F 1 R 2
One-eighth-inch top rail around platform.

P-1603-DIS Iron (R)
8⅜ x 2¹³⁄₁₆ x ⅞   12 oz
A-10 F 1 R 2
One-eighth-inch top rail around platform. Nickel finish eroded.

P-788-DIS Iron (R)
10¼ x 4¼ x 1⅝   3 lbs 2½ oz
Splayed cleats. F 2   R 2
Large gate-mark on rim. One-quarter-inch
top rail around platform.

P-1784-DIS Iron (O)
7¾ x 2⅝ x 1⅛   6½ oz
H-C 9   F 1   R 2
Front and side guides on platform. Nickel
finish.

P-111-DIS Iron (R)
10 x 4⅜ x 1   1 lb 4¾ oz
A-9   F 1   R 3
Three-eighths-inch top rails front and
sides of platform. Rear cleat as stop.

E-424-DIS Iron (R)
8⅝ x 3¾ x 1⁷⁄₁₆   12 oz
A-2   F 1   R 2
One-eighth-inch top rail around platform.
Nickel finish.

P-786-DIS Iron (O)
7½ x 2¼ x 1   6¾ oz
H-C 9   F 1   R 2
One-eighth-inch top rail around platform;
extended guides on each side rail. Nickel
finish eroded.

P-865-DIS Iron (O)
8½ x 2¹¹⁄₁₆ x 1⅜   11½ oz
A-10   F 1   R 2
On reverse, "Patent Appld. For, 7319." A
device for locking the iron stand in place
on reverse; probably the basis for patent.
One-eighth-inch top rail around platform.

P-19-DIS Iron (C)
8⅛ x 4 x 1¹⁄₁₆   11 oz
A-10   F 1   R 2
Two gate-marks on rim; extensive
backcoping.

P-17-DIS Iron (C)
9⅜ x 4⅛ x 1¼   13 oz
A-3   F 1   R 2

P-213-DIS Iron (C)
8½ x 3⅝ x ¾   9 oz
A-15   F 1   R 2
Extensive backcoping.

P-303-DIS Iron (C)
8 x 3½ x ⅞ 7 oz
A-10 F 1 R 2
Two gate-marks on rim; filing.
Extensive backcoping.

E-65-DIS Iron (C)
8¼ x 3¹³/₁₆ x ⅞ 8 oz
A-3 F 1 R 2
Gate-mark on rim; filing.
Extensive backcoping.

P-195-DIS Iron (C)
8⅝ x 3⅞ x ⅞ 7½ oz
A-4 F 1 R 2
Two gate-marks on rim; filing.
Extensive backcoping.

P-1252-DIS Iron (C)
8⅝ x 3¾ x ⅞ 9½ oz
A-9 F 1 R 2
On face, "1894." Gates on rim filed.
Extensive backcoping.

P-578-DIS Iron/wood (C)
9¾ x 3⅝ x 1⅛ 9½ oz
A-10 F 1 R 2
Two gate-marks on rim; filing.

P-698-DIS Brass (R)
9¼ x 4⅛ x 1¼ 15 oz
A-3 F 1 R 2
Three-sixteenths-inch top rails front and
sides of platform. Backcoping on reverse
of floral pattern.

P-1725-DIS Brass (R)
9⅝ x 4⅛ x ⅞ 13¾ oz
H-C 6 F 1 R 2
One-quarter-inch strap at rear of
platform; backcoping.

E-36-DIS Iron (O)
7½ x 3⅜ x ⅝ 7½ oz
A-15 F 1 R 2
Two large gate-marks on rim; extensive
backcoping.

E-75-DIS Iron (C)
8⅞ x 3⅞ x ⅞ 9 oz
A-10 F 1 R 2
One-eighth-inch rail around platform;
extensive backcoping.

  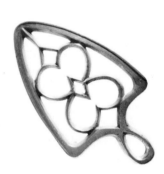

E-85-DIS Iron (C)
9¾ x 4¼ x 1¼ 13½ oz
A-10 F 1 R 2
On face, "3." One-sixteenth-inch top rail around platform.

E-343-DIS Iron (C)
9¼ x 3⅞ x 1¼ 10 oz
A-10 F 1 R 2
Extensive backcoping.

E-1-DIS Iron (C)
8⅞ x 3¾ x 1 8 oz
A-10 F 1 R 2

P-1837-DIS Iron (R)
6½ x 3¼ x ⅝ 4½ oz
A-5 F 1 R 2
Large gate-mark on rim; extensive backcoping.

P-465-DIS Iron (O)
8⅝ x 4 x ⅞ 7½ oz
A-3 F 1 R 2
Two gate-marks on rim; filing. One-eighth-inch top rail around platform.

P-1281-DIS Iron (O)
7⅞ x 3¾ x 1 6 oz
A-3 F 1 R 2
One gate-mark on rim; filing.

D-7-DIS Iron (R)
6 x 2¾ x 1¼ 7 oz
A-10 F 1 R 2
Gate-marks on handle and rim.

P-14-DIS Iron (O)
7½ x 3⅞ x 1⁵⁄₁₆ 8½ oz
A-2 F 1 R 2
Two gate-marks on rim. One-sixteenth-inch top rails front and sides of platform.

P-412-DIS Brass (R)
8⅜ x 4⅞ x 1½ 1 lb 1 oz
A-20 F 1 R 2
Shallow rails, front and sides.

 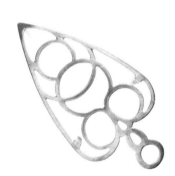 

P-681-DIS Brass (R)
8⅛ x 4¼ x ¾ 14 oz
A-12 F 1 R 2
One-sixteenth-inch top rails front and
sides of platform.

P-1347-DIS Brass (VR)
9⅝ x 4⅜ x 1⅜ 1 lb
B-18 F 1 R 2
Legs are splayed. One-eighth-inch top rail
at rear of platform.

P-1820-DIS Brass (R)
9⅛ x 4¾ x 1½ 14¾ oz
A-2 F 1 R 2

P-1354-DIS Brass (R)
8⅝ x 4¼ x 1½ 15½ oz
A-8 F 1 R 2
End of handle dated, "1840." Painted
black; front leg splayed.

P-533-DIS Brass (VR)
9½ x 4 x 1¼ 10 oz
N-10 F 1 R 2
One-quarter-inch rim around bottom of
platform extended to form three supports.

P-24-DIS Bronze (VR)
8 x 4 x 1¾ 12 oz
A-2 F 1 R 2

P-1843-DIS Iron (O)
8½ x 3¹³⁄₁₆ x ¹⁵⁄₁₆ 7¼ oz
A-21 F 1 R 2
Two gate-marks on rim. One-sixteenth-
inch top rails front and sides of platform.

P-1560-DIS Iron/wood (R)
10½ x 4 x 1¾ 10 oz
N-2 F 1 R 2
One-quarter-inch rail on bottom of
platform.

E-448-DIS Iron (O)
11 x 4⅜ x 1 1 lb
A-10 F 1 R 2
One-eighth-inch top rails front and sides
of platform.

  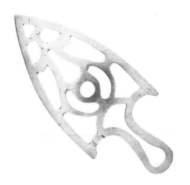

  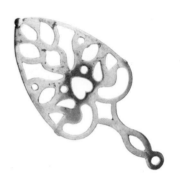

 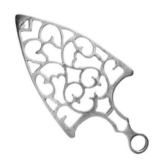 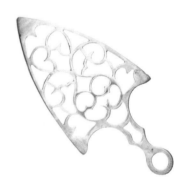

E-468-DIS Brass (R)
9⅝ x 4⅜ x 1½   12 oz
F-18 F 1 R 2
Measurement includes tang; wood handle missing.

E-28-DIS Iron (O)
6¹³/₁₆ x 3⁷/₁₆ x ¹¹/₁₆   5 oz
A-15 F 1 R 2
Gate-marks on rim; extensive backcoping.

E-528-DIS Iron (R)
9⅛ x 4⅝ x 1⅛   1 lb 3 oz
D-10 F 1 R 2
Reverse draft; old casting.

E-501-DIS Brass (R)
8⅞ x 4½ x 1⅜   1 lb 5 oz
A-9 F 1 R 2

P-1102-DIS Brass (R)
10⅜ x 4⅛ x 1   1 lb 7 oz
O-11 F 1 R 2
One-eighth-inch top rails front and sides of platform.

P-95-DIS Brass (R)
7 x 3½ x 1¹/₁₆   4½ oz
A-3 F 1 R 2

P-1017-DIS Brass (R)
7¾ x 3⅜ x __   9¾ oz
A-4 F 1 R 2
Reverse draft.

P-577-DIS Bronze (R)
9½ x 4¾ x 1½   1 lb 1 oz
A-2 F 1 R 2

P-567-DIS Brass (R)
8¼ x 4 x 1⅛   7½ oz
A-24 F 1 R 2

P-596-DIS Brass (VR)
9½ x 4¼ x 1¼   15 oz
C-10   F 1   R 2

P-58-DIS Brass (R)
8⅞ x 3½ x ⁹⁄₁₆   5½ oz
N-19   F 1   R 2

P-231-DIS Brass (VR)
8⅝ x 3¾ x 1¼   10½ oz
A-10   F 1   R 2

P-126-DIS Brass/wood (VR)
11¾ x 4⅞ x 1⅝   1 lb 5 oz
A-18   F 1   R 2
One-half-inch scalloped rail around
bottom of platform.

P-800-DIS Brass (R)
10⅛ x 4 x 1¼   9¾ oz
A-2   F 1   R 2

P-1093-DIS Brass/wood (R)
10¼ x 4¾ x 1¼   12 oz
A-8   F 1   R 2

P-1740-DIS Brass (R)
9 x 3⅝ x 1   7 oz
N-19   F 1   R 2
On reverse, "1299930."

P-193-DIS Brass (R)
8¼ x 3½ x 1   6¾ oz
N-19   F 1   R 2

P-164-DIS Brass (R)
9⁹⁄₁₆ x 4⅜ x ⅞   7 oz
A-19   F 1   R 2

P-60-DIS Brass (R)
7½ x 3¼ x ⅞   9 oz
Three supports are formed by brass bolts
screwed into platform and filed smooth.
F 1 R 2

P-449-DIS Brass (R)
7¾ x 3½ x 1⅛   9¾ oz
A-4 F 1 R 2

P-585-DIS Brass (R)
9¾ x 4 x 1⁹/₁₆   13¾ oz
H-18 F 1 R 2

P-813-DIS Brass (R)
9½ x 4⅜ x 1¼   15¾ oz
A-2 F 1 R 2

P-682-DIS Brass (VR)
9¼ x 4¼ x ⅞   14½ oz
A-10 F 1 R 2

P-51-DIS Brass (R)
8½ x 3⁹/₁₆ x 1   7½ oz
N-10 F 1 R 2

P-173-DIS Brass (R)
8¼ x 4 x 1⅜   10 oz
A-2 F 1 R 2

P-232-DIS Brass (R)
6⅞ x 3⅜ x 1⅛   8½ oz
A-19 F 1 R 2

P-1325-DIS Brass (R)
6⅞ x 3⅝ x 1⅛   13½ oz
A-3 F 1 R 2
Front leg replaced with copper pin and
rear left is brass pin.

  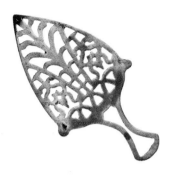

P-584-DIS Brass (R)
8 7/16 x 4 x 1 3/4   15 1/2 oz
D-19 F 1 R 2
Three-eighths-inch rim on bottom of platform.

P-55-DIS Brass (R)
9 7/8 x 4 1/2 x 1 5/8   15 oz
A-19 F 1 R 2

P-942-DIS Brass (R)
8 5/8 x 4 x 1 1/4   6 1/2 oz
D-18 F 1, R 2
Legs terminate in a cylindrical post about one-eighth-inch from end.

P-388-DIS Brass (R)
8 3/4 x 4 3/8 x 1 1/2   15 oz
D-18 F 1 R 2

P-1180-DIS Brass (R)
8 1/2 x 4 1/4 x 1 3/8   12 oz
A-19 F 1 R 2

P-816-DIS Brass (R)
9 3/8 x 4 3/8 x 1 1/4   1 lb 5 oz
D-9 F 1 R 2
One-quarter-inch top rails front and sides of platform

P-921-DIS Brass (VR)
8 1/8 x 4 1/4 x 1 1/4   11 oz
B-9 F 1 R 2

D-1-DIS Iron (R)
8 7/8 x 4 3/8 x 1 1/2   12 oz
D-9 F 1 R 2

P-219-DIS Brass (R)
8 1/8 x 4 1/8 x 1 9/16   11 1/2 oz
A-10 F 1 R 2

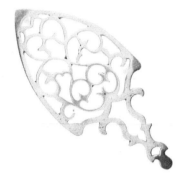

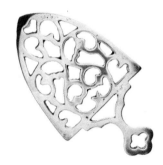
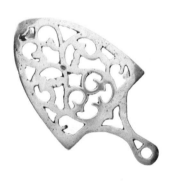

P-61-DIS Brass (VR)
8⅛ x 3⁹/₁₆ x 1⅛   8½ oz
A-10 F 1 R 2

P-937-DIS Brass (R)
8⅛ x 3⅞ x 1½   12 oz
A-10 F 1 R 2
Casting reveals legs were riveted to
pattern.

P-744-DIS Brass (R)
8⅜ x 4¼ x 1¼   1 lb 2½ oz
A-9 F 1 R 2
Three-sixteenths-inch top rails front and
sides of platform.

P-296-DIS Brass (R)
8⅝ x 4⅜ x 1½   12 oz
A-18 F 1 R 2

P-1162-DIS Brass (VR)
10½ x 4⅞ x 1⁵/₁₆   1 lb 2 oz
H-9 F 1 R 2
Front leg shorter than rear ones.

P-1024-DIS Brass (R)
7¾ x 4½   1 lb 2½ oz
Legs cut off; they probably were an inch
or longer.
F 1 R 2

P-216-DIS Brass (R)
9⅞ x 4½ 1⅜   1 lb 8 oz
A-2 F 1 R 2

P-595-DIS Brass (R)
8½ x 4³/₁₆ x 1¼   1 lb ½ oz
A-19 F 1 R 2

P-568-DIS Brass (O)
8¼ x 4⅝ x 1½   1 lb 2¾ oz
A-9 F 1 R 2

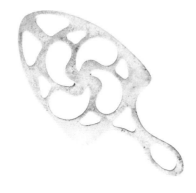  

E-450-DIS Brass (R)
9¾ x 4½ x 1¾   1 lb 13 oz
A-9 F 1 R 2

P-767-DIS Iron (R)
8 x 3⅞ x 1⁵/₁₆   13½ oz
D-9 F 1 R 2
Either pitted or rough casting.

E-74-DIS Iron (R)
9½ x 4¾ x 1¼   13½ oz
A-8 F 1 R 2
On reverse, "No. 2 T. Johnson." Note
similarity of handle to horseshoe trivets.
One-quarter-inch front guide and three
cleats on top side rails.

P-130-DIS Brass (VR)
9 x 4⅜ x 1⅝   1 lb 1½ oz
B-18 F 1 R 2
One-quarter-inch top rails front and sides
of platform. Legs are extensions of rim.

P-1980-DIS Brass/wood (VR)
12⅝ x 4½ x 1¾   1 lb 4 oz
N-18 F 1 R 2

E-437-DIS Iron (O)
8 x 5⅛ x 1⅛   1 lb 12½ oz
Cleats. F 1 R 2
On reverse, "Kenrick No. 11." Three-
quarters-inch top side rails on platform.
Small break in geometric pattern lower
left.

P-623-DIS Brass (O)
9⅞ x 4⅜ x 1¼   15½ oz
H-18 F 1 R 2
One-quarter-inch scalloped top rails on
front and sides of platform.

P-1574-DIS Brass (R)
11¾ x 6⅜ x 1½   1 lb 4½ oz
Rim extended into splayed supports
which are included in the width
measurement. One-quarter-inch scalloped
top rails front and sides of platform.

P-393-DIS Iron/wood (O)
11⅝ x 4¼ x 1   13½ oz
H-10 F 1 R 2
Three-sixteenths-inch top rails front and
sides of platform.

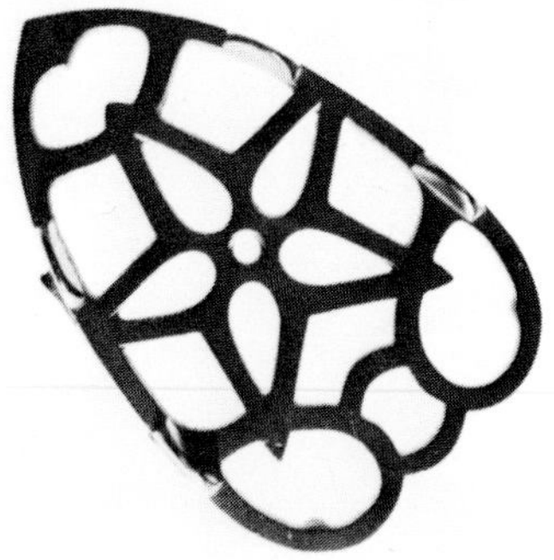
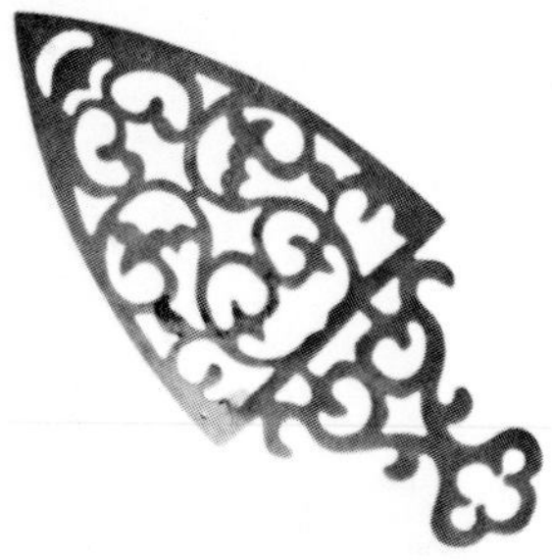
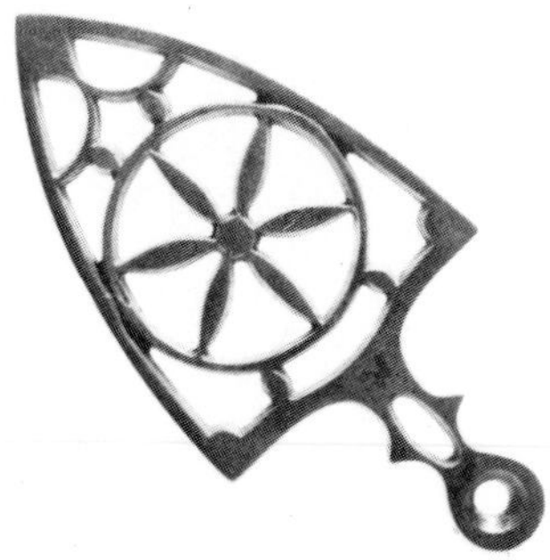
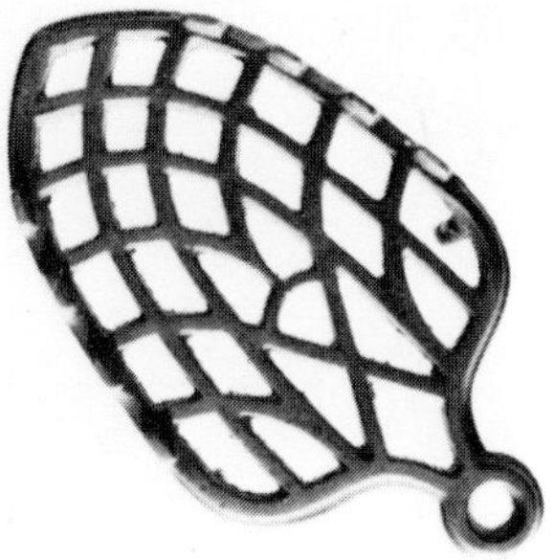
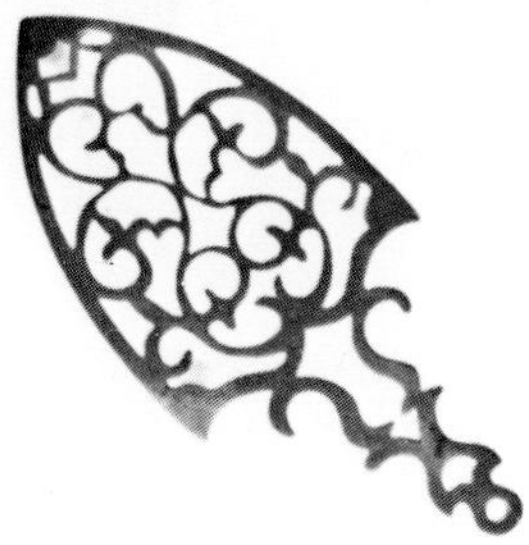
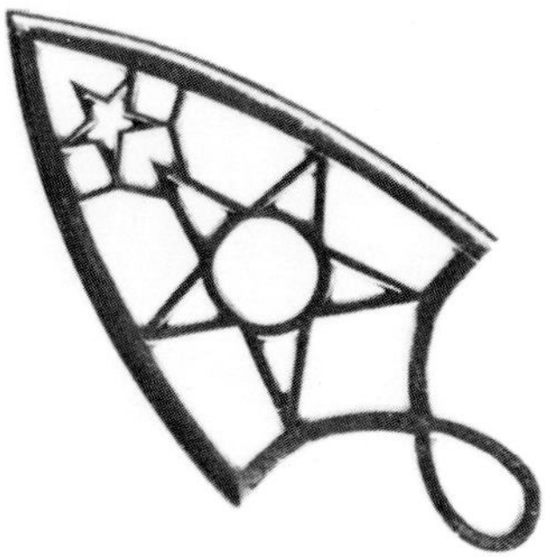
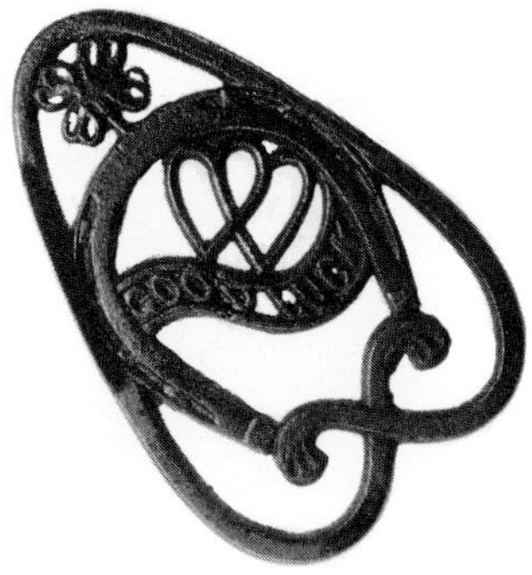
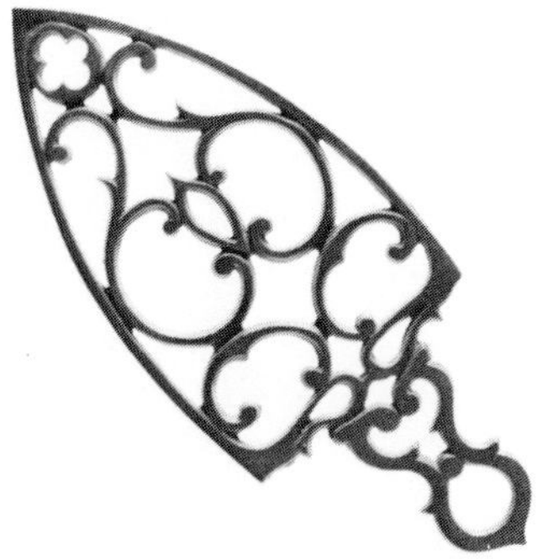
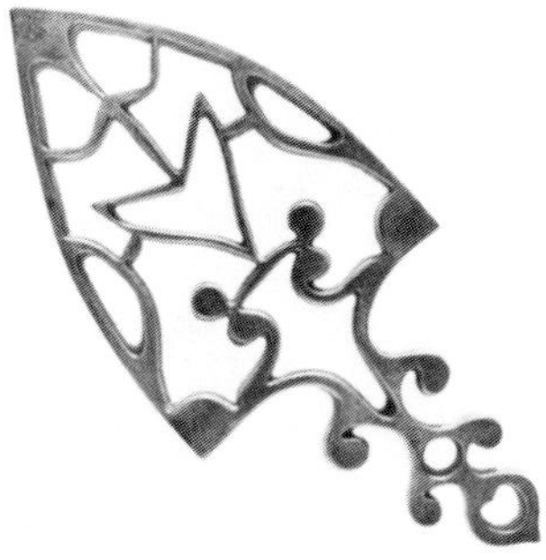

E-363-DIS Iron (R)
$6\frac{7}{8}$ x $4\frac{1}{2}$ x $\frac{3}{4}$ 12 oz
A-14 F 1 R 2
Two gate-marks on rim. Two seven-sixteenths-inch guides on top side rails of platform.

E-436-DIS Brass (R)
$8\frac{11}{16}$ x $5\frac{1}{4}$ x 1 1 lb 4 oz
A-8 F 2 R 2
Four scalloped guides on side rails of platform.

CW-3-DIS Iron (R)
$5\frac{5}{8}$ x $3\frac{1}{8}$ x $\frac{7}{8}$ $7\frac{3}{4}$ oz
A-3 F 1 R 2
On face, "Good Luck." Five-sixteenths-inch top side rails on platform.

E-503-DIS Brass (R)
8 x $3\frac{5}{8}$ x $1\frac{5}{8}$ 13 oz
A-2 F 1 R 2

E-510-DIS Brass (R)
$7\frac{7}{8}$ x $3\frac{1}{2}$ x $1\frac{5}{8}$ 10 oz
F 1 R 2

P-590-DIS Iron (O)
9 x $3\frac{5}{8}$ x $\frac{7}{8}$ 6 oz
A-5 F 1 R 2
Two gate-marks on rim. Delicate casting.

P-1152-DIS Iron (R)
8 x $3\frac{7}{8}$ x $1\frac{3}{16}$ 9 oz
A-18 F 1 R 2
Two gate-marks on rim; filing.

E-47-DIS Iron (R)
$8\frac{1}{8}$ x $4\frac{1}{8}$ x $1\frac{1}{16}$ $8\frac{1}{2}$ oz
A-9 F 1 R 2
Gate-marks on rim. One-sixteenth-inch top rails front and sides of platform.

P-940-DIS Brass (VR)
$9\frac{1}{8}$ x 4 x 2 1 lb 1 oz
A-1 F 1 R 2
One-quarter-inch top rails front and sides of platform.

P-97-DIS Brass (VR)
8⅞ x 3½ x 1¼   8½ oz
A-19 F 1 R 2

P-1103-DIS Brass (VR)
9 x 3¾ x 1¼   9½ oz
A-2 F 1 R 2

P-671-DIS Brass (R)
7¼ x 3⅛ 1¼   6 oz
A-17 F 1 R 2

P-1075-DIS Brass (R)
7¾ x 3¾ x ⅞   9½ oz
A-18 F 1 R 2

P-1345-DIS Brass (VR)
8½ x 3¾ x 1⅛   10½ oz
A-19 F 1 R 2

P-154-DIS Brass (R)
8¹³/₁₆ x 4⅜ x 1   10 oz
Front C-10 Rear A-10 F 1 R 2

P-897-DIS Brass (R)
9½ x 4¹/₁₆ x 1⁵/₁₆   11½ oz
K-9 F 1 R 2

P-912-DIS Brass (R)
8¼ x 3⅝ x 1¼   9¾ oz
A-19 F 1 R 2

P-812-DIS Brass (R)
9½ x 4⅜ x 1¼   1 lb ½ oz
A-2 F 1 R 2

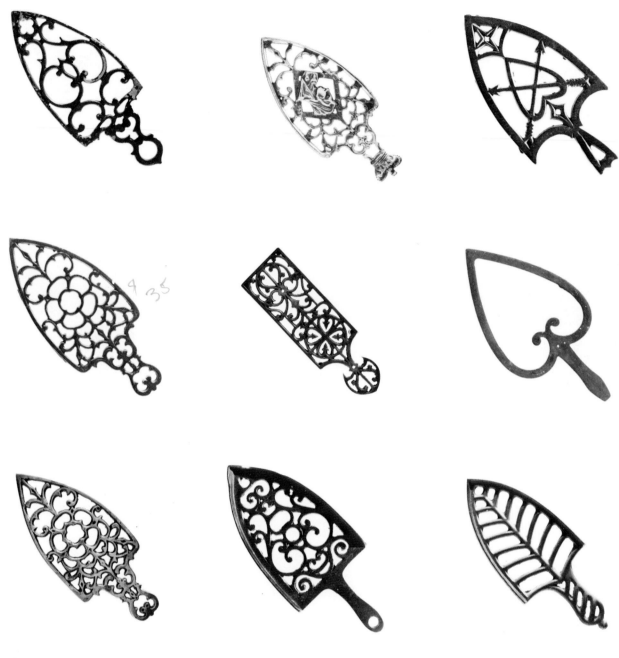

P-550-DIS Brass (R)
8⅝ x 3½ x ¾   6¾ oz
A-5 F 1 R 2

P-106-DIS Iron (C)
8⅜ x 3⅝ x ⅞   7½ oz
A-3 F 1 R 2
Two cast-marks on rim.

P-566-DIS Brass (O)
8⅜ x 3½ x 1⅛   9½ oz
A-19 F 1 R 2

P-1960-DIS Brass (R)
8 x 3⁷⁄₁₆ x 1¼   10½ oz
D-3 F 1 R 2
On face, "Diamond Jubilee 1827."
Backcoping on handle and portrait.

P-1197-DIS Brass (VR)
7¼ x 2¼ x ⅞   5 oz
A-25 F 2 R 2

P-2000-DIS Brass (R)
10⅛ x 4⅜ x 1⁹⁄₁₆   1 lb 1 oz
A-1 F 1 R 2
Three-eighths-inch top rails front and
sides of platform. Enlarged cleat at front.

P-735-DIS Iron (O)
9 x 4½ x 1⅝   14 oz
D-2 F 1 R 2
Two gate-marks on rim.

P-1022-DIS Iron (VR)
7⅛ x 3½ x ¹³⁄₁₆   4½ oz
F-5 F 1 R 2
Reverse draft.

P-440-DIS Iron (R)
10⅝ x 4½ x 1¼   15½ oz
A-10 F 1 R 2
One-quarter-inch top rails front and sides
of platform. Nickel finish eroded. Another
trivet of the same design in the Paley
Collection has green enamel finish.

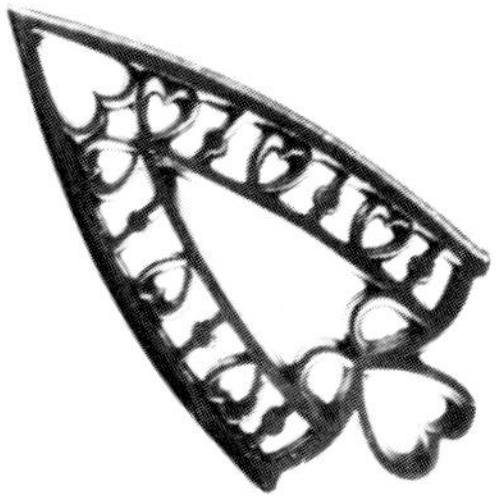

  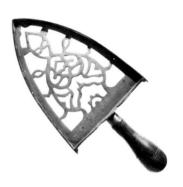

P-400-DIS Brass (R)
9⅝ x 4⅜ x 1⅛   1 lb 1 oz
A-19 F 1 R 2

E-458-DIS Brass (R)
9½ x 4¼ x 1½   12½ oz
E-18 F 1 R 2

P-659-DIS Brass (O)
9¾ x 4½ x 1⅛   15½ oz
A-9 F 1 R 2

P-1271-DIS Brass/wood (VR)
10⅛ x 3⅞ x ⅞   14 oz
A-19 F 1 R 2
One-quarter-inch rim around bottom of
platform.

P-697-DIS Brass (VR)
10 x 4¹³/₁₆ x 1   13¾ oz
F 1 R 2
Rim extended into splayed supports
terminating in ball feet.

P-1468-DIS Brass (VR)
9½ x 4¹/₁₆ x 1   9 oz
A-10 F 1 R 2

E-339-DIS Iron (R)
6¼ x 3⅞   10 oz
Legs cut off.   F 1 R 2

P-1757-DIS Brass/wood (VR)
11 x 5⅛ x 1½   1 lb 2 oz
J-18 F 1 R 2
Platform is brass secured by riveted strap
iron frame. Legs are extensions of frame;
handle attached to the backplate.

P-170-DIS Brass (VR)
6¾ x 3¼ x ⅞   3½ oz
Front N-4 Rear F-4 F 1 R 2

P-728-DIS Brass (R)
8½ x 3⅝ x 1⁷/₁₆ 11 oz
A-17 F 1 R 2

P-1077-DIS Brass (R)
10⅛ x 4⅞ x ⅞ 13¾ oz
Rim extended into splayed cleats.
F 1 R 2
One-half-inch scalloped rim around
bottom of platform

P-661-DIS Brass (O)
9 x 3⅝ x 1⅛ 10½ oz
A-10 F 1 R 2

P-707-DIS Brass (R)
8½ x 3½ x 1 8¼ oz
A-19 F 1 R 2
Extensive backcoping.

P-1092-DIS Brass (R)
8¾ x 4 x 1¼ 11½ oz
F-19 F 1 R 2

P-252-DIS Brass (R)
8⅛ x 3½ x 1¹/₁₆ 9½ oz
A-19 F 1 R 2
On face, "Salter 102."

P-233-DIS Brass (R)
7⅞ x 3½ x 1 10 oz
A-19 F 1 R 2

P-660-DIS Brass (R)
8½ x 4 x 1⅜ 12½ oz
D-19 F 1 R 2

P-1649-DIS Brass (R)
7¾ x 4³/₁₆ x 1⅛ 9¼ oz
A-19 F 1 R 2

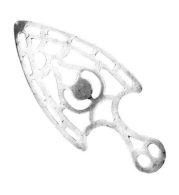

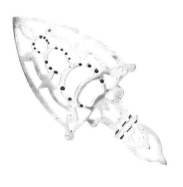

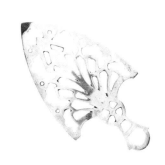

P-49-DIS Brass (R)
10 x 4¼ x 1¹/₁₆   1 lb 7½ oz
Rim extended into splayed cleats.
F 1   R 2
On reverse, "Falkirk No. 5."
One-quarter-inch scalloped rim on bottom
of platform and handle.

P-132-DIS Brass (VR)
8¾ x 4 x 1⅛   11 oz
J-C 7   F 1   R 2
Legs are extensions of platform bent
down into supports.

P-926-DIS Brass (R)
10⅛ x 4⅝ x 1¾   1 lb 3½ oz
A-2   F 1   R 2

P-1614-DIS Brass (R)
11⅛ x 4¼ x 1¼   14½ oz
A-19   F 1   R 2
On face, "ED VII."

P-678-DIS Brass (R)
11 x 4⅛ x 1   13 oz
A-19   F 1   R 2

P-218-DIS Brass (R)
6⅝ x 3½ x ⅞   3½ oz
H-10   F 1   R 2

P-528-DIS Brass (R)
9⅛ x 4¹/₁₆ x 1¾   1 lb 4½ oz
A-10   F 1   R 2

P-417-DIS Brass (VR)
9 x 4¼ x ¾   5½ oz
H-13   F 1   R 2

P-712-DIS Brass (R)
8½ x 4¼ x 1¼   13½ oz
A-19   F 1   R 2

E-412-DIS Iron (O)
9¼ x 3¾ x 1⁹/₁₆ 12½ oz
A-9 F 1 R 2
Machine grinding.

P-230-DIS Iron (O)
7 x 3¾ x 1⅜ 9 oz
Three cleats. F 1 R 2
On face, "Carron." On reverse, "2."

P-115-DIS Iron (C)
6¼ x 3¼ x 1 5½ oz
A-19 F 1 R 2
On face, "British Make." Large gate-mark
on rim; filing.

P-679-DIS Brass (R)
8 x 4¼ x 1½ 13¾ oz
A-18 F 1 R 2

P-163-DIS Brass (O)
7⅝ x 3¾ x ¾ 4½ oz
H-19 F 1 R 2
On reverse of ring on handle, "2400."
Scalloped rim around bottom of platform.

P-437-DIS Brass (VR)
10⅞ x 4¹⁵/₁₆ x ⅞ 14¾ oz
Rim extended into supports.
F 1 R 2
Scalloped top rail around platform.

P-1199-DIS Brass (O)
8¾ x 4 x ¾ 6½ oz
H-15 F 1 R 2
On face, "A Gentleman In Kharki."

P-70-DIS Brass (VR)
8⅞ x 4³/₁₆ x 1¼ 13¾ oz
A-8 F 1 R 2
On face, "Peace and plenty."

E-525-DIS Iron (O)
10 x 4³/₁₆ x 1 1 lb 2 oz
A-11 F 1 R 2
On face, "CSA Richmond 1922." One-
sixteenth-inch top rails front and sides of
platform. Souvenir trivet.

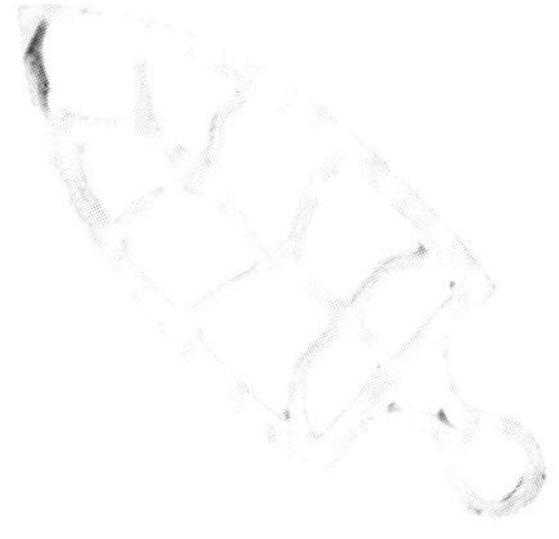

E-348-DIS Iron (O)
8¼ x 3⁷/₁₆ x ¹³/₁₆   8 oz
A-11 F 1 R 2
Gate-marks on rim; machine grinding.

P-1590-DIS Iron (R)
6½ x 3½ x ⁹/₁₆   4½ oz
A-23 F 1 R 2
Gate-mark on rim; extensive backcoping.

E-357-DIS Iron (O)
8⅞ x 5 x ½   8 oz
A-13 F 1 R 2

P-11-DIS Iron (C)
7⅝ x 3¾ x ¾   6 oz
A-5 F 2 R 2
Machine grinding.

P-710-DIS Iron (R)
7⅞ x 4¼ x ¹⁵/₁₆   5 oz
A-10 F 1 R 2
Badly corroded.

E-129-DIS Iron (O)
7 x 3¼ x ¹⁵/₁₆   6 oz
A-10 F 1 R 2
Backcoping on reverse of handle.

P-172-DIS Brass (R)
8½ x 4 x 1⅛   11½ oz
A-10 F 1 R 2

E-423-DIS Aluminum (R)
10¼ x 4 x 1¼   7½ oz
A-2 F 1 R 2
One-quarter-inch rails front and sides of platform.

E-431-DIS Aluminum (R)
8¾ x 3⅞ x 1¹/₁₆   4 oz
A-3 F 1 R 2
Two front guides

P-762-DIS Tin/wood (R)
14 x 5 x 1
F 1   R 2
Stamped and bent; handle riveted. Three-eighths-inch top rails front and sides of platform.

E-000-DIS Stamped metal (R)
11⅝ x 4¼ x 1⅝
Pre-made riveted legs. F 1   R 2
One-quarter-inch top rails front and sides of platform. Unusual piece; platform is stamped thin steel plate. Riveted legs are pre-made round tapered shafts with bulbous terminals. Rim is separately made and attached by notching. Handle is riveted to platform.

P-1339-DIS Tin (R)
11⅞ x 4¼ x 1¹/₁₆
F 1   R 2
Stamped and bent. Five-eighths-inch

decorative top rails front and sides of platform.

E-471-DIS Tin (O)
10 x 4⅝ x ⅞
F 1   R 2
Stamped and bent. Three-eighths-inch scalloped top side rails on platform.

P-1448-DIS Tin (R)
9¾ x 4⅝ x 1
F 1   R 2
On face, "ZE."
Stamped and bent.

P-749-DIS Tin (VC)
9¼ x 4⅝ x 1
F 1   R 2
On face, "UCM." Seven-sixteenths scalloped top rails on sides of platform.

P-844-DIS Tin (R)
8 x 5½ x ⅞
F 1   R 2
Stamped and bent riveted supports. One-inch top rails on front and sides of platform.

P-1714-DIS Tin (R)
7½ x 4 x ⅞
F 2   R 2
Stamped and bent. One-eighth-inch top rails front and sides of platform.

P-1379-DIS Tin (R)
7½ x 4¹/₁₆ x ⅞
F 2   R 2
Stamped and bent. One-quarter-inch top rails front and sides of platform.

  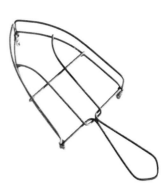

P-1763-DIS Tin (R)
7½ x 4 x ¾
F 2 R 2
Stamped and bent.

P-1606-DIS Tin (R)
6½ x 4½ x ⅞
F 1 R 2
On face, "Pat'd." Stamped and bent. One-eighth-inch top rails front and sides of platform.

P-1693-DIS Tin (R)
6¹¹⁄₁₆ x 4⅜ x 1
F 1 R 2
Stamped and bent.

P-1572-DIS Tin (R)
7⅛ x 4½ x ⅞
F 1 R 2
Stamped and bent.

P-1728-DIS Tin (R)
6½ x 4 x 1½
F 1 R 2
Stamped and bent; riveted supports. One-quarter-inch top rail around platform.

P-1653-DIS Tin (R)
6⅜ x 4⅝ x ¾
F 1 R 2
Stamped and bent. One-eighth-inch top rail around platform.

P-1012-DIS Wire (R)
11⅜ x 4½

P-138-DIS Wire (R)
10½ x 5¾
Wire wrapped around posts; center wire is bent down into an additional support.

P-474-DIS Wire (R)
11½ x 4¾

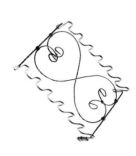

P-1399-DIS Wire (R)
10⅛ x 5

P-879-DIS Wire (R)
8 x 5
Wires are brought together and fastened
with metal clips to strengthen supports.

P-536-DIS Wire (R)
7¾ x 4¼
Twisted wire, braided posts with oval
soldered feet.

P-1161-DIS Wire (R)
7¾ x 3⅝

P-537-DIS Wire (R)
7¾ x 5¼

P-245-DIS Wire (R)
8½ x 5
Rubber tubing on feet to prevent
scratching of surfaces.

P-1646-DIS Wire (R)
7 x 5

P-1766-DIS Wire (R)
6½ x 4⅝
Coiled wire rim guides.

P-1715-DIS Wire (R)
5 x 3¼
Perhaps a toy iron stand.

Manufacturers' Iron Stands

Historically, trivet and stand designs remained relatively unchanged. New England and Pennsylvania styles stayed the same with few exceptions, notably Rimby's *Tulips* and *Twelve Hearts* and a few other round stands which were never copied in the same size, or weight as the originals. Also, stove and plaque trivets were not reproduced. In the later part of the nineteenth century, new designs were added to the classifications of Multi-Purpose Trivets; Decorative Iron Stands; and Tea, Coffee and Table Stands. However, it was the old traditional designs that were most frequently reproduced.

In contrast, the design of Manufacturers' Iron Stands was in constant flux between 1865 and 1930. Changes in design resulted from technical development of irons themselves, production factors and marketing competition. Some stand shapes conformed to size and contour of new commercial iron styles, while others retained traditional decorative elements. Older design concepts were gradually supplemented with initials, monograms, trademarks, slogans or company names.

Most iron stands were designed for specific models. Supports were much shorter, sizes and shapes were more varied, and many stands had clearly defined rails, guide cleats or posts on the platform. Also, handles began to disappear. Most iron rests from this period do not have handles. Added to the traditional spade and heart-shaped stands were double-pointed ones; many unusual design styles were patented by manufacturers.

Stands made by the Sensible Company exemplified new trends. Ober stands were unique to that company, designed as iron rests but advertised as also being suitable for coffee or tea pots. The round and square Ober designs are typical of manufacturers' iron stands, but because they had no handles, guides or cleats, they are shown in the tea, coffee and table stand section.

To a great extent, function replaced decoration and cost was clearly a factor as many stands were stamped metal, steel, or aluminum. Few brass or bronze stands were produced; nickel-plate was the new elegance in trivet finishes. Nickel surfaces were either matt finished or highly polished. During this era, American design was the predominant influence.

The nineteenth century saw further developments to sadirons. Cool handles, detachable handles, heat shields and various patented devices continuously improved the design of sadirons. Self-heating irons were investigated and there were alcohol, kerosene, gasoline, naphtha or carbide-acetylene, gas and electric irons. Electric steam irons were introduced early in the twentieth century.

Also, there were numerous specialty models such as pleaters, fluters, and an array of commercial irons with stands to be used by tailors and launderers. Irons used by housewives were generally much smaller than commercial ones. Some large commercial stands weighed as much as three to six pounds. Small traveling irons, complete with carrying cases, also became popular. A number of iron stands produced in this period were mounted on slate bases. At a later date, tin heat shields and abestos pads were used.

E-430-MIS Iron (R)
8⅛ x 4¹³/₁₆ x ¹⁵/₁₆ 7 oz
A-3 F 1 R 2
On face, "W." One-sixteenth-inch top rails front and sides of platform. Backcoping by repeated drilling of small round holes.

P-1475-MIS Iron (R)
8 x 3¾ x ⅞ 7½ oz
A-4 F 1 R 2
On face, "C."

P-1476-MIS Iron (VR)
7⅞ x 3¾ x ⅞ 6 oz
A-4 F 1 R 2
On face, "F." One-sixteenth-inch top rails front and sides of platform.

Most of the iron stands cast in the nineteenth century were produced by independent gray iron foundries. Iron stand patterns were kept on hand to be modified for different companies. Frequently, the same models were customized for different dealers. It is not uncommon to find the same basic design with a variety of company identifications or commerical messages.

In the twentieth century, the design of iron rests became more utilitarian and less decorative. Many were exceedingly plain and uninteresting; only the most dedicated collectors include them in their collections.

P-1470-MIS Iron (O)
8½ x 4 x 1   11 oz
A-3 F 1 R 2
On face, "W." Six guide cleats on top side rails of platform.

E-420-MIS Iron (O)
8¼ x 3⅞ x ¹¹/₁₆   7½ oz
A-9 F 1 R 2
On face, "W." One-sixteenth-inch top rails front and sides of platform. Backcoping by drilling rather than routing.

P-174-MIS Iron (VR)
7¾ x 3½ x 1   8 oz
A-10 F 1 R 2
On face, "K." Two gate-marks on rim. One-sixteenth-inch top rails front and sides of platform.

P-41-MIS Iron (O)
8 x 4¹³/₁₆ x 1   7 oz
A-10 F 1 R 2
On face, "D." Gate-mark on rim. One-sixteenth-inch rails front and sides of platform.

E-125-MIS Iron (R)
7¾ x 3⅝ x ¹⁵/₁₆   8 oz
A-10 F 1 R 2
Shallow top rails front and sides of platform; backcoping.

P-319-MIS Iron (R)
9¾ x 4⅞ x ⅞   11½ oz
A-3 F 1 R 2
On face, "W." Gate-marks on rim. One-eighth-inch top rails front and sides of platform. Backcoping on reverse of handle.

P-1861-MIS Iron (O)
7¾ x 3¾ x ¾   7¼ oz
A-19 F 1 R 2
On face, "B." Two gate-marks on rim.

P-1151-MIS Iron (R)
7½ x 4³/₁₆ x ⅝   12½ oz
A-15 F 2 R 2
On face, "WF." Gate-marks on rim; machine grinding. Three-sixteenths-inch top side rails on platform. Rotating drum at rear of platform.

P-38-MIS Iron (O)
7½ x 4⅝ x ¾   9½ oz
A-11 F 1 R 2 S 2
On face, "G." On reverse, "Smarts Brockville." Two gate-marks at rear of platform; machine grinding. One-quarter-inch top rails front and sides of platform. Nickel finish.

P-690-MIS Iron (O)
6¾ x 5 x ¾   11 oz
A-11 F 1 R 2 S 2
On face, "G." On reverse, "Smarts
Brockville." Machine grinding. One-
quarter-inch top side rails on platform.
Nickel finish.

P-15-MIS Iron (C)
7¼ x 4¼ x ⅝   5¾ oz
A-9 F 1 R 1 S 2
On face, "T." Two gate-marks on rim.
Made in Guelph, Ontario; T is for Taylor
(Hankenson).

P-16-MIS Iron (O)
7¹/₁₆ x 4¼ x ⅝   5¾ oz
A-9 F 1 R 1 S 2
On face, "TF." Two gate-marks on rim.
TF stands for Taylor-Forbes; made later
than T stand (Hankenson).

E-78-MIS Iron (R)
8⅜ x 3¾ x ⅞   3 oz
A-20 F 1 R 2
On face, "S."

D-4-MIS Iron (VR)
8 x 4⁵/₁₆ x Front¾   Rear 1⁹/₁₆
Front C-2 Rear O-2 F 1 R 2
On face, "SS." Unusual swivel strap handle, which locks on either side. Stand tilts
forward. Seven-sixteenths-inch to three-
sixteenths inch tapered top side rails on
platform.

P-1118-MIS Iron (R)
7⅜ x 4⅜ x ⅞   13¾ oz
A-15 F 2 R 1
On face, "RNH." Two gate-marks on rim.
Three-quarters-inch top guide rails on
sides of platform.

P-461-MIS Iron (R)
8¼ x 3¾ x 1   4 oz
A-19 F 1 R 2
On face, "L & Co."

P-748-MIS Iron (R)
8 x 3½ x ¹³/₁₆   2¾ oz
A-6 F 1 R 2
On face, "S & CO." Two gate-marks on
rim; filing.

E-81-MIS Iron (VR)
7⅞ x 3½ x ⅞   4 oz
A-20 F 1 R 2
On face, "JA & CO."

P-662-MIS Iron (R)
9¼ x 4 x ¾ 8¾ oz
A-15 F 2 R 2
On face, "Pat Apld For." Gate-mark on rim. Rotating wooden drum at rear of stand with small wire clip to hold drum in trough.

P-534-MIS Iron (O)
6¾ x 3½ x 9/16 4½ oz
A-21 F 1 R 2

E-427-MIS Aluminum (R)
9⅜ x 5 x 1 8¾ oz
C-8 F 1 R 2
Five-sixteenths-inch top side rails on platform.

P-109-MIS Iron (C)
5³/₁₆ x 4⅛ x ¹¹/₁₆ 7 oz
A-15 F 1 R 2
Two gate-marks at rear of platform. Three-sixteenths-inch top side rails on platform. Nickel finish.

P-1346-MIS Iron (O)
5⁵/₁₆ x 4 x ¹¹/₁₆ 6½ oz
A-15 F 1 R 2
Two gate-marks at rear of platform. Three-sixteenths-inch top side rails on platform. Nickel finish.

E-39-MIS Iron (R)
5½ x 4³/₁₆ x ¹¹/₁₆ 8 oz
A-14 F 1 R 2
On face, "Hope." One-quarter-inch top side rails on platform.

E-6-MIS Iron (O)
5⅞ x 4½ x ⅞ 9 oz
A-10 F 1 R 2
On face, "Kerr & Coombes Hamilton Ont." Two gate-marks at rear of platform. Three-eighths-inch top side rails on platform.

P-615-MIS Iron (O)
6 x 4⅝ x ¾ 10¾ oz
M-C 3 F 1 R 2
Two gate-marks at rear of platform. Five-sixteenths-inch top side rails on platform. Supports formed by ornamental cleats extending from rim.

D-905-MIS Iron (R)
6 x 4½ x ⅞ 10½ oz
A-10 F 1 R 2
Three-eighths-inch top side rails on platform.

P-1533-MIS Iron/wood (O)
9¾ x 3½ x 1⅛ 10½ oz
A-19 F 1 R 2
On face, "F W London." On reverse, "Pat Applied For." One-eighth-inch top rail around platform.

P-223-MIS Iron (R)
11⅝ x 4⅜ x 1⅛ 1 lb. 1 oz
H-23 F 1 R 2
One-eighth-inch top rails front and sides. Nickel finish.

E-395-MIS Iron (O)
10¾ x 4½ x 1 12½ oz
Front scalloped cleat C-7 Rear E-8
F 1 R 2

P-535-MIS Iron (R)
7 x 3¹⁵⁄₁₆ x 2 1 lb
A-8 F 1 R 2
Three-eighths-inch top rails front and sides of platform. Nickel finish.

E-922-MIS Iron (R)
7¼ x 4⅛ x 1⅛ 12½ oz
A-8 F 1 R 2
Pronounced gate-marks; machine grinding. One-quarter-inch top rail around platform.

P-200-MIS Bronze (R)
7¹⁵⁄₁₆ x 4⅞ x ¾ 1 lb 1 oz
A-11 F 1 R 2 S 2
One-quarter-inch top side rails on platform.

E-491-MIS Iron (O)
7⅞ x 3½ x 1⅛ 13½ oz
A-10 F 1 R 2
On reverse, "44." One-quarter-inch top rails front and sides of platform.

P-222-MIS Iron (O)
6½ x 4¼ x ⅞ 12 oz
A-19 F 1 R 2
Top rail around platform.

P-321-MIS Iron (R)
6⅝ x 4¼ x 1¼ 13 oz
A-3 F 1 R 2
Nickel finish eroded.

P-1489-MIS Iron (R)
8½ x 3⅞ x ¹⁵⁄₁₆   7½ oz
A-4 F 1 R 2
On face, "Fox & Co St Louis."
Two gate-marks on rim. One-sixteenth-inch top rails front and sides of platform.

E-72-MIS Iron (R)
9⅛ x 4 x 1   12 oz
A-10 F 1 R 2
On face, "S.R. Fox & Co. St. Louis Mo."
On reverse, "No 1." One-eighth-inch top rail around platform.

E-365-MIS Iron (R)
9¼ x 4⅛ x 1⅛   12 oz
A-8 F 1 R 2
On face, "American Butt Co." One-eighth-inch top rail around platform.

P-10-MIS Bronze (R)
9³⁄₁₆ x 4 x 1⅛   15½ oz
A-3 F 1 R 2
On face, "New England Butt Co. Prov. R.I." Two gate-marks on rim. One-eighth-inch top rail around platform.

P-1781-MIS Iron (R)
9¹⁄₁₆ x 4 x 1¼   11¾ oz
A-4 F 1 R 2
On face, "Nashua Lock Co. Nashua N.H." Gate-marks on rim. One-eighth-inch top rail around platform.

P-1541-MIS Iron (O)
8⅞ x 3⅞ x 1½   14½ oz
A-2 F 1 R 2
On face, "Pat Oct 18 1879." Gate-marks on rim. One-eighth-inch top rail around platform. Paley collection includes about nine trivets of this design with different advertising messages.

E-87-MIS Iron (O)
9 x 3¾ x ⅞   10½ oz
A-10 F 1 R 2
On face, "Ives & Allen Manufacturers Montreal." Small piece broken off heart at the top.

CW-2-MIS Iron (R)
10⅛ x 6 x ¹⁵⁄₁₆   1 lb 2 oz
Rim extended into splayed supports.
F 1 R 2
On face, "Rub while the iron is hot." Measurement includes splayed supports.

E-31-MIS Iron (O)
6 x 4¼ x ⅞   11 oz
A-11 F 1 R 2
Five-sixteenths-inch top side rails on platform.

P-23-MIS Iron (R)
7 x 4⅝ x ⅞   15½ oz
A-19 R 2
On reverse, "Pat Pending."
Hinged front guide also serves as front
support. One-quarter-inch top side rails
on platform.

P-1952-MIS Iron (O)
6¾ x 5⅛ x ¾   15½ oz
Front M-C 4 Rear C-M 10 F 1 R 2
On reverse, "Rd. No. 653885/16."
One-eighth-inch top side rails with addi-
tional stops at front and rear.

P-1115-MIS Iron (R)
7½ x 4⅝ x 1   1 lb
A-10 F 1 R 2
On face, "Ill." Two gate-marks at rear of
platform. Cleat guides at front, sides and
rear.

P-1289-MIS Iron (R)
6¾ x 3⅞ x 1   14½ oz
A-19 F 1 R 2 S 2
On face, "Hot Cross." On reverse, Rd
440891." Large gate-mark on rim. Five-
sixteenths-inch top rail on right side of
platform.

P-626-MIS Iron (VR)
6¾ x 4½ x ⅞   9½ oz
A-19 F 1 R 2
On face, "Patent Applied For." One-
eighth-inch top rails front and sides of
platform.

P-1742-MIS Iron (R)
8½ x 4¹⁵/₁₆ x 1⅛   1 lb 3 oz
A-10 F 1 R 2
On face, "GE Co S F CAL." Three-sixteenths-inch top side rails on platform.

P-271-MIS Iron (O)
5¾ x 4⅜ x ⅝   8 oz
Front M-C 1 Rear J-C 6 F 1 R 2
On face, "Rochester Sad Iron." Two gate-
marks at rear of platform. Two guide
cleats on sides of platform.

E-453-MIS Iron/brass (R)
9¼ x 4¾ x 1⅛   1 lb 5½ oz
A-9 F 1 R 2
Brass posts riveted to cast-iron platform.
Five-eighths-inch top side rails on
platform.

P-275-MIS Iron (R)
9½ x 4⅞ x 1   15½ oz
A-3 F 1 R 2
Gate-marks on rim. Five-eighths-inch top
side rails on platform.

216

 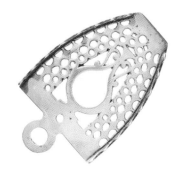 

 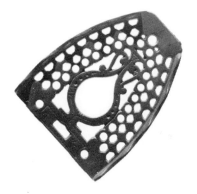 

E-331-MIS Iron (VR)
8 x 3¾ x 1   12¾ oz
A-9 F 2 R 2
On reverse, "Champion Pat Pdng Self Heating Sad Iron Co   Kansas City Mo." Cup on handle for wax to keep iron from sticking. Three-sixteenths-inch top front guide rails on platform.

E-457-MIS (R)
8½ x 4⅜ x ⁵⁄₁₆   15 oz
Extended curved cleats. F 1   R 1
On reverse, "DHSO."

P-5-MIS Iron (VC)
6⅛ x 4½ x ⅞   11 oz
A-10 F 1 R 2
Two gate-marks at rear of platform. Five-sixteenths-inch top side rails on platform.

P-1254-MIS Iron (O)
6 x 4½ x ½   9 oz
A-15 F 1 R 2
Two gate-marks at rear of platform. Two three-sixteenths-inch top guide cleats on each rail.

P-1140-MIS Brass (R)
7⅛ x 4⅜ x ⅞   11 oz
A-9 F 1 R 2
One-quarter-inch top scalloped side rails on platform.

P-1537-MIS Iron (O)
5½ x 4⅜ x ¾   9 oz
A-15 F 1 R 2
On reverse, "Brighton 8." Two gate-marks at rear of platform. One-quarter-inch top scalloped side rails on platform.

E-16-MIS Iron (VC)
5¾ x 4½ x ¾   10 oz
A-11 F 1 R 2
Four gate-marks at rear of platform which has incised decorative treatment. Three-sixteenths-inch top side rails on platform.

E-344-MIS Iron (VC)
5⅞ x 4½ x ¾   9½ oz
A-10 F 1 R 2
One-quarter-inch top scalloped side rails on platform.

E-62-MIS Iron (O)
5⅞ x 4⅝ x ⅞   10 oz
A-10 F 1 R 2
On face, "Less & Drake Newark NJ USA." One-quarter-inch top scalloped side rails on platform.

P-175-MIS Iron (C)
7⅛ x 4⅛ x ⅜   8¾ oz
A-16 F 1 R 1 S 2
On face, "Best on Earth."

P-1036-MIS Iron (C)
7⅜ x 3⅞ x ⅝   9½ oz
A-15 F 1 R 1 S 2
On face, "J.T. Co. From Producer to Consumer," trademark. Gate-marks on rim; machine grinding. Nickel finish eroded.

E-93-MIS Iron (C)
7 x 4 1/16 x ⅜   8 oz
A-15 F 1 R 1 S 2
Two one-eighth-inch top guides on each side rail of platform.

P-1253-MIS Iron (O)
7⅛ x 4 1/16 x 7/16   9 oz
A-15 F 1 R 1 S 2
On face, "Simmon's Special." Machine grinding. Nickel finish eroded.

P-263-MIS Iron (C)
7 x 4 x 9/16   9 oz
A-15 F 1 R 1 S 2
On face, "Dubuque Potts." Gate-marks on rim; machine grinding.

E-335-MIS Iron (R)
6⅞ x 3⅞ x ½   9½ oz
A-14 F 1 R 1 S 2
On face, "Richmond CAL." Two guide cleats on each side of platform.

E-2-MIS Iron (O)
7½ x 4⅜ x ½   9 oz
A-15 F 1 R 1 S 2
On face, "Simmon's Special." One-sixteenth-inch top rail around platform with two guide cleats on each side rail. Nickel finish.

E-352-MIS Iron (C)
7⅛ x 4⅛ x ½   9½ oz
A-15 F 1 R 1 S 2
On face, "Dubuque Potts." Two guide cleats on each side of platform.

E-70-MIS Iron (O)
7½ x 4¼ x 9/16   9½ oz
A-15 F 1 R 1 S 2
On face, "J.S. H & Co. Crown." Nickel finish.

 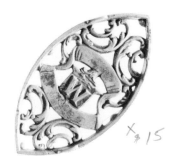 

P-311-MIS Iron (O)
7¼ x 4 x ⅞   9¼ oz
A-5 F 1 R 1 S 2
On face, "L." Gate-marks on rim; machine grinding.

E-330-MIS Iron (C)
7⅜ x 4¼ x ⁹⁄₁₆   10½ oz
A-15 F 1 R 1 S 2
On face, "Best on Earth." Two guide cleats on each side of platform. Nickel finish.

E-432-MIS Iron (C)
7½ x 4 x ⅞   9 oz
A-3 F 1 R 1 S 2
One-sixteenth-inch rail around platform. Nickel finish.

E-338-MIS Iron (VC)
7⁹⁄₁₆ x 4 x ½   8 oz
A-15 F 1 R 1 S 2
On face, "W The Royal." One-sixteenth-inch rail around platform; two guide cleats on each side rail.

P-433-MIS Iron (C)
7¾ x 4⅛ x ½   9¼ oz
A-5 F 1 R 1 S 2
On face, "W" "The Peerless." One-eighth-inch top rail around platform. Nickel finish eroded.

E-96-MIS Iron (C)
7⅝ x 4¹⁄₁₆ x ⅝   8 oz
A-15 F 1 R 1 S 2
On face, "W" with small fox. One-sixteenth-inch top rail around platform; two guides on each side rail.

P-404-MIS Iron (C)
7⅞ x 4⅛ x ⅝   10¼ oz
A-15 F 1 R 1 S 2
On face, "Humphrey Gas Iron General Specialty Company." Two gate-marks on rim; filing. One-eighth-inch top rail around platform.

P-264-MIS Iron (O)
7⅛ x 3⅞ x ⁵⁄₁₆   6¼ oz
A-16 F 1 R 1 S 2
On face, "J.R. Clark Co. Minneapolis." Gate-marks on rim.

P-709-MIS Iron (O)
8⅛ x 4¾ x ¾   13¼ oz
A-14 F 1 R 1 S 2
On face, "Consolidated Gas Iron Co. Imperial." One-eighth-inch top rail around platform. Nickel finish eroded.

 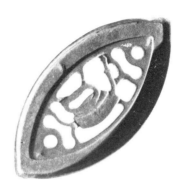 

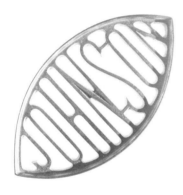 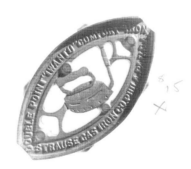 

P-1438-MIS Iron (O)
7¹⁵/₁₆ x 4⅛ x ⅞   13½ oz
A-9 F 2 R 2
On face, "New York Pressing Iron Co New Ideal Double End." Large gate-mark on rim. Three-sixteenths-inch top side rails on platform.

P-757-MIS Iron (R)
7⅜ x 3¾ x ⅞   8¼ oz
A-4 F 1 R 1 S 2
One-sixteenth-inch top rail around platform. Extensive backcoping; nickel finish.

P-1669-MIS Iron (O)
7¾ x 4¼ x ⁹/₁₆   10¼ oz
A-15 F 1 R 1 S 2
On face, "Johnson." Gate-marks on rim; machine grinding. Three-sixteenth-inch top rail around platform.

E-408-MIS Iron (C)
7¼ x 4¹/₁₆ x 1³/₁₆   1 lb 3½ oz
M-C 7 F 2 R 2
Three-sixteenths-inch top side rails on platform.

E-355-MIS Iron (C)
7⅞ x 4 x 1   11 oz
A-9 F 1 R 1 S 2
Three-eighths-inch top side rails on platform; one-sixteenth-inch rails front and rear. Nickel finish eroded.

P-262-MIS Iron (C)
7⅜ x 4 x 1⅜   1 lb 2 oz
G-C 7 F 2 R 2
On face, "I Want U Comfort Iron. Strause Gas Iron Co Phila Pa USA." Gate-marks on rim; machine grinding. One-quarter-inch top side rails on platform.

E-381-MIS Iron (R)
8 x 4¼ x ¹¹/₁₆   14 oz
A-11 F 1 R 1 S 2
On face, "UNEEDA UGI Co Philadelphia Pa." Seven-sixteenths-inch top rail around platform. Reverse draft.

P-1840-MIS Iron (O)
7⅞ x 4³/₁₆ x ¾   1 lb
Four cleats. F 2 R 2
On face, "Sunshine-Jasper Co. New York USA. Sunshine Home Gas Iron No. 6 Iron Stand." Gate-marks on rim; filing. Five-sixteenths-inch top scalloped side rails on platform. Beautiful stand.

P-756-MIS Iron (O)
7⅞ x 4³/₁₆ x ¹⁵/₁₆   1 lb 3½ oz
Scalloped cleats. F 2 R 2

P-48-MIS Iron (C)
6½ x 4 x 1⅛ 12½ oz
A-9 F 1 R 2
On face, "Strause I Want U Iron The McClary Mfg Co London Ont." Gate-marks at rear of platform; machine grind-ing. Five-sixteenths-inch top rail around platform.

E-13-MIS Iron (C)
6½ x 4 x 1⅛ 10 oz
A-9 F 1 R 2
On face, "I Want U Comfort Iron Strause Gas Iron Co Phila Pa USA." One-eighth to one-quarter-inch tapered top rail around platform.

P-383-MIS Iron (C)
6½ x 4 x 1⅛ 12½ oz
A-9 F 1 R 2
On face, "The B & H Peerless Gas Iron Phila Pa." One-quarter-inch tapered top side rails on platform.

E-121-MIS Iron (C)
6½ x 4 x 1³/₁₆ 13 oz
A-9 F 1 R 2
On face, "I Want U Comfort Iron Strause Gas Iron Co Phila Pa USA." One-eighth to one-quarter-inch tapered top rail around platform. Another version of this design, "C. Gefrorer & Son, Inc Phila Pa USA."

E-25-MIS Iron (C)
6½ x 4 x ¾ 13½ oz
A-11 F 1 R 2
On face, "C. Gefrorer & Son Inc Phil'a Pa USA. The Comfort Iron." Three-six-teenths-inch top rail around platform.

E-120-MIS Iron (C)
5½ x 4 x 1 13 oz
A-9 F 1 R 2
One-eighth to one-quarter-inch tapered top rail around platform. Nickel finish.

P-620-MIS Iron (C)
6½ x 4 x 1⅛ 11½ oz
A-9 F 1 R 2
One-quarter-inch top side rails on plat-form. Machine grinding.

P-1143-MIS Iron (O)
9 x 4½ x 1½ 2 lbs 4 oz
A-9 F 1 R 2
On face, "I Want U Comfort Iron Strause Gas Iron Co Phila. Pa. U.S.A." One-eighth-inch top rail around platform with one-quarter-inch side rails.

E-478-MIS Iron (C)
8⅞ x 4¼ x 1½ 1 lb 15 oz
A-9 F 1 R 2
On face, "I Want U Comfort Iron Strause Gas Iron Co Phila Pa USA." Five-six-teenths-inch top rails sides and back of platform. Nickel finish.

E-433-MIS Iron (C)
7¹/₁₆ x 4³/₁₆ x 1   14 oz
A-9 F 1 R 2
On face, "Rosenbaum Mfg Co New York
U Need It Gas Iron." One-sixteenth to
one-quarter-inch tapered top rail around
platform. Nickel finish.

P-640-MIS Iron (O)
7 x 4½ x 1⅛   1 lb 1 oz
A-11 F 1 R 2
On face, "Rev O Noc Gas Iron." One-
quarter-inch tapered top rails front and
sides of platform.

E-562-MIS Iron (O)
6⅜ x 4¼ x 1   8 oz
A-9 F 1 R 2
On face, "Gunn Quality Gas Iron Co.
Phila Pa USA Gunn Quality Gas Iron."
One-quarter-inch top side rails on
platform.

E-396-MIS Iron (C)
6½ x 4 x ⅞   14 oz
A-9 F 1 R 2
On face, "Eastern Iron Co Phila Pa."
One-eighth to one-quarter-inch tapered
top rail around platform. Nickel finish.
Another version of this design has "Gunn
Quality Gas Iron Co Philadelphia Pa."
on face.

P-1029-MIS Iron (R)
8¾ x 4¾ x 1⅜   2 lbs 15½ oz
Ornamented splayed cleats. F 1 R 2
On face, "L'Ami-Des Teintupiers. Paris."
On reverse, "AE 1 26." Scalloped rim on
bottom of platform. One-quarter-inch top
rail around platform.

P-1393-MIS Iron (O)
7¼ x 4⁵/₁₆ x ⅞   9½ oz
A-10 F 1 R 2
On face, "Ideal 1915 New York Pressing
Iron Co." One-eighth-inch top rails front
and sides of platform.

P-1255-MIS Iron (O)
7⅛ x 4⅛ x 1⅛   12½ oz
A-8 F 1 R 2
On face, "The Real Gas Iron." Filing on
rim. One-quarter-inch top rails front and
sides of platform.

D-3-MIS Brass (R)
6⁷/₁₆ x 4⅜ x 1½   12 oz
Cleats. C-6 F 2 R 2
On face, "B T-H." Three-sixteenths-inch
top side rails on platform. Break in right
rail.

P-1256-MIS Iron (O)
6¾ x 4⅛ x 1⅛   12¾ oz
A-9 F 1 R 2
On face, "Stead." Gate-marks at rear of
platform; machine grinding. Three-
eighths-inch top rail around platform.

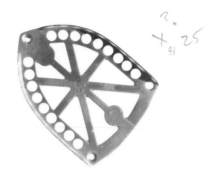

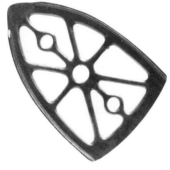

P-1522-MIS Iron (R)
6⅝ x 5½ x ¾   10 oz
A-15 F 1 R 2
On face, "F." Some filing.

P-67-MIS Iron (VC)
6 x 4⁷⁄₁₆ x ¾ 8½ oz
A-10 F 1 R 2
One-quarter-inch top side rails on
platform.

P-1920-MIS Iron (O)
6¾ x 4⁵⁄₁₆ x ⁹⁄₁₆ 7¾ oz
A-15 F 1 R 2
Two gate-marks on rim. Three-sixteenths-
inch top side rails on platform.

E-37-MIS Iron (O)
5¾ x 4¼ x ¾   8 oz
A-11 F 1 R 2
Gate-marks at rear of platform. Five-sixteenths-inch top side rails on platform.

E-35-MIS Iron (O)
6 x 4⅜ x ⅞   8 oz
A-10 F 1 R 2
On face, "H.R. Ives & Co. Montreal."
Three-eighths-inch top side rails on
platform.

E-95-MIS Iron (VC)
6¼ x 4½ x ¹⁵⁄₁₆ 10 oz
A-10 F 1 R 2
On face, "Enterprise Mfg Co Philadelphia." Gate-marks at rear of platform.
Three-eighths-inch top side rails on
platform.

E-114-MIS Iron (O)
6 x 4⅜ x ⅝ 9 oz
A-15 F 1 R 2
Gate-marks at rear of platform; machine
grinding. Three-eighths-inch top side rails
on platform.

E-5-MIS Iron (R)
6⅜ x 4¾ x ⅞   13 oz
A-3 F 1 R 2
Three-eighths-inch top side rails on platform. Hole in platform center is pipe
fitting for securing stand to surface.

E-42-MIS Iron (VC)
5¹³⁄₁₆ x 4¼ x ¾   11 oz
A-15 F 1 R 2
Gate-marks at rear of platform; machine
grinding. One-quarter-inch top side rails
on platform.

  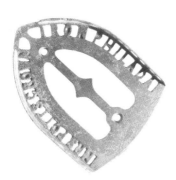

E-10-MIS Iron (O)
5⅞ x 4⅜ x ¹⁵/₁₆   12 oz
A-9 F 1 R 2
Three-eighths-inch top scalloped side rails
on platform.

E-48-MIS Iron (VC)
6 x 4¼ x 1   11 oz
On face, "Mrs Potts Crown Iron Philad."
Three-eighths-inch top side rails on platform.

P-299-MIS Iron (O)
5¾ x 4¹/₁₆ x ¹¹/₁₆   9½ oz
A-19 F 1 R 2
Two gate-marks at rear of platform. Front
foot shorter than rear ones. One-quarter-
inch top side rails on platform.

E-139-MIS Iron (VC)
6⅛ x 4½ x ⅞   9½ oz
A-10 F 1 R 2
Two gate-marks at rear of platform.
Three-eighths-inch top side rails on
platform.

P-279-MIS Iron (C)
6⅛ x 4½ x ¹⁵/₁₆   10 oz
A-3 F 1 R 2
Two gate-marks at rear of platform.
Three-eighths-inch top side rails on
platform.

E-140-MIS Iron (C)
6 x 4⁷/₁₆ x ⅞   9½ oz
A-10 F 1 R 2
Two gate-marks at rear of platform.
Three-eighths-inch top side rails on
platform.

P-1155-MIS Iron (C)
6 x 4½ x ⅝   9¾ oz
A-15 F 1 R 2
Two gate-marks at rear of platform; machine grinding. Five-sixteenths-inch top
side rails on platform.

E-98-MIS Iron (VC)
6⅛ x 4½ x ¹⁵/₁₆   9½ oz
A-10 F 1 R 2
On face, "Mrs Potts Crown Iron Philadelphia." Two gate-marks at rear of
platform. Three-eighths-inch top side rails
on platform.

P-8-MIS Iron (C)
6³/₁₆ x 4½ x ⅞   9 oz
A-4 F 1 R 2
On face, "Enterprise Mfg Co Philadelphia." Two gate-marks at rear of
platform. Five-sixteenths-inch top side
rails on platform.

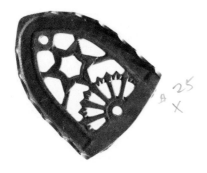

P-160-MIS Iron (O)
6 x 4⅜ x ⅞   10¾ oz
A-11 F 1 R 2
On face, "The Griswold Mfg Co Erie Pa Classic." Five-sixteenths-inch top side rails on platform. Machine grinding.

E-22-MIS Iron (VC)
6¹/₁₆ x 4⁷/₁₆ x ⅞   10 oz
A-9 F 1 R 2
Three-eighths-inch top side rails on platform.

E-17-MIS Iron (O)
6 x 4½ x ¹¹/₁₆   9 oz
A-11 F 1 R 2
Two gate-marks at rear of platform. One-quarter-inch sharply scalloped top side rails on platform.

E-370-MIS Iron (C)
6⅛ x 4⅜ x ⅞   11 oz
A-10 F 1 R 2
On face, "Ypsilanti Mfg Co Ypsilanti Mich." Three-eighths-inch top side rails on platform.

E-117-MIS Iron (VC)
6 x 4¼ x ⅞   11 oz
A-10 F 1 R 2
On face, "The Cleveland Foundry Co." One-quarter-inch top side rails on platform.

E-94-MIS Iron (O)
6 x 4⁷/₁₆ x ¹¹/₁₆   8 oz
A-11 F 1 R 2
Five-sixteenths-inch top scalloped side rails on platform.

E-45-MIS Iron (O)
5⅞ x 4⅜ x ¹¹/₁₆   8 oz
A-11 F 1 R 2
On reverse, "1604." One-eighth-inch top side rails each with two five-sixteenths-inch guide cleats on sides, front and rear of platform.

E-21-MIS Iron (O)
6⅛ x 4⅜ x ¾   13 oz
A-15 F 1 R 2
Three-eighths-inch top scalloped side rails on platform.

E-134-MIS Iron (C)
6¹/₁₆ x 4½ x ¹¹/₁₆   9 oz
A-15 F 1 R 2
Three-eighths-inch top scalloped side rails on platform.

P-569-MIS Iron (O)
6⅛ x 4⅛ x ⅝   8¾ oz
A-15 F 1 R 2
Two gate-marks at rear of platform. One-quarter-inch top side rails on platform.

P-63-MIS Iron (C)
5⅞ x 4⅜ x ¾   12 oz
A-11 F 1 R 2
On face, "N.R. Streeter & Co. Groton, N.Y." Two gate-marks at rear of platform. Five-sixteenths-inch top side rails on platform.

E-710-MIS Iron (O)
6 x 4¼ x ¾   8½ oz
A-11 F 1 R 2
One-quarter-inch top side rails on platform.

P-298-MIS Iron (VC)
5⅝ x 4¼ x ¾   8 oz
A-11 F 1 R 2
On face, "Royal." Two gate-marks at rear of platform. One-quarter-inch top side rails on platform. Nickel finish.

E-41-MIS Iron (O)
6 x 4⁷/₁₆ x ¹¹/₁₆   11 oz
A-12 F 1 R 2
On face, "Colebrookdale Iron Co. Potts-town. Pa." Five-sixteenths-inch top side rails on platform.

E-133-MIS Iron (O)
6 x 4⅜ x ¾   9½ oz
A-11 F 1 R 2
On face, "Colebrookdale Iron Co. Potts-town Pa." Two gate-marks at rear of platform; machine grinding. Three-eighths-inch top side rails on platform.

E-14-MIS Iron (VC)
6 x 4⅜ x ¾   10 oz
A-11 F 1 R 2
On face, "Colebrookdale Iron Co. Potts-town Pa." Three-eighths-inch top side rails on platform.

E-38-MIS Iron (C)
5⅝ x 4¼ x ¾   10 oz
A-11 F 1 R 2
On face, "Royal." One large gate-mark at rear of platform. One-quarter-inch top side rails on platform.

E-128-MIS Iron (C)
5¾ x 4³/₁₆ x ¾   11 oz
A-11 F 1 R 2
On face, "Union Mfg. Co. Boyertown Pa Victory 700." Five-sixteenths-inch top side rails on platform.

P-71-MIS Iron (O)
6 x 4⁷/₁₆ x ¹¹/₁₆ 8½ oz
A-19 F 1 R 2
On face, "J.B. Lewis Hamilton Ont." Two gate-marks at rear of platform. Five-sixteenths-inch top side rails on platform.

P-882-MIS Iron (O)
5¾ x 4⅜ x ¾ 10½ oz
A-11 F 1 R 2
On face, "The Pugh Mfg Co." Two gate-marks at rear of platform. Five-sixteenths-inch top side rails on platform.

P-235-MIS Iron (O)
5¾ x 4⅜ x ¾ 10 oz
A-11 F 1 R 2
On face, "Jameson Pugh Co." Two gate-marks at rear of platform. Five-sixteenths-inch top side rails on platform.

E-34-MIS Iron (O)
5½ x 4¼ x ⅞ 6 oz
A-11 F 1 R 2
One large gate-mark at rear of platform. One-quarter-inch top side rails on platform.

E-107-MIS Iron (C)
6 x 4¼ x ⅞ 9 oz
A-9 F 1 R 2
Five-sixteenths-inch top side rails on platform.

E-53-MIS Iron (O)
6 x 4⁵/₁₆ x ⅞ 9 oz
A-11 F 1 R 2
Three-eighths-inch top side rails on platform.

E-9-MIS Iron (O)
5¹⁵/₁₆ x 4⁷/₁₆ x ¹¹/₁₆ 9 oz
A-19 F 1 R 2
On face, "J.B. Lewis Hamilton Ont." Two gate-marks at rear of platform. Three-eighths-inch top side rails on platform.

E-366-MIS Iron (C)
5¾ x 4⅜ x 1³/₁₆ 8½ oz
A-19 F 1 R 2
Two gate-marks at rear of platform. One-quarter-inch top side rails on platform.

E-340-MIS Iron (C)
5⅜ x 4⅛ x ¾ 10 oz
A-11 F 1 R 2
One-quarter-inch top side rails on platform.

E-127-MIS Iron (O)
5½ x 4¼ x ¾   6 oz
A-15 F 1 R 2
One-quarter-inch top side rails on platform. Nickel finish.

E-66-MIS Iron (O)
6⅜ x 4 x ¾   8 oz
A-4 F 1 R 2
One-quarter-inch top side rails on platform.

E-113-MIS Iron (C)
6 x 4½ x ¾   9½ oz
A-11 F 1 R 2
Three-eighths-inch top side rails on platform. Nickel finish.

P-1313-MIS Iron (VC)
6⅛ x 4½ x ¹¹/₁₆   10¾ oz
A-11 F 1 R 2
On face, "E," "Enterprise Mfg Co Phil'a. U.S.A." On reverse, "3791." Two gate-marks at rear of platform. Three-eighths-inch top side rails on platform.

P-1328-MIS Iron (O)
6 x 4⅜ x ⅞   10½ oz
A-19 F 1 R 2
On face, "E." Two gate-marks at rear of platform. Five-sixteenths-inch top side rails on platform.

P-306-MIS Iron (O)
6 x 4¼ x ⅝   12 oz
A-19 F 1 R 2
On face, "E," "Economy Syracuse N.Y." Three-eighths-inch top side rails; machine grinding.

E-137-MIS Iron (O)
5⅞ x 4¼ x ⅞   11 oz
A-3 F 1 R 2
On face, "St Louis Mo." Three-eighths-inch top side rails on platform.

E-4-MIS Iron (VC)
6⅛ x 4⅜ x ⅝   12 oz
A-14 F 1 R 2
On face, "E," "Enterprise Mfg Co Phil'a. USA." Gate-marks at rear of platform. Three-eighths-inch top side rails on platform. Similar design identified on face, "Pleuger & Henger Mfg Co St Louis Mo."

E-108-MIS Iron (O)
6¹/₁₆ x 4⅜ x ⅝   8 oz
A-15 F 1 R 2
On face, "B." One-quarter-inch top side rails on platform.

P-66-MIS Iron (VC)
6 x 4¼ x ¾ 8 oz
A-13 F 1 R 2
On face, "B & D." Two gate-marks at rear of platform. Two one-quarter-inch top guides on each rail of platform.

P-291-MIS Iron (C)
8 x 4¼ x ⅝ 10 oz
A-15 F 1 R 2
On face, "H Co," "The W.H. Howell Co Geneva Ill, USA."

P-782-MIS Iron (R)
6½ x 4¹³/₁₆ x 1 1 lb 14½ oz
Cleats. F 1 R 2
On face, "Mc B & O." Supports are five cleats on each side of reverse. Repeated on the bottom forming a scalloped rail on top and supports on reverse.

P-1268-MIS Iron (C)
6 x 4¼ x ⅝ 9¾ oz
A-15 F 1 R 2
On face, "F," "Fanner Mfg Co. Cleveland O." Gate-marks show filing. Five-sixteenths-inch top side rails on platform.

P-1496-MIS Iron (O)
7⅞ x 5⅜ x 1⅝ 2 lbs ½ oz
H-C 10 F 1 R 2
On face, "F Troy Beauty." One-quarter-inch top rail around platform.

E-55-MIS Iron (C)
5⅞ x 4⁵/₁₆ x ¾ 9½ oz
A-10 F 1 R 2
On face, "W." Three-eighths-inch top side rails on platform. Nickel finish.

E-119-MIS Iron (C)
6³/₁₆ x 4¹/₁₆ x ¾ 8 oz
A-11 F 1 R 2
On face, "C." One-quarter-inch top side rails on platform.

E-92-MIS Iron (O)
6½ x 4⅛ x 1¹/₁₆ 10 oz
A-9 F 1 R 2
On face, "C." One-quarter-inch top side rails on platform.

P-304-MIS Iron (VC)
6 x 4⅛ x ¾ 9¾ oz
A-11 F 1 R 2
On face, "C." Two gate-marks at rear of platform. One-quarter-inch top side rails on platform.

P-1226-MIS Iron (O)
6⅛ x 4¼ x ¹³/₁₆ 9¾ oz
H-C 3 F 1 R 2
On face, "XX." Five-sixteenths-inch top side rails on platform.

E-40-MIS Iron (O)
6 x 4⅛ x ¾ 8 oz
A-11 F 1 R 2
On face, "XX." One-quarter-inch top side rails on platform.

E-30-MIS Iron (O)
5⅞ x 4¼ x ¹¹/₁₆ 11 oz
A-11 F 1 R 2
On face, "S," "Laclede Mfg Co. St Louis Mo." Two gate-marks at rear of platform. Three-eighths-inch top side rails on platform.

P-571-MIS Iron (O)
5¾ x 4¼ x ¾ 10½ oz
A-19 F 1 R 2
On face, "AF," "American Foundry & Mfg Co St Louis MO." Two gate-marks on rim; finning. One-quarter-inch top scalloped side rails on platform.

E-33-MIS Iron (C)
5¾ x 4³/₁₆ x ¾ 9½ oz
A-11 F 1 R 2
On face, "P&H," "Pleuger & Henger Mfg Co St Louis Mo." One-quarter-inch top scalloped side rails on platform.

E-132-MIS Iron (O)
6¾ x 4⅛ x ½ 9 oz
A-14 F 1 R 2
On face, "A S." Three-eighths-inch top side rails on platform. Nickel finish.

P-1487-MIS Iron (O)
5¾ x 4⅜ x ⅝ 8 oz
A-15 F 1 R 2
On face, "S Simmons Hdw Co St Louis." Two gate-marks at rear of platform. Two one-eighth-inch top cleats on side rails of platform.

E-126-MIS Iron (C)
5¾ x 4¼ x ¹¹/₁₆ 10 oz
A-12 F 1 R 2
On face, "R." Two one-quarter-inch top guide rails front and rear of platform.

E-115-MIS Iron (VC)
6 x 4⁷/₁₆ x ⅞ 12½ oz
A-11 F 1 R 2
On face, "Ferro Steel Cleveland." One-quarter-inch top side rails on platform.

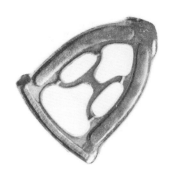  

P-268-MIS Iron (C)
5⅞ x 4⅜ x ¹¹/₁₆ 8 oz
A-15 F 1 R 2
On face, "WH Howell Co Geneva Ill." Two gate-marks at rear of platform. Shallow guide cleats at front and rear of platform.

E-124-MIS Iron (VC)
5⅞ x 4⅜ x ⅝ 7 oz
A-11 F 1 R 2
Two gate-marks at rear of platform. Two one-eighth-inch guide cleats on each side rail of platform.

E-118-MIS Iron (O)
5¹⁵/₁₆ x 4⅜ x ⅞ 13 oz
A-11 F 1 R 2
On face, "The WH Howell Co Geneva Ill." Three-eighths-inch top scalloped side rails on platform. Another version inscribed, "M.F. & Co Chicago."

E-32-MIS Iron (VC)
5⅞ x 4⅜ x ¹¹/₁₆ 7 oz
A-15 F 1 R 2
On face, "WH Howell Co. Geneva Ill." Front guide and rear cleats.

E-7-MIS Iron (VC)
5½ x 4⅛ x ⅝ 5 oz
A-14 F 1 R 2
Front guide and rear cleats.

E-99-MIS Iron (C)
5⅞ x 4⅛ x ¾ 8 oz
A-15 F 1 R 2
On face, "The William Howell Co. Geneva Ill." Shallow top cleats front and back of platform.

P-112-MIS Iron (C)
5⅞ x 4⅜ x ¾ 9 oz
A-12 F 1 R 2
On face, "W.H. Howell Co. Geneva Ill." Two gate-marks at rear of platform. Top guide cleats at front and rear of platform.

P-1486-MIS Iron (O)
5⅞ x 4⅜ x ¾ 9 oz
A-17 F 1 R 2
On face, "Bartlett & Co. Hibbard Spencer Our Very Best." Two gate-marks at rear of platform. Top guide cleats at front and rear of platform.

E-29-MIS Iron (R)
5⅞ x 4¼ x ¹⁵/₁₆ 14 oz
A-9 F 1 R 2
On face, M.F. & Co. Chicago." Seven-sixteenths-inch top scalloped side rails on platform.

 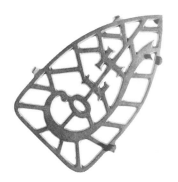 

P-900-MIS Iron (O)
5⅜ x 3¹⁵/₁₆ x ⅝   10 oz
A-14 F 1 R 2
On face, "Stoves and Ranges Cinderella
Never Fails." Three one-eighth-inch cleats
on each side rail of platform. Nickel
finish.

P-903-MIS Iron (O)
5⅝ x 4¹/₁₆ x ⁹/₁₆   9 oz
A-14 F 2 R 2
On face, "Victor Stoves & Ranges." One-
quarter-inch top side rails on platform.
Nickel finish.

P-518-MIS Iron (C)
6⅞ x 4⅜ x ¾   1 lb
O-C 2 F 2 R 2
On face, "GE." One-quarter-inch top side
rails on platform. Nickel finish eroded.

P-273-MIS Iron (O)
6¾ x 4½ x ½   7 oz
A-14 F 1 R 2
On face, "Colt." Two top guide posts on
each side of platform. Nickel finish.

P-1107-MIS Iron (R)
7 x 4¹/₁₆ x ⁹/₁₆   7¾ oz
A-15 F 1 R 1 S 2
On face, "The Gem." Nickel finish.

P-1787-MIS Iron (O)
6½ x 3½ x ¹¹/₁₆   8½ oz
A-15 F 1 R 2
On face, "Acme." On reverse, "102." One-
quarter-inch top front guide. Nickel
finish.

P-409-MIS Iron (O)
6¾ x 4⅛ x ⅞   9½ oz
A-11 F 1 R 2
On face, "Vulcan." On reverse, "674 V
3820." One-eighth-inch top rail around
platform. Nickel finish.

P-1483-MIS Iron (R)
10½ x 3⁹/₁₆ x ⅞   10¾ oz
H-23 F 1 R 2
On face, "Omega." Three-sixteenths-inch
top rails front and sides of platform.
Front leg shorter.

P-1488-MIS Iron (O)
6 x 4 x ⅝   8 oz
Front H-C 2 Rear N-17 F 1 R 2
On face, "Clefton." Gate-marks at rear of
platform.

P-1604-MIS Iron (O)
7½ x 4¾ x ¾   12 oz
A-7 F 1 R 2
On face, "Gem."
Two gate-marks at rear of platform; machine grinding. One-quarter-inch top rail around platform.

P-1591-MIS Iron (O)
6⅝ x 4⅝ x 1¹/₁₆   12¾ oz
A-9 F 1 R 2
On face, "British." One-quarter-inch top rails front and sides of platform. Nickel finish.

P-1249-MIS Iron (O)
6¹³/₁₆ x 4 x ¾   15 oz
A-14 F 1 R 2
On face, "Mesco." One-eighth to three-eighths-inch tapered top rails front and sides of platform. Nickel finish.

P-1049-MIS Iron (O)
7⅛ x 4⅛ x 1⅝   1 lb 2 oz
H-C 10 F 1 R 2
On face, "A-Best-O." Three-sixteenths-inch top rails front and sides of platform.

P-142-MIS Iron (O)
7¼ x 4⅛ x 1⅛   1 lb ½ oz
A-15 F 1 R 2
On face, "HGI," "Humphrey Gas (Iron) Mfg By General Specialty Co." One-quarter-inch top rails on front and sides of platform. Nickel finish.

P-1901-MIS Iron (O)
6⅝ x 4⅝ x 1   14½ oz
A-9 F 1 R 2
On face, "Davis." On reverse, "Wide." Five-sixteenths-inch top rails front and sides of platform. Nickel finish.

P-1782-MIS Iron (R)
12 x 4⅞ x ¹³/₁₆   1 lb 9½ oz
Front: pointed cleat.
Rear: H-C 8 F 1 R 2
On face, "OSI," "OEWA Wien." Three-eighths-inch top rails front and sides of platform. Nickel finish.

P-907-MIS Iron (O)
6¾ x 2¹⁵/₁₆ x ⅞   4¾ oz
A-10 F 1 R 2
On face, "MIA." Gate-marks on rim. One-eighth-inch top side rails on platform.

E-407-MIS Iron (R)
8½ x 3¼ x ¾   9 oz
A-10 F 1 R 2
On face, "2 Matador." One-eighth-inch top rail around platform. Nickel finish.

E-23-MIS Iron (O)
$5^{11}/_{16}$ x $4^1/_8$ x $^3/_4$ $9^1/_2$ oz
A-12 F 1 R 2
On face, "Witt Nashville Tenn." One-eighth-inch top side rails with two one-quarter-inch guides on rails.

E-477-MIS Iron (C)
$6^7/_8$ x $4^7/_{16}$ x $2^1/_8$ 1 lb 6 oz
O-8 F 1 R 2
On face, "GE." Three-eighths-inch top side rails on platform.

E-100-MIS Iron (O)
$5^5/_8$ x $4^1/_8$ x $^9/_{16}$ 10 oz
A-12 F 1 R 2
On face, "Stoves and Ranges Cinderella Never Fail." One-quarter-inch top side rails on platform. Nickel finish.

E-490-MIS Iron (C)
$6^3/_4$ x $4^1/_8$ x $1^3/_8$ 14 oz
Front C 6 Rear H-C 10 F 1 R 2
On face, "Vulcan," (trademark). One-quarter-inch top guides and rails rear and sides of platform. Rear left cleat broken.

E-123-MIS Iron (R)
$5^1/_8$ x $3^5/_8$ x $^5/_8$ 5 oz
Splayed Cleats. F 2 R 2
On face, "Harper" (twice).

E-753-MIS Iron (R)
$7^1/_2$ x $3^3/_8$ $10^1/_2$ oz
Front leg two and one-eighth inches; Rear feet three-quarters-inch. F 1 R 2
On face, "The Crownall." On reverse, "Rd No 349247." One-quarter-inch top rear stops on platform.

E-558-MIS Iron (O)
$7^3/_4$ x $4^7/_8$ x $1^3/_8$ 1 lb $8^1/_2$ oz
A-9 F 1 R 2
On face, "Salter."
One-half-inch top side rails and rear stop on platform. Nickel finish.

E-364-MIS Iron (C)
$6^1/_2$ x $4^1/_2$ x 1 1 lb
A-10 F 1 R 2
One-quarter-inch top rails front and sides; one-eighth-inch top rail at rear of platform. Nickel finish.

E-385-MIS Iron (O)
$6^3/_8$ x 4 x 1 12 oz
A-11 F 1 R 2
Three-eighths to one-sixteenth-inch tapered top rails and guides on platform. Nickel finish eroded.

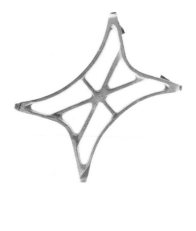

P-293-MIS Iron (C)
5 x 3¾ x ¾ 5 oz
D-5 F 2 R 2

P-636-MIS Iron (O)
5½ x 4⅛ x ⅞ 6 oz
D-15 F 2 R 2
On face, "Marvel." Machine grinding.

P-40-MIS Iron (C)
5⅞ x 3⁹/₁₆ x ¾ 7 oz
A-15 F 2 R 2
On face, "Sensible." Two gate-marks on rim. Two one-eighth-inch top guide cleats on each side of platform. Appears to be opening for stove-lid lifter.

E-8-MIS Iron (R)
5⅞ x 3 x ⅞ 6 oz
A-11 F 2 R 2
On face, "EM Co." Two three-sixteenths-inch top cleats front and rear. Appears to be provision for stove-lid lifter.

P-223-MIS Iron (R)
9⅜ x 4¾ x 1 11 oz
M-C 6 cleats on one side; M-C 10 cleats on the other side. F 2 R 2
On face, "Centennial A & R.O.A. Phila. Pa." Top guide posts front and back; top cleats on sides of platform.

E-332-MIS Iron (O)
5 x 3¾ x ⅞ 8 oz
D-11 F 2 R 2
Top guides are extensions of posts.

P-769-MIS Iron (O)
5 x 3½ x ⅝ 6¼ oz
A-15 F 2 R 2
Gate-marks on rim.

E-494-MIS Iron (O)
7 x 4¾ x ⅝ 12 oz
Supports are rounded extensions of platform. F 1 R 2
On face, "R & F Co Ld." Fifteen-six-teenths-inch top front and rear guides on platform. Nickel finish.

E-409-MIS Iron (R)
6⅜ x 4¹⁵/₁₆ x Front ½ Rear 1¹/₁₆
Splayed cleats; holes for securing to surface. On face, "Safe Stand." On reverse, "Pat Apl 20 1915." One-quarter-inch top side rails on platform; platform recessed at rear as a stop.

E-565-MIS Iron (O)
8 x 5 x 1¼   1 lb 10 oz
A-9 F 1 R 2
Three-sixteenths-inch top rails front and
sides of platform.

P-619-MIS Iron (O)
8⅜ x 5¾ x 2   1 lb 15 oz
A-9 F 2 R 2
Two gate-marks at rear of platform.
Seven short guide posts on each rail of
platform.

P-120-MIS Iron (O)
6⅜ x 4¹/₁₆ x ½   7¾ oz
A-25 F 1 R 2
One-eighth-inch top side rails on
platform.

P-147-MIS Iron (O)
5⅞ x 3½ x ½   7½ oz
A-25 F 2 R 2
Reverse draft.

P-480-MIS Iron (O)
7⅝ x 4½ x ⁹/₁₆   7½ oz
A-14 F 1 R 2
On reverse, "Frank P. Hazelton Boston
Mass Asbestos." Two gate-marks at rear
of platform. One-quarter-inch top side
rails front and sides of platform.

E-131-MIS Iron (C)
6⁵/₁₆ x 4½ x 1   15 oz
A-10 F 1 R 2
On reverse, "106." One-half-inch top rails
front and sides with one-quarter-inch rail
at rear of platform. Nickel finish eroded.

P-1922-MIS Iron (C)
5½ x 3¼ x ⅞   8¾ oz
A-15 F 2 R 2
Post in center. Gate-marks on rim; machine grinding. One-quarter-inch top
guide cleats on each side of platform.
Nickel finish.

E-497-MIS Iron (C)
7¾ x 4½ x ⅞   15 oz
A-14 F 1 R 2
One-quarter-inch top front stop with
one cleat same height on each side of
platform.

P-1688-MIS Iron (C)
5⅞ x 2⅞ x ⅝   8½ oz
A-14 F 1 R 2
Machine grinding. Nickel finish.

E-495-MIS Iron (O)
6¾ x 4½ x ¹¹/₁₆ 9 oz
A-15 F 1 R 2 S 2
On face, "Skel Gas."
Two three-sixteenths-inch top guide cleats on each rail of platform.

P-515-MIS Iron (C)
5⅞ x 3⁹/₁₆ x ⅞ 9¾ oz
A-16 F 1 R 2
One-quarter-inch top cleats on side rails of platform. Nickel finish.

E-506-MIS Iron (C)
6¼ x 4⅛ x 1¹³/₁₆ 14 oz
A-9 F 1 R 2
One-quarter-inch top front guide and one guide cleat on each side rail of platform.

P-932-MIS Iron (C)
8¾ x 4⅞ x ⅞ 13¼ oz
A-7 F 1 R 2
On reverse, "75C."
Large gate mark on rim; machine grinding. One-quarter-inch top rails front and sides of platform.

E-502-MIS Iron (C)
6⅜ x 4¼ x ⅞ 14 oz
A-14 F 1 R 2
One-quarter-inch top rails front and sides of platform.

E-564-MIS Iron (C)
6¾ x 3⅝ x 1¹¹/₁₆ 12½ oz
O-8 F 1 R 2

E-563-MIS Iron (C)
7¼ x 4³/₁₆ x 1 12½ oz
M-C 7 F 1 R 2
Five-sixteenths-inch top side rails on platform.

E-19-MIS Iron (C)
7⅞ x 4¼ x 1¹/₁₆ 11 oz
A-9 F 1 R 1 S 2
Three-sixteenths-inch top side rails on platform.

E-560-MIS Iron (C)
7¼ x 4 x 1⅛ 12½ oz
A-10 F 1 R 2
One-quarter-inch top side rails on platform.

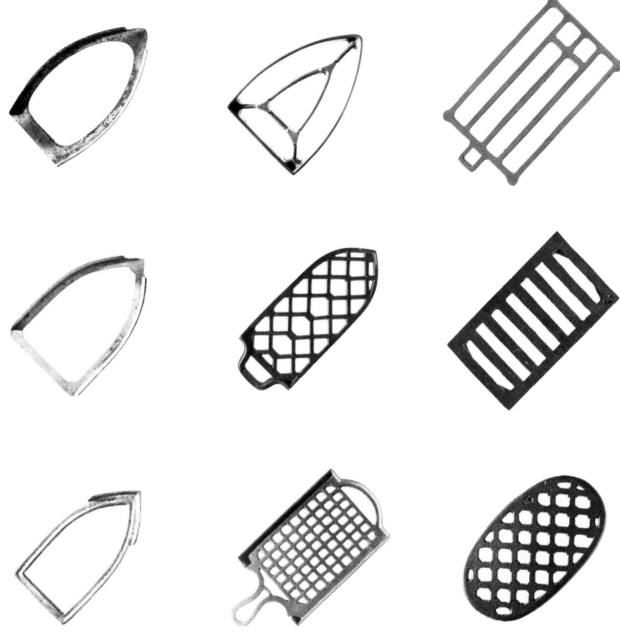

E-560-MIS Iron (C)
7¼ x 4 x 1⅛   13 oz
A-8 F 1 R 2
Five-sixteenths-inch top side rails on platform.

E-472-MIS Iron (O)
6⅞ x 4⅜ x 1 7½ oz
A-8 F 1 R 2

E-561-MIS Iron (O)
7 x 3⅝ x ⅝ 6 oz
A-14 F 1 R 2
Three-sixteenths-inch top front guide on platform. Nickel finish.

E-499-MIS Iron (O)
6¾ x 4⅝ x ¾   14 oz
Front C-2 Rear D-11 F 1 R 2
On reverse, "360." One-quarter-inch top rail around platform. Nickel finish.

E-556-MIS Iron (O)
8⅝ x 3⅜ x ⅝   9 oz
A-15 F 1 R 2
One-eighth-inch top front and rear guides on platform.

P-1206-MIS Iron (VR)
9¹/₁₆ x 4⅜ x ¾   12½ oz
D-15 F 2 R 2
Two gate-marks on rim; machine grinding. One-eighth-inch top rails front and sides of platform. Nickel finish.

E-419-MIS Iron (O)
6¾ x 3¾ x 1⅛   12½ oz
A-9 F 2 R 2

E-446-MIS Iron (R)
6¾ x 3¾ x 2   2 lbs 7½ oz
Cleats M-C 7 F 2 R 2

E-438-MIS Iron (R)
8¼ x 4¾ x ⁹/₁₆   14 oz
C 2-M F 1 R 1 S 2
On reverse, "89."

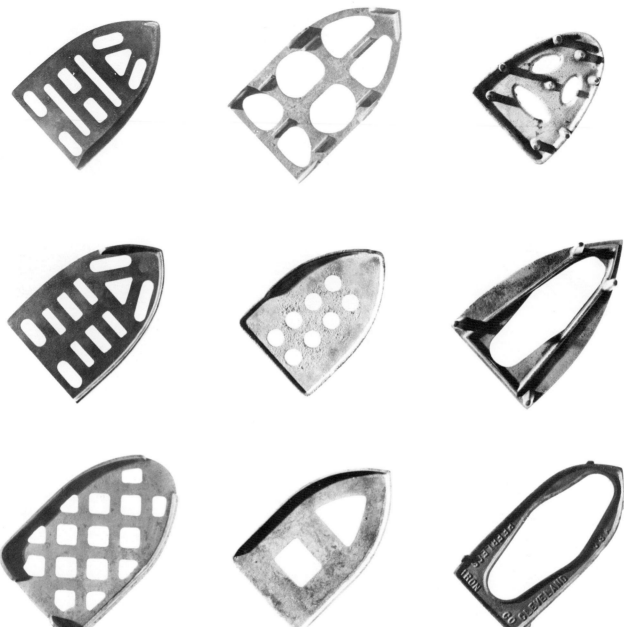

P-1481-MIS Iron (O)
6⅝ x 4⅜ x ¾   15½ oz
Post supports front and back with cleats
on the sides. F 1 R 1 S 2
On reverse, "U 9974." One-quarter-inch
top rails front and right side of platform.

E-552-MIS Iron (C)
9 x 6⅛ x 1   3 lbs
Post at front and rear with mounting
holes; one support cleat on each side.
F 1 R 2 S 2
On reverse, "W 1041." Three-eighths-inch
top front stop and right side rail on platform. May have had slate base.

E-401-MIS Iron (C)
6⅞ x 4⅜ x 1   1 lb
A-9 F 2 R 2
Five-sixteenths-inch top rails front and
sides of platform. Nickel finish.

E-403-MIS Iron (O)
6¾ x 3¾ x 1¼   13 oz
H-C 7 F 1 R 2
Three-eighths-inch top front rail; guide
cleats on each side of platform. Nickel
finish eroded.

E-557-MIS Iron (O)
7 x 4¾ x 1⅛   15½ oz
A-9 F 1 R 2
One-quarter-inch top rail around platform; large guide on left rail. Corroded.

E-546-MIS Iron (O)
7¾ x 4⁹⁄₁₆ x 1⅝   1 lb 7 oz
A-18 F 1 R 2
One-quarter-inch tapered top rails front
and sides of platform.

E-493-MIS Iron (O)
5¾ x 4¾ x ⅞   1 lb 8 oz
A-9 F 1 R 2
Eight posts on top of platform. Outer
posts were guides and inner posts hold
iron above platform surface. Nickel finish.

E-484-MIS Iron (R)
7¼ x 4½   1 lb 9½ oz
A reversible stand. One side, B-2 two
inches. Other side, Notched cleats two
and three-quarters inches. Inside leg of
notch is shorter than outside leg. Inside
post held the iron; outside post was a
guide. Stand was made for two different
models of iron.

E-359-MIS Iron (O)
7 x 3½ x ⅞   7½ oz
A-4 F 1 R 2
On face, "Peerless Iron Co. Cleveland
USA." One-sixteenth-inch top rail around
platform.

P-1495-MIS Iron (O)
6¾ x 4⅛ x ¾   14 oz
A-14   F 1   R 2
On face, "Lincoln." Large gate-mark on
rim; machine grinding. One-eighth-inch
top guides front, with three scalloped
cleat guides on sides, and rear corner cleat
on right of platform. Interesting design.

E-547-MIS Iron (O)
7½ x 5 x 1½   2 lbs 2 oz
Sleeves that fit seven-eighths-inch
diameter posts. F 1   R 2
One-quarter-inch top rail around platform. Nickel finish.

E-508-MIS Iron (R)
6⅞ x 5 x ¾   2 lbs 2 oz
Front large cleat. Rear R-C 2   F 1   R 2
One-quarter-inch top rails front and sides
of platform.

E-524-MIS Iron (O)
7⅝ x 4¹⁵/₁₆ x 2   3 lbs 8 oz
Three splayed supports; drilled to be
secured to surface. F 1   R 2
On reverse, "NYPICO 954." Three-
eighths-inch top guide rail on right side of
platform.

E-548-MIS Iron (O)
7½ x 5 x 1   2 lbs 14 oz
A-16   F 1   R 2
On face, "Empire Laundry Machinery Co.
Boston." One-quarter-inch top rail around
platform.

E-549-MIS Iron (O)
6⅝ x 4 x 1⅜   1 lb 4½ oz
Cleats. F 1   R 2
Three-sixteenths-inch top front guide
with three guide cleats on each side rail of
platform.

P-1153-MIS Iron (VR)
8⅛ x 5⅝ x 1⅛   3 lbs 4½ oz
A-14   F 1   R 2
On face, "Mfd for John Randles Inc. 208-
210 Water St. N.Y. City. Phone Beekman
3-2595." Illustration of a washing machine. Nickel finish eroded.

E-349-MIS Iron (R)
6¼ x 4¹¹/₁₆ x ¹⁵/₁₆   15 oz
A-10   F 1   R 2
On face, "We give one of these stands
with each set of our cold handle sadirons.
Chalfant Manf. Co. Philada." One-half-
inch top side rails on platform.

P-1332-MIS Iron (R)
6⁹/₁₆ x 4⅜ x ¹¹/₁₆   1 lb ½ oz
Scalloped cleats. F 1   R 2
On face, "Sunshine's Home Iron-Stand.
Patent Applied For. Made by Household
Gas Iron Co. New York." Filing on rim.
Bottom and top of trivet identical; guide
cleats become supports when stand is
turned over. Interesting design.

E-544-MIS Iron (C)
7½ x 5 x 2½   2 lbs 9 oz
H-C 7 F 1 R 2
On face, "Schreiber & Goldberg New York." Three-sixteenths-inch rail around platform.

E-550-MIS Iron (O)
6½ x 4½ x 1½   15 oz
Cleats. F 1 R 2
On face, "The Guaranteed Stand Cleveland. O. USA." Scalloped front rail with stops at rear of platform. Nickel finish.

E-551-MIS Iron (R)
7 x 4½ x 1¼   2 lbs 1 oz
K-11 F 1 R 2
Two three-quarters-inch cleats on each side; two and three-eighths-inch posts at rear of platform; short post at front hold iron elevating it above platform surface.

E-546-MIS Iron (C)
7¾ x 4⅝ x 1⅝   1 lb 8 oz
A-18 F 1 R 2
On face, "Sunshine Jasper Company New York." One-quarter to three-sixteenths-inch top tapered rails front and sides of platform. Nickel finish.

E-413-MIS Iron (R)
5¹¹/₁₆ x 3⅞ x ⅝   15½ oz
A-16 F 1 R 2
Large gate-mark at left rear of platform. Opening at rear may be for stove-lid lifter.

E-485-MIS Iron/slate (C)
7¼ x 4⁵/₁₆ x 1⁵/₁₆   2 lbs 7 oz
A-14 F 2 R 2
On face, "Simplex Patent." Five-sixteenths-inch top front guide with three guide cleats on right rail and two guide cleats on left rail of platform. Nickel finish.

E-452-MIS Iron/slate (O)
6 x 4⅛ x 2   2 lbs 4 oz
A-7 F 1 R 2
On face, "P." Three-eighths-inch top front and right side rails on platform. Slate screwed to stand. Nickel finish.

E-511-MIS Iron/slate (O)
5⅞ x 2¹⁵/₁₆ x 1⅜   1 lb 8 oz
A-14 F 1 R 2
On face, "Simplex." Base has four A-15 feet attached to slate. Screws go through slate into legs of stand. Three-eighths-inch side rails on platform.

E-492-MIS Iron/slate (O)
7 x 4½ x 1¼   2 lbs 9 oz
A-16 F 1 R 2
On face, "Simplex." Stand attached to slate with screws. Five-sixteenths-inch top side cleats with two one-eighth-inch rear stop cleats on platform. Nickel finish.

Plaque and Motto Trivets

It is doubtful whether plaque trivets legitimately should be classified with conventional trivets, but collectors such as Hankenson, Paley and others have consistently included them. It is clear that plaque trivets were meant for wall display or decoration rather than utilitarian purposes. Therefore, it was not customary to put feet on them. Although the surfaces were highly modeled and irregular, most plaque trivets had short cleats on top so that when laid face down, the back was flat and the top cleats provided supports. Nevertheless, it seems doubtful plaque trivets were extensively used for iron rests or stands as some collectors claim.

Trivets made as wall plaques had a hole or loop for hanging them on the wall. Others had a wire support so they could stand, tripod fashion, on a table or mantelpiece.

Many plaque trivets featured horseshoe designs, and the majority were decorated with lodge emblems. These differed from other trivets and stands since many were painted in bright colors. A number of plaque trivets were iron castings, either gilded or nickel-plated, or were made of brass. Some of the smaller ones probably were used as paperweights. Designs with an American eagle perching on the crown of the horseshoe were popular.

Horseshoe plaque trivets generally were poured through the ends of the horseshoe so tips of the eagle wings were at the opposite end of the mold. The molten iron did not always flow evenly into the wing tips, so in poor castings they may appear broken or rounded.

Other plaque trivets carried inscriptions such as "Home Sweet Home," "Good Luck" or fraternal identifications. The production of plaque trivets appears to have peaked around the 1880's and 1890's.

Motto trivets are not well represented in this catalogue. Short proverbs, biblical verses, or folk homilies were cast in letterforms as openwork iron stands with decorative embellishment and very short legs. Some motto trivets were produced in the latter part of the nineteenth century, but most of them were made as souvenirs and novelties from the 1930's through the 1950's.

Most motto trivets had both hanging holes and short, stubby feet. On occasion, motto trivets could have been taken down from the wall and used on tables as stands for hot dishes.

Mitto trivets from Wilton Products catalogue.

P-1286-PT Iron (R)
6½ x 4⅛ 13½ oz
On face, "O.U.A.M." On reverse, "Pat Apl'd For By Hoag." Original finish. Backcoping on horseshoe; tripod wire.

P-1363-PT Brass (R)
7 x 6½ 1 lb 6½ oz
On face, "FLT." Original finish; gilding over brass. Deep backcoping.

P-386-PT Iron (R)
6½ x 4 1 lb 1½ oz
Illegible inscription. Backcoping on horseshoe.

P-2010-PT Iron (R)
9 x 8¼ 1 lb 8¾ oz
On face, "Good Luck." Original finish; backcoping on horseshoe.

P-1183-PT Iron (R)
6½ x 6¼ 1 lb 8 oz
Nickel finish; backcoping on horseshoe.

P-1293-PT Iron (O)
6½ x 3⅞ 1 lb
On face, "O of F." Gilt finish; backcoping on horseshoe.

P-657-PT Brass (R)
6⅜ x 4 1 lb
On face, "G.A.R." Backcoping on horseshoe; tripod wire.

P-1125-PT Iron (R)
6½ x 4 1 lb 3½ oz
On face, "G.A.R." Backcoping on horseshoe.

P-1007-PT Iron (R)
6¾ x 4⅛ 1 lb 1 oz
On face, "Good Luck." Backcoping on horseshoe; tripod wire.

P-1699-PT Iron (R)
6½ x 4 14¾ oz
On face, "GAR." Nickel finish eroded; tripod wire.

P-1587-PT Iron (R)
5½ x 3½ 9 oz
On face, "IOOF FLT." Nickel finish; backcoping on horseshoe.

P-354-PT Iron (O)
6¾ x 4 1 lb 2 oz
On face, "FLT IOOF." Gilt finish eroded; backcoping on horseshoe.

P-1189-PT Iron (O)
6⅞ x 4¼ 14¾ oz
On face, "FLT." Gilt finish eroded; loop for hanging. Backcoping on horseshoe. Sharp casting.

P-197-PT Iron (O)
6½ x 4 1 lb ½ oz
On face, "Luck." Backcoping on horseshoe.

P-512-PT Iron (O)
6½ x 4 1 lb
On face, "Good Luck." Tip of right wing broken. Nickel finish eroded; tripod wire. Backcoping on horseshoe.

P-1184-PT Iron (O)
6½ 4 1 lb ½ oz
Backcoping on horseshoe.

P-1547-PT Iron (O)
6½ x 4¼ 1 lb 6 oz
On face, "AOUW GH." Nickel finish eroded; backcoping on horseshoe.

P-2024-PT Iron (O)
6¾ x 4¼ 1 lb ½ oz
On face, "Good Luck." Gilt finish eroded; backcoping on horseshoe.

P-641-PT Iron (O)
6½ x 4   1 lb
On face, "Good Luck." Nickel finish eroded; backcoping on horseshoe.

P-1005-PT Iron (R)
6¾ x 4¼   1 lb 3½ oz
On face, "FLT IOOF." Repainted; backcoping on horseshoe.

P-208-PT Iron (O)
6¾ x 4¼   1 lb ½ oz
On face, "Knights of Pythias FCB." On reverse, "Pat'd Apl'd For." Painted black; hanging loop. Backcoping on horseshoe.

P-408-PT Iron (R)
6⅜ x 4   1 lb
On face, "Home Sweet Home." Painted black; tripod wire. Backcoping on horseshoe.

P-1576-PT Iron (R)
3⅝ x 2⅞   8½ oz
On face, "FLT IOOF." On reverse, "1923." Original finish.

P-209-PT Iron (R)
6¾ x 4¼   15½ oz
On face, monogram "AR." On reverse, "Pat Apl'd For." Extremely sharp casting; painted black. Loop for hanging; backcoping on horseshoe.

P-1924-PT Iron (R)
6½ x 4   14 oz
On face, "O.U.F." Original finish.

P-975-PT Iron (R)
6½ x 4⅛   13 oz
On face, "GAR." Original finish; backcoping on horseshoe.

P-765-PT Iron (O)
6½ x 4⅛   14¾ oz
On face, "F & AM." Painted black; tripod wire. Backcoping on horseshoe.

245

P-1263-PT Brass (O)
6 x 5   1 lb 3½ oz
On face, "FLT IOOF." Extensive back-coping.

E-333-PT Iron (R)
6 x 6⅜   1 lb 9 oz
On face, "God Bless Our Home." Shallow backcoping.

P-902-PT Iron (R)
6¼ x 4   13¾ oz
On face, "Happy New Year." On reverse, "Pat Apl'd For By C.J. Hoag." Tripod wire; backcoping on horseshoe.

P-369-PT Iron (R)
6 x 3⅞   1 lb 1 oz
Front cleat; A-10 on rear. On reverse, "Patented." Nickel finish and gilding.

P-201-PT Iron (O)
6¼ x 3⅜   11¼ oz
On face, "Good Luck Forget Me Not." Nickel finish eroded; extensive back-coping.

E-389-PT Iron (R)
6½ x 6⅝   1 lb 2 oz
On face, "God Bless Our Home." Shallow backcoping.

P-655-PT Iron (R)
6½ x 6½   1 lb 1¾ oz
On face, "Home Sweet Home 1888 GL." Original gilt finish; backcoping on horseshoe.

P-1280-PT Iron (R)
6 x 6   1 lb 5 oz
On face, "God Bless Our Home TOTE." Original finish; top of "S" broken. Back-coping on horseshoe.

P-1279-PT Iron (R)
6 x 6⅛   1 lb 5¾ oz
On face, "God Bless Our Home 1892."

P-721-PT Iron (R)
6 x 5⅞   1 lb ¾ oz
On face, "God Bless Our Home 1888 GL."
Extensive backcoping.

P-1330-PT Iron (R)
6½ x 6¼   1 lb 4 oz
On face, "Home Sweet Home 1908 GL."
Painted black; tripod wire.

P-2018-PT Iron (VR)
5⅞ x 5¼   1 lb 3½ oz
On face, "Erin Go Braugh."

P-1351-PT Iron (VR)
7½ x 5¼   1 lb 7 oz
On face, "Good Luck." Painted black;
extensive backcoping.

P-656-PT Iron (O)
4¾ x 4   12 oz
On face, "Good Luck My Boy." Gilt finish
eroded; tripod wire.

P-362-PT Iron (VR)
5⅞ x 5³⁄₁₆   1 lb 6 oz
On face, "Luck." Nickel finish; extensive
backcoping.

P-413-PT Iron (R)
5 x 4¼   12 oz
Painted black; Backcoping on horseshoe.

P-1087-PT Iron (R)
4 x 3   4½ oz
On face, "GAR." Gilt finish.

P-1404-PT Iron (R)
4½ x 3⅞   6½ oz
On face, "Good Luck." Horseshoe nails
were added after the casting; one has
fallen out.

The Small Ones

This classification includes toy trivets for doll houses, little girls' stands, miniature trivet reproductions and samples carried by salesmen. Some collectors also include stands for travel, or ribbon and lace irons.

Small trivets and stands were made almost as long ago as large ones. As with standard-sized trivets, the earliest miniatures were hand-fabricated and reflected period styles. In the late nineteenth century up to the 1930's, toy irons and stands were widely marketed.

Around the turn of the century, penny toys made of iron were popular. There were tiny kitchen utensils or tools and some trivets, irons and stands. The smallest miniatures were exquisitely crafted doll house furnishings.

At the same time, marketing sadirons was extremely competitive and salesmen often covered large territories. It was impractical for them to carry sample cases of full-size ironware. Instead they carried miniature examples of different irons and stands replicating their products. Many of these salesmen's samples have found their way into collections as miniatures.

Also, there were intermediate-size trivets and stands somewhat smaller than standard ones which were produced for travel or as commercial specialty irons. Smaller irons also were used for pressing ribbons and lace. However, they were usually enough larger than toy irons that they were not confused with miniature trivets and stands.

Manufacturers made small replicas of their commercial styles to be used as premiums, as give-a-ways, or for sale as toys for young girls. A woman purchasing an iron might receive a miniature of the iron complete with a stand for her daughter. The "Girl's Iron" soon was separately advertised in trade publications. The marketing technique was to encourage the daughter to buy the same brand of iron when the time came for her to set up housekeeping.

In the twentieth century, manufacturers of trivet reproductions began to make popular designs in small sizes. Most of these were handled, multi-purpose stands approximately four inches in length. The small trivets were marketed as decorative wall hangings and sold in sets of four to six miniatures.

A number of collectors specialize in acquiring miniatures. For more information on small trivets and stands, see *Tuesday's Children; Collecting Little Irons and Trivets* and *Early Tuesday Morning; More Little Irons and Trivets* published by Judy and Frank Politzer.

The small trivets, rests and stands illustrated here are from the Ellwood Collection, but the Paley Collection at Shelburne Museum also includes a substantial number of miniatures.

Girl's Iron.

Toy Sadiron.

Acme Toy Sadiron.

The Monitor Toy Sadiron.

Girl's Iron.

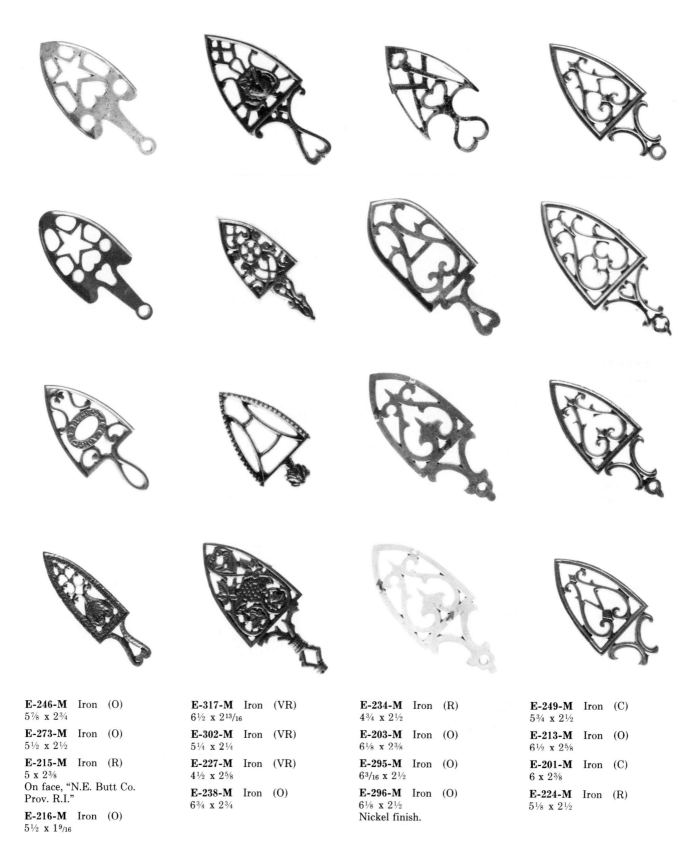

E-246-M Iron (O)
5⅞ x 2¾

E-273-M Iron (O)
5½ x 2½

E-215-M Iron (R)
5 x 2⅜
On face, "N.E. Butt Co.
Prov. R.I."

E-216-M Iron (O)
5½ x 1⁹⁄₁₆

E-317-M Iron (VR)
6½ x 2¹³⁄₁₆

E-302-M Iron (VR)
5¼ x 2¼

E-227-M Iron (VR)
4½ x 2⅝

E-238-M Iron (O)
6¾ x 2¾

E-234-M Iron (R)
4¾ x 2½

E-203-M Iron (O)
6⅛ x 2⅜

E-295-M Iron (O)
6³⁄₁₆ x 2½

E-296-M Iron (O)
6⅛ x 2½
Nickel finish.

E-249-M Iron (C)
5¾ x 2½

E-213-M Iron (O)
6½ x 2⅝

E-201-M Iron (C)
6 x 2⅜

E-224-M Iron (R)
5⅛ x 2½

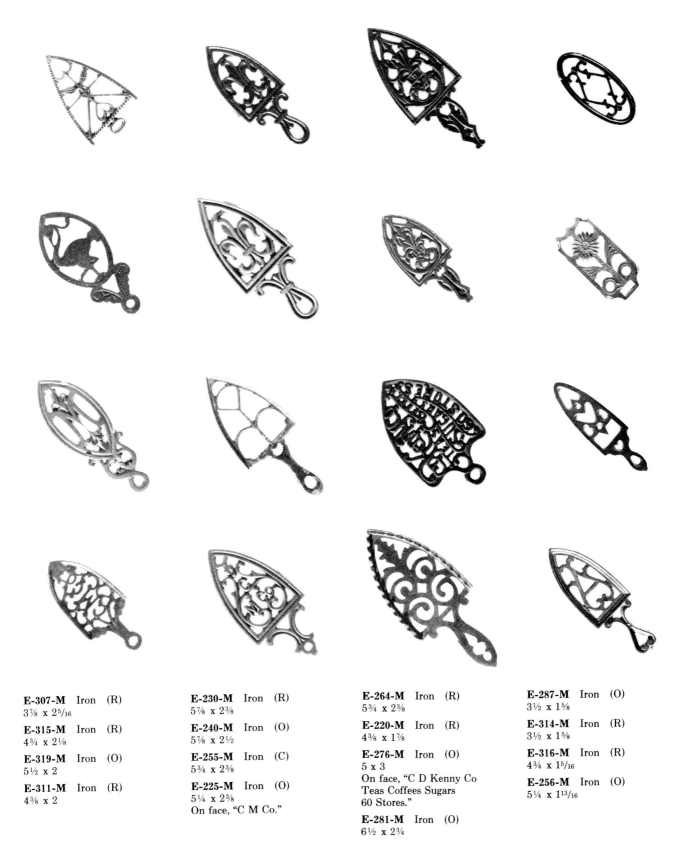

E-307-M Iron (R) 3⅞ x 2⁵⁄₁₆	**E-230-M** Iron (R) 5⅞ x 2⅜	**E-264-M** Iron (R) 5¾ x 2⅜	**E-287-M** Iron (O) 3½ x 1⅝
E-315-M Iron (R) 4¾ x 2⅛	**E-240-M** Iron (O) 5⅞ x 2½	**E-220-M** Iron (R) 4⅜ x 1⅞	**E-314-M** Iron (R) 3½ x 1⅝
E-319-M Iron (O) 5½ x 2	**E-255-M** Iron (C) 5¾ x 2⅜	**E-276-M** Iron (O) 5 x 3 On face, "C D Kenny Co Teas Coffees Sugars 60 Stores."	**E-316-M** Iron (R) 4¾ x 1⁵⁄₁₆
E-311-M Iron (R) 4⅜ x 2	**E-225-M** Iron (O) 5¼ x 2⅜ On face, "C M Co."	**E-281-M** Iron (O) 6½ x 2¾	**E-256-M** Iron (O) 5¼ x 1¹³⁄₁₆

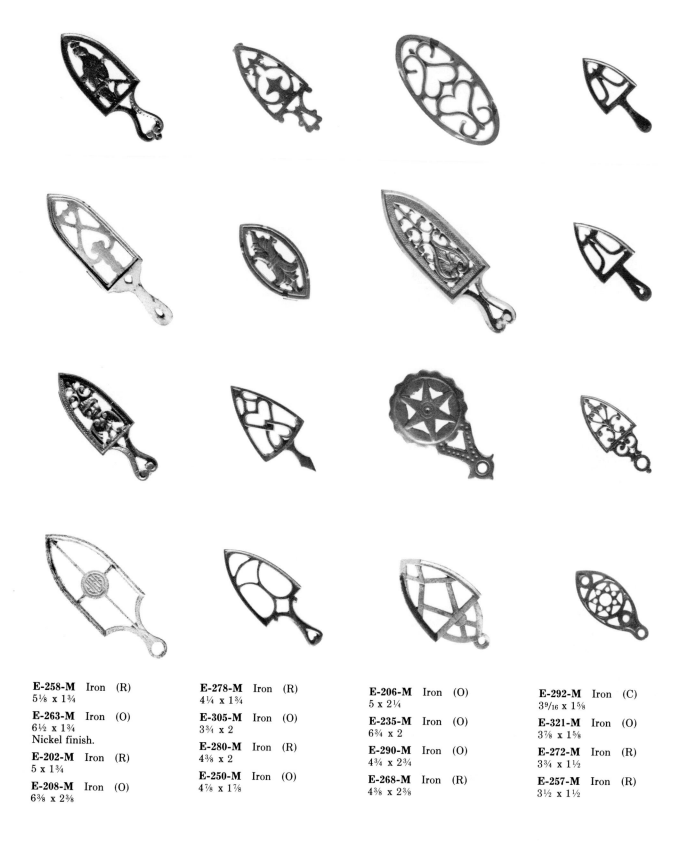

E-258-M Iron (R)
5⅛ x 1¾

E-263-M Iron (O)
6½ x 1¾
Nickel finish.

E-202-M Iron (R)
5 x 1¾

E-208-M Iron (O)
6⅜ x 2⅜

E-278-M Iron (R)
4¼ x 1¾

E-305-M Iron (O)
3¾ x 2

E-280-M Iron (R)
4⅜ x 2

E-250-M Iron (O)
4⅞ x 1⅞

E-206-M Iron (O)
5 x 2¼

E-235-M Iron (O)
6¾ x 2

E-290-M Iron (O)
4¾ x 2¾

E-268-M Iron (R)
4⅜ x 2⅜

E-292-M Iron (C)
3⁹/₁₆ x 1⅝

E-321-M Iron (O)
3⅞ x 1⅝

E-272-M Iron (R)
3¾ x 1½

E-257-M Iron (R)
3½ x 1½

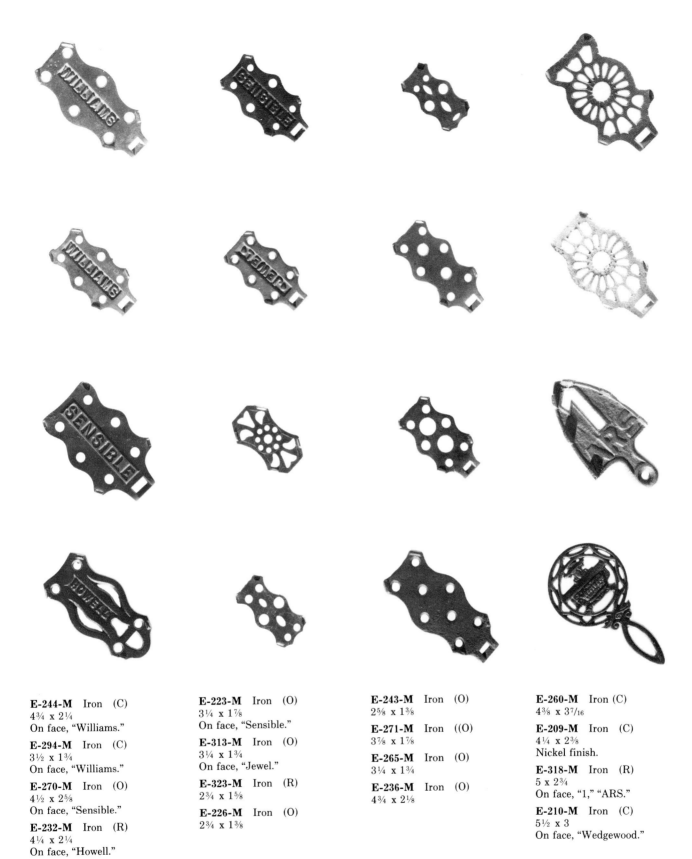

E-244-M Iron (C)
4¾ x 2¼
On face, "Williams."

E-294-M Iron (C)
3½ x 1¾
On face, "Williams."

E-270-M Iron (O)
4½ x 2⅝
On face, "Sensible."

E-232-M Iron (R)
4¼ x 2¼
On face, "Howell."

E-223-M Iron (O)
3¼ x 1⅞
On face, "Sensible."

E-313-M Iron (O)
3¼ x 1¾
On face, "Jewel."

E-323-M Iron (R)
2¾ x 1⅝

E-226-M Iron (O)
2¾ x 1⅜

E-243-M Iron (O)
2⅝ x 1⅜

E-271-M Iron ((O)
3⅞ x 1⅞

E-265-M Iron (O)
3¼ x 1¾

E-236-M Iron (O)
4¾ x 2⅛

E-260-M Iron (C)
4⅜ x 3⁷⁄₁₆

E-209-M Iron (C)
4¼ x 2⅜
Nickel finish.

E-318-M Iron (R)
5 x 2¾
On face, "1," "ARS."

E-210-M Iron (C)
5½ x 3
On face, "Wedgewood."

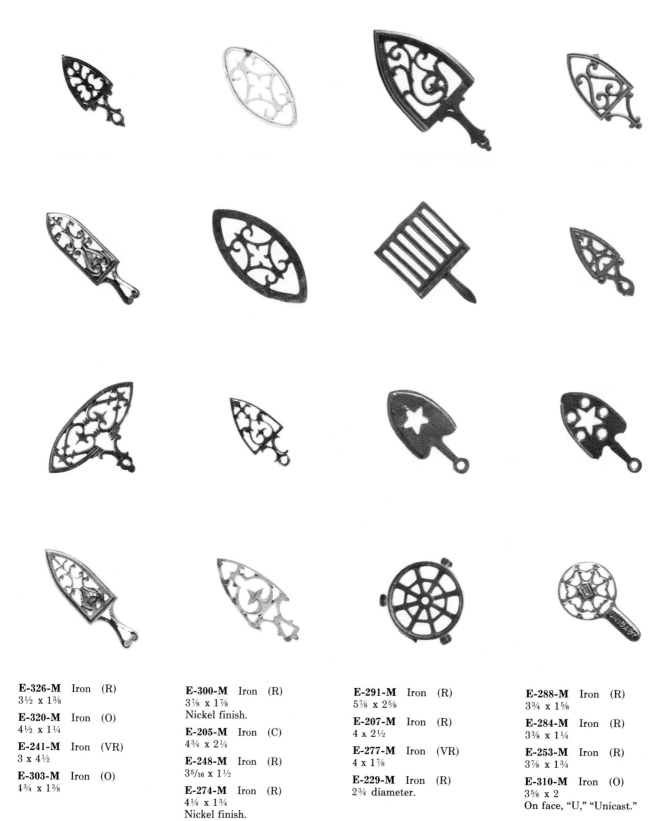

E-326-M Iron (R)
3½ x 1⅜

E-320-M Iron (O)
4½ x 1¼

E-241-M Iron (VR)
3 x 4½

E-303-M Iron (O)
4¾ x 1⅜

E-300-M Iron (R)
3⅞ x 1⅞
Nickel finish.

E-205-M Iron (C)
4¾ x 2¼

E-248-M Iron (R)
3⁵⁄₁₆ x 1½

E-274-M Iron (R)
4¼ x 1¾
Nickel finish.

E-291-M Iron (R)
5⅞ x 2⅝

E-207-M Iron (R)
4 x 2½

E-277-M Iron (VR)
4 x 1⅞

E-229-M Iron (R)
2¾ diameter.

E-288-M Iron (R)
3¾ x 1⅝

E-284-M Iron (R)
3⅜ x 1¼

E-253-M Iron (R)
3⅞ x 1¾

E-310-M Iron (O)
3⅝ x 2
On face, "U," "Unicast."

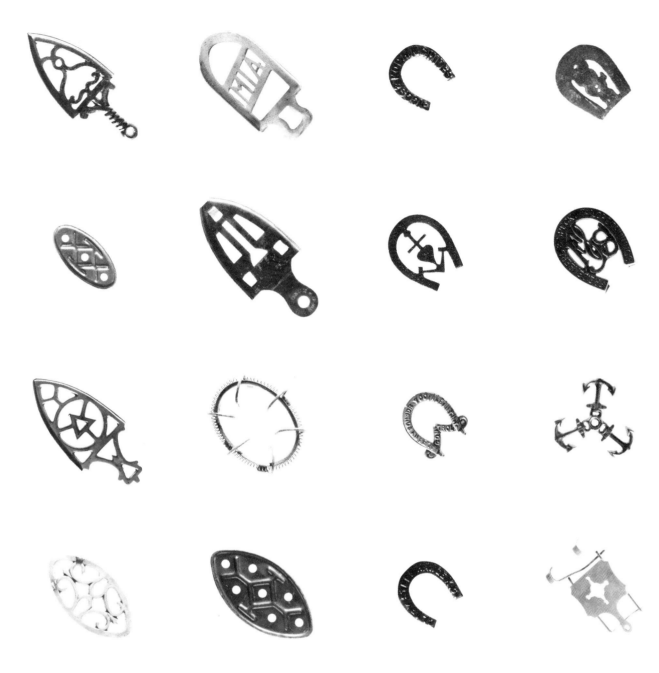

D-6-M Iron (VR)
5⅝ x 2¼

E-306-M
Stamped Metal (C)
3 x 1½

E-267-M Iron (R)
5¼ x 2⅜
Nickel finish.

E-245-M Iron (O)
3⅞ x 2
Nickel finish.

E-266-M Iron (O)
4¾ x 2¼
On face, "MIA."

E-247-M
Stamped Metal (O)
5⅜ x 2½
On face, "Bonum Geschutzt."

E-144-M
Stamped Metal/wire (R)
3½ x 2¾

E-254-M
Stamped Metal (C)
4⁹⁄₁₆ x 2¼

E-162-M Iron (R)
2 x 2
On face, "Biggs & Koch
K C Hides: Good Luck."

E-143-M Iron (R)
2⅝ x 2¼

E-174-M Iron (R)
2⅜ x 2⅛
On face, "The Stove That
Pays For Itself. Good Luck.
Albany Foundry Co. Albany
NY Control." Nickel finish.

E-242-M Iron (R)
2⅛ x 2
On face, "Good Luck
Clark Steel Range K.C."

E-322-M Iron (O)
2½ x 2⅛

E-173-M Iron (R)
3⅛ x 2½
On face, "F & S,"
"Freidenberg & Speck
Tailors' Trimmings."

E-145-M Brass (R)
3-inch diameter.

E-189-M Brass (R)
4⅞ x 3¼
Handcrafted.

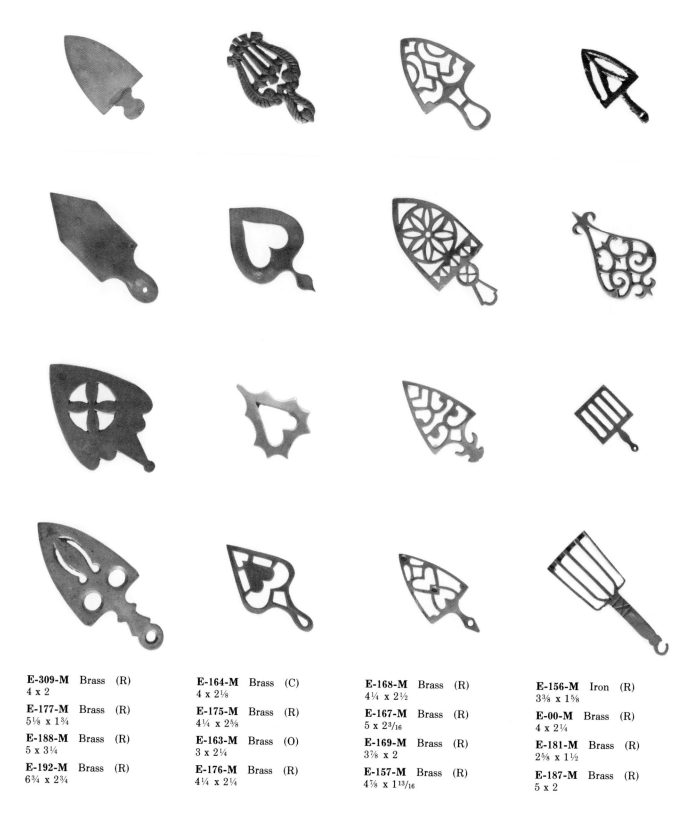

E-309-M Brass (R) 4 x 2	**E-164-M** Brass (C) 4 x 2⅛	**E-168-M** Brass (R) 4¼ x 2½	**E-156-M** Iron (R) 3⅜ x 1⅝
E-177-M Brass (R) 5⅛ x 1¾	**E-175-M** Brass (R) 4¼ x 2⅝	**E-167-M** Brass (R) 5 x 2³/₁₆	**E-00-M** Brass (R) 4 x 2¼
E-188-M Brass (R) 5 x 3¼	**E-163-M** Brass (O) 3 x 2¼	**E-169-M** Brass (R) 3⅞ x 2	**E-181-M** Brass (R) 2⅝ x 1½
E-192-M Brass (R) 6¾ x 2¾	**E-176-M** Brass (R) 4¼ x 2¼	**E-157-M** Brass (R) 4⅞ x 1¹³/₁₆	**E-187-M** Brass (R) 5 x 2

Author's note. *This is the first comprehensive book on trivets and stands to be published. The nearly thirteen hundred catalogue entries are by no means all inclusive, rather they were selected to exemplify traditional trivet and stand designs found in America between 1840 and 1950. The number of catalogue entries was further limited by the book size, number of pages, and production costs.*

Many trivets and stands from the Paley and Ellwood collections were not photographed because differences to those shown in the book were so slight that inclusion would have made them repetitious. Other designs, particularly in the Manufacturers' Iron Stands section, were left out because they simply lacked interest. Unfortunately, some noteworthy designs could not be recorded because the trivets or stands were unavailable. In researching articles and trade books, trivets were pictured which could not be found. Examination of foundry records and patterns revealed designs for which no examples could be traced. Also, restrictions connected with photographing and cataloguing private collections prevented access to some interesting trivets.

Over the past five years, when the most intensive preparation for publication took place, more trivets and stands intermittently became available and, as much as possible, these were incorporated. Finally, it became necessary to halt this practice because it was complicating the already difficult task of finalizing text and catalogue. It is certain there are many trivets and stands that are not represented, and before this book goes on the market other uncatalogued designs will undoubtedly surface.

Collecting of illustrative materials was done throughout the research. At the time it was difficult to know which images would be used, or exactly how they would be used. The objective was to accumulate as much related visual material as possible to establish a historical and technical perspective on the design and manufacture of trivets and stands.

Photographing the trivets presented special problems, such as removing shadows so openwork was made clear and shapes were not distorted by photographic angle. The photographs were taken from directly above the trivet or stand which was placed on a light-table to eliminate shadows. A raking light placed at one side highlighted surface relief. Brass and nickeled stands were particularly difficult to photograph due to their reflective surfaces. There was such a range of small to large that it was impossible to show comparative sizes photographically. Photographs were taken over a period of time, at various locations, and several photographers participated. Each photographer worked a little differently in terms of camera, lighting and print quality.

The majority of line illustrations were printed from reprographic copies, and in most instances, this was adequate. However, in the chapter on trivet makers and distributors, copies made from half-tone illustrations taken from company catalogues were poor-quality. An attempt was made to obtain the original catalogue photographs, but often they had been discarded or lost. Even though the prints are rough, they are sufficient to identify the designs.

Final decisions were made at the time of rough paste-up when text, captions, illustrations and catalogue entries were put into page format for the first time. The need for a number of adjustments became apparent. Classifying and sequencing of catalogue entries had to be finalized. This was a period of doubts, hard decisions, and some regrets, but also it was a time for feeling a sense of accomplishment.

In hindsight, the New England and Pennsylvania category is a geographical and period grouping, while other classifications are mainly based on func-

tion, and only incidentally on period. Decorative iron stands probably should not be mixed with New England and Pennsylvania Trivets or Multi-Purpose Stands. More attention should have been given to grouping similar designs for purposes of comparison. Some similarities did not become obvious until the book was well into production. To make changes at that point would have been cost prohibitive.

The publication took nine years to research and write, and it was almost a year in actual production. The research was fascinating, but at the same time, the amount of information and images was staggering. Sorting through approximately thirty-five hundred trivets to make a selection was agonizing in itself. The technical and historical materials were unfamiliar in the beginning. Absorbing and weaving this information into text proved to be more difficult than expected.

Compiling the book was further complicated because the publisher was in Ohio, the printing representative in Michigan, the editor in Vermont, the printer in Missouri and the author in Arizona.

Even with its recognized shortcomings, it is hoped that the book will contribute to greater appreciation for these little known utensils called trivets and stands. RRK

VIII. GLOSSARY OF TERMS

All definitions are given within the context of subjects dealt with in this book.

Acanthus. *Akanthos.* An ornamentation patterned after the leaves of the Acanthus, a prickly herb from the Mediterranean region.

Adjustable Table Stand. Table stand with a divided platform mounted on runners so that surfaces can slide apart to support large platters or serving dishes. Usually nickel-plated, silver, silver-plated or made of metal alloy. Surface ornamentation often is either etched or stamped open-work.

Akroter. An architectural capping ornament used on vertical elements such as columns.

Allegorical. Reference to the use of a figurative treatment of one subject to explain another; illustrating a spiritual or abstract meaning by using symbolic forms possessing similar qualities.

Alloy. Combination of two or more metals.

Aluminum. A bluish silver malleable metal characteristically lightweight and resistant to corrosion. In 1886, Charles Hall, of Oberlin, Ohio, perfected a process for economical production of aluminum.

Andiron. One of a pair of metal bars with short legs used in the hearth to support a fire grate or logs. Sometimes called a "firedog."

Antefix. An architectural capping ornament used on horizontal elements such as beams.

Arabesque. A form of ornamentation consisting of an interlocking pattern of flowers, foliage, fruit or geometric elements.

Artifact. A product of human workmanship.

Artificial Objects. Victorian term referring to things made by man, "inventions of man's mind," such as symbols or creatures of fantasy and mythology.

Artisan. An artist trained in some mechanical art or trade; a craftsman.

Back-Coping. Routing out the reverse of a pattern in the thicker parts of the casting thereby reducing the amount of metal required and the weight of the final casting. The process strengthens the casting by equalizing the thickness of metal where thick and thin parts are joined.

Bar-Iron. Pig-iron that has been refined so that it loses its brittleness, becomes malleable and is suitable for smithing.

Bellows. An instrument often fashioned of wood, leather and metal tubing that works like an artificial lung by alternate expansion and contraction drawing in air and expelling it through a tube. It was used by a molder to clean out mold cavities and blow off the parting surface in the casting process, and by a blacksmith to supply air to the forge.

Bench Molding. Process of casting small, loose, or single patterns in a flask.

Bench Rammer. A wooden hand tool with a tapered wedge on one end and a cylindrical head on the other, often having a heavy iron band around either end to prevent the wood from splitting, used by the molder to compact the sand.

Binders. Additives, such as wood or cereal flours, pulverized animal dung or clay, blended with casting sands to promote cohesion and porosity. When molten metal is poured into the mold, the sand is heated, additives burn out allowing gases or steam to escape, and casting quality is improved.

Black Lead. An extremely fine particle form of carbon having a soft, greasy, appearance; also called graphite.

Blast. Forceful flow of compressed air from some form of blower into the cupola or furnace; initially a bellows, later blowing tubs or cylinders operated by water or steam power.

Bloom. A bar of wrought iron from the forge or puddling furnace; a measurement of wrought or bar-iron.

Bloomery. A furnace or forge where wrought iron is made.

Blotch. An imperfection on the surface of a casting caused by improper ramming of the sand around the pattern in the mold-making process, frequently the result of ramming too far from the pattern.

Bottom Board. A board placed on top of the drag after the sand is rammed. The drag is turned over and mold board removed exposing the pattern.The bottom board then rested underneath supporting the flask.

Box Iron. A seventeenth-century pressing iron with a cavity into which a hot "lug" of iron was inserted. Early box irons were heated with hot charcoal that rested on a small grill inside the iron or brass box. Box irons were used into the twentieth century.

Bracketed Trivet. A type of trivet with a wing-nut assembly on the bottom of the platform for attaching the trivet to the fire-bar of a parlour or bedroom fireplace.

Brass. An alloy of copper and zinc.

Bronze. An alloy of copper and tin.

Butt. In reference to a type of separable door hinge. In the nineteenth century, a number of factories specialized in butt hinges.

Carbon. An element formed naturally, as diamonds and graphite; a constituent of coal, petroleum, asphalt, limestone and other carbonates; present in all organic compounds. Carbon darkens the color of iron. It is used in making a high quality of steel.

Casting. Metal object formed by pouring molten metal into a mold cavity and allowing it to solidify.

Cast-Iron. A commercial alloy of iron, carbon and silicon that is cast in a mold. It becomes hard, brittle, nonmalleable, and cannot be hammered without breaking. However, it is more easily fusible than steel.

Cast-Mark. An irregular extrusion resulting from breaking off the downspout or gate from the casting.

Cathedral Stands. Extended, narrow, iron rests with parallel sides and a pointed end as in a cathedral window. Points are formed with either straight or curved lines. A few stands for cathedral-shaped irons were made rectangular. (Hankenson used the term differently to describe a somewhat different style of stand.)

Cereal or Stove Trivets. Stands with short stubby feet scarcely a quarter-inch high, usually having an opening for insertion of a stove-lid lifter. Designed for use on iron ranges to prepare foods that scorch easily such as cereals, gravies, or sauces.

Chased; Chasing. In reference to smithing, ornamentation of metal surfaces by incising, parallel grooves, hatch-work, hammering, filing or chiseling in a decorative treatment.

Chippendale. Eighteenth-century furniture designer whose name has become synonymous with styles he introduced.

Chopper. A hand tool used to cut off gates.

Cleats. Flat supports; often extensions of the rim. Cleats were sometimes used as guides on the top edge of the platform to prevent the iron from sliding off the rest.

Coke. A fuel, distilled from wood or coal through a controlled burning with low oxygen, used in the smelting of iron.

Colliers. Workmen who made the charcoal used in iron furnaces.

Compass Flower. Design element resembling a flower

constructed with a compass by overlapping circles; may have three, four, five or six petals. Sometimes referred to as a "star."

Cope. The top half of the flask used in sand casting.

Core. Body of sand or other investment material used to form holes or openings of a desired shape in castings. The core is necessary to make constant wall castings as in the making of bells, pipe, or hollow-wares such as pots, pans or kettles; any parts of the sand mold that are made separately and placed within the principal mold.

Cross-Bar. A swing-bar extending from the side of a hearth or fireplace. Used in the hearth to suspend pots or skewers in cooking; used in the fireplace mainly for tea kettles. Sometimes called a "fire-bar."

Crucible. Silicon carbide or ceramic deep bowl-shaped container in which to hold and smelt metal.

Cupola. A smaller furnace resembling a blast furnace used for melting metals in foundries or steelworks.

Cutting. The process of replenishing casting sand with moisture and additives. The term comes from the way the shovel is used in blending the sand and additive mixture.

Dead-Head. A loose pattern which could be inserted into a vacant area of a sand mold when making other castings. Another procedure used "cassette" patterns. These patterns had a groove around the edge used to lock a number of cassette patterns into a metal frame. The frame, with cassette patterns locked in place, was used to make molds much the same as a matchplate pattern. The molder cut runners and gates in the sand for both dead-head and cassette patterns.

Decoration. In reference to Victorian usage, applied ornamentation in repeating pattern or in combination with others. (See ornament.)

Decorative Iron Stands, Rests. Iron rests of old traditional generic styles, usually having rails or guides but not designed for a particular model or type of iron.

Distelfink. The mythical bird of paradise. Frequently used in German folk art.

Double-Point. A style of pressing iron or iron rest that is ovular and pointed at both ends.

Downspout. The channel formed in the sand mold from the top of the cope to the pattern made with a sprue-pin, sprue-cutter or wedge.

Draft. The taper made on the edge of the pattern to facilitate withdrawing it from the sand mold. Tapers normally slanted from the bottom towards the top; occasionally a reverse draft was used when more metal went into the cope.

Drag. Bottom of the flask when it is in position for pouring; sometimes called a "nowel."

Draw-Pin; Draw-Hook, Draw-Screw (sometimes called a Lifting Screw). Instruments used to draw the pattern from the mold.

Draw-Plate. An attachment to a pattern with a threaded hole to receive a Draw-Screw; used to lift a pattern from the mold.

Drawing. Removing the pattern from the mold or extracting the core box from the shaped core.

Eastlake. Late nineteenth-century furniture style, characterized by sturdy, rectangular lines, associated with Charles Eastlake, English painter and art critic. In 1868, Eastlake published *Hints on Household Taste;* influential in the United States during the 1870's.

Element. In reference to design, a segment of a design composition.

Embossed. Raised in relief from the surface; embellished with raised work.

Emery. A dark granular variety of corundum, effectively used for grinding metal or glass.

Enamel. A vitreous composition usually opaque for coating the surface of metal, glass, or pottery, and baked under intense heat into a hard, impervious, surface.

Facing Sand. A special mixture of coating sand made to withstand the erosion or high temperature of molten iron; sometimes a coating mixture to produce a particular surface finish.

Feet. Trivet or stand supports less than one inch in length.

Fender. A low metal guard railing ten to fourteen inches high placed in front of the fireplace. Frequently decorative and often made of brass.

Fender Trivet. A stand with hooks on the front of the platform to attach to the fender railing. Sometimes the hooks were extended to the length of the rear legs so the fender trivet also could sit level on a flat surface. Other fender trivets had hooks and no legs and could only be used on a fender or cross-bar. Most fender trivets had handles and many had an adjustable platform that could be moved closer or farther from the heat. The majority of fender trivets were made of brass, but a few were made of iron or sheet metal and rod. All were hand-crafted implements.

Some fender trivets were called "cross-bar trivets." The distinction being that cross-bar trivets had hooks with square corners and fender trivets had curved ones. Perhaps the square or curved hooks worked equally well on either the fender or cross-bar.

Ferric Oxide. The black chemical coating produced by natural oxidization of iron over a long period of time.

Ferrous Oxide. The bright orange chemical coating produced by a recent oxidization of iron.

Fillers. Workmen responsible for loading the cold blast furnace with charcoal, ore and limestone.

Fins. Projections on a casting caused by imperfect fit between the cope and drag molds. Fins resulted from a shift of the pattern caused by improper ramming. Sometimes called "flashings."

Fireback. A heavy iron plate, often ornamented with relief designs, covering the back of the fireplace to reflect the heat and protect the masonry.

Flask. A two-part frame which holds the sand in which a casting mold is made.

Flatback. In reference to making a mold where the face of the pattern is in the drag and the cope surface is at the parting-line between the cope and drag.

Floral. Pertaining to or imitating flowers.

Floriated. Having floral design elements.

Fluter. A pressing iron used to form decorative pleats in cloth.

Foliated. Having design elements resembling leaves.

Folk Art. The tradition based art of the common people; art of the largest proportion of a civilization, which determines the group character and tends to preserve its designs and customs relatively unchanged.

Follow-Board. A board that conforms to the contour of the pattern and forms the parting surface.

Footman. A four-legged stand used in the fireplace for warming pots or kettles. Resembles a small table, usually made of brass or iron; similar to, but smaller than a waiter. Most were ten to fourteen inches high.

Forge. A smithy where metal is worked, such as a blacksmith shop where iron is wrought or refined.

Founder. Overseer of an iron furnace supervising loading the furnace, pouring, closing down, or other furnace operations, and having full responsibility for the quality of iron produced.

Founding. The making of metal castings.

Foundry. A metal casting works. They began as independent firms around 1820 and were well established in America by the 1850's.

Fraktur. A Germanic letterform, either printed or calligraphic.

Fret. An ornamental treatment consisting of straight lines or bars arranged in symmetrical patterns forming a lattice or decorative network. Also referring to the Greek key border design.

Fylfot. Another word for swastika.

Furnace. In metallurgy, a place where metals are smelted or reduced to a molten state.

Gate; In-Gate. A channel through which molten metal flows into the mold cavity.

Gated Pattern. A multiple pattern with runners, gates and well attached.

Georgian. A period style covering the years 1714 to 1830 coinciding with the successive reigns of the English kings named George.

Gilded; Gilt. On trivets, usually a gold paint on iron, often with a japanned finish over the gilt.

Gothic. The letter style commonly used to imprint company names or stock numbers on iron castings. Gothic letters of uniform thickness, without serifs and condensed.

Grate. A frame box of crossed or parallel iron bars used in a fireplace to hold fuel above the hearth floor to improve the draft.

Gray-Iron *(Grey-Iron is the English spelling).* A grade of pig-iron favored by foundries for casting.

Green-Sand. A naturally bonded sand used for sand casting. The most significant deposits were found near Albany, New York.

Guides. Cleats, rails or posts on iron rests projecting above the platform surface to prevent the iron from sliding off the platform.

Guide Posts. Posts on the top edge of the platform to position the iron in place and to prevent it from sliding off the rest.

Guttermen. Workmen who cleared away the slag from the furnace and dug channels for the casting of pig-iron.

Gutters. Shallow channels at the joint or parting line in the sand mold to act as relief vents to carry away escaping gases.

Handbook. A manual of instructions on how to do a specific task describing materials, tools, technical procedures and ornamentation; usually with illustrations on decoration, craft, construction, or production methods.

Hoop Iron. Thin, flexible bands of refined iron.

Incised. Cut or depressed below the surface; having a carved or engraved configuration or inscription.

Inorganic Model. Victorian design reference to a sub-division of organic; inanimate things found in nature such as snowflakes, waves, clouds, mountains or similar material representations.

Intermediate Pattern. A model made from a smoothed trivet, or one sculpted in wood, plaster, or wax; usually cast in white metal, finished and used to make the production pattern in iron, brass, bronze or lead. Today, intermediate patterns for small castings are often made of plastic.

Iron. A silver-white metallic element, malleable, ductile, and readily oxidized in moist air. Found almost universally in combined forms, it constitutes about 5 percent of the earth's crust. Iron melts at 2,795 degrees F., has a specific gravity of 7.86 and weighs 491 lbs. per cubic foot.

Ironmasters. Owners or overseers of iron plantations operating during the eighteenth and nineteenth centuries in America.

Ironmonger. A dealer in iron goods or hardware.

Japanned. Having a high gloss lacquer finish, as first used by the Japanese. An asphaltum varnish was applied to the metal over a painted or decorated surface, and it was baked on with heat. Japanning was a popular finish on trivets between 1880 and 1920 in America.

Jenny Lind. A Swedish singer who travelled widely in this country around the middle of the nineteenth century performing in eastern music halls and western mining camps. Several trivet patterns having an allegorical female figure were named for her.

Kitchen Stands and Trivets (classified as Early New England and Pennsylvania Trivets.) A category established by the author which includes trivets from the period between 1840 and 1865 found in the New England and Pennsylvania regions, but not necessarily made there. Includes kitchen and round stands and iron rests. Most handled and round stands have large platforms approximately six or seven inches in diameter, and are heavy (weighing two to four pounds). Iron rests also are larger and heavier. The majority of trivets and stands from this period have sprue-or wedge-marks on the reverse. A few stands are considerably smaller and were used for small kettles, plates or coffee pots.

Kitsch. The overly sentimental and romantic vulgarity appealing to an unsophisticated taste.

Legs. Trivet or stand supports which are an inch or more in length.

Lifter. A hand tool used in the sand molding process to remove loose sand from a mold cavity.

Ligature. A symbol consisting of two or more overlapping letterforms; a monogram.

Loam. Essentially clay; in sand-casting, the mixture of sand, clay and venting material principally used in making clay molds.

Loop Handle. A trivet handle formed in an open loop with the ends merging into the platform rim.

Loose Pattern. A production pattern, which is freely positioned in the flask, in comparsion to a matchplate pattern which is locked into the cope and drag.

Lyre. A "U" shaped stringed instrument similar to a harp used by the ancient Greeks. The characteristic shape often was used for trivets, or as a decorative element in design.

Machine Grinding. Using a high-speed emery grinding wheel to remove excess metal. Machine grinding leaves parallel striated markings usually found on the trivet platform rim or reverse.

Malleable. Capable of being extended, bent or shaped by beating with a hammer or by the pressure of rollers.

Manufacturers' Iron Stands. Iron rests carrying advertising, trademarks, monograms, model or company names which were made and distributed by manufacturers. Also, stands of functional design, which were produced for specific iron brands or models, without handles and having rails, guide posts, cleats or stops on the platform surface.

Master Pattern. A model carved in wood, but sometimes sculpted in wax, clay or plaster, used to make either an intermediate pattern or production pattern in sand casting.

Matchplate. A pattern on a plate the size of the flask with the face of the trivet and runners on the drag side and the legs and well on the cope side.

Mild Steel. Steel which is low in carbon content.

Mold. The impression or cavity left in the sand by the pattern.

Mold Board. The board that fits the bottom of the drag upon which the pattern is placed to make the mold.

Motif. A design theme; a principal ornament.

Mottled Iron. A grade of pig-iron mainly used for forging or making steel.

Motto Trivet. A trivet design embellished with cast letterforms of a proverb, motto or platitude.

Multi-Purpose Trivets and Stands. All handled stands without rails, guides or posts on the platform. Even though the triangular shape of iron rests suggests their use in pressing, the flat surface permits the stand to be used for other purposes.

Nickel. A hard, malleable, ductile metal, nearly silver-white; often used as plating on other metals because it is capable of high polish and corrosion resistant.

Nickel Plate. Nickel finish electroplated on to another metal; popular on iron trivets in the latter part of the nineteenth and early twentieth centuries.

Non-Ferrous. In reference to metals other than iron.

Olivine. A Chrysolite mineral which does not contain silica used today as a replacement for green-sand.

Open-Work. Any decorative work cut or pierced to show openings through its surface.

Organic. A Victorian design reference to natural forms derived from animate subjects such as plants, animals, insects, humans or other living things.

Ornament. In Victorian terminology, a two-dimensional design element based on natural plant forms.

Pakton. A metal alloy of zinc, copper and nickel resembling silver in appearance, first developed by the Chinese.

Pan Handle. A solid, flat, trivet handle having a terminal with a hanging hole in a round, diamond, or other simple shape. The surface of the handle may have decoration such as chasing.

Parting-Line. The division of the mold where the cope and drag meet and part.

Pattern. In casting, the model from which a mold is made. In design, the consistent repetition of a design motif. In the making of trivets, there could be as many as three patterns: a master pattern carved in wood, sculpted in wax, clay or plaster, an intermediate pattern made of white metal, and a production pattern used to produce a large number of castings.

Pattern Book. A manual of decorative illustrations used by artisans practicing various handicrafts, trades or professions. The book usually illustrated ornaments or artifacts by time period, culture, profession, or some other classification.

Paw Feet. Supports resembling lion feet on a group of round table stands of English origin, which were popular in America during the nineteenth century. The paw feet were most associated with the English Regency period.

Permeability. In reference to sand mixtures used for casting having the texture and additives to ventilate gases and steam.

Plaque Trivet. A decorative metal casting, modelled on the face and flat on the reverse, usually without any supports, made to hang on the wall or to stand up with a wire support. Plaque trivets had a large number of horseshoe designs with symbols of fraternal organizations. Eagles and other patriotic motifs also were used. Many were cast in brass. Plaque trivets often were heavy and when laid face down, the flat back became the platform for an iron or pot.

Plate. A smooth flat surface. Sometimes the platform of a trivet is referred to as the "plate."

Plate Mill. An industrial plant specializing in the manufacture of sheet or plate metal; sometimes called a "rolling mill."

Platform. The raised surface or main body of a trivet or stand supported by three or more supports.

Platter Trivet. An oval table stand designed specifically for serving platters, usually ten or more inches long, and often adjustable. (See Adjustable Table Stand.)

Post. A cylindrical, untapered metal trivet leg or guide.

Potter. An artisan who works with clay and ceramic firing. In the iron industry, a molder was called a "potter" until the eighteenth century.

Pouring. Filling the mold cavity with molten metal.

Production Pattern. The pattern used for production of castings; usually made of iron, sometimes brass, white metal, lead, or combination of the three, i.e., a pattern may be white metal with well and runners of brass or lead.

Puddling. The process of heating and stirring pig-iron in the furnace to convert it into malleable iron suitable for smithing.

Quill. A tool consisting of a fibrous material with a wire spine used by molders to dampen the joint around the edges of the pattern preparatory to lifting the pattern from the mold. Squeezing the wet material caused water to run down the wire to the joint moistening the sand so it would not crumble.

Quad. A kitchen or table stand with four supports.

Rails. A raised projection around the top contour of an iron rest to prevent the iron from slipping off the platform. Rails may be partial (front, sides or back) or they may encircle the entire platform.

Rammer. Compressed air or hand tool used to compact sand around the pattern.

Regency. An English period style from 1811 to 1820. On trivets, "paw" feet were the most characteristic element from the Regency style.

Reproductions. In reference to trivets made after 1930, replicating old traditional designs.

Reduction. Converting scrap metal to a molten state; sometimes called "melting."

Refining. The process of converting pig-iron into wrought iron or steel. It is a process of changing polyglot, crystalline, structure into parallel grain through repeated heating and hammering, or rolling or stirring in the furnace.

Registered. Reference to an English patent notice.

Relief. Reference to ornament, design or letters raised above the surface.

Rest. A stand for a pressing iron.

Returns. Scrap metal composed of runners, wells, down-spouts or defective castings returned to the furnace for reduction and reuse.

Reverse. The back of a trivet or stand platform.

Riddle. The circular sieve used by the molder to sift fine sand over and around the pattern in the flask.

Rim. The outer edge of a trivet platform.

Roll-Over. After tamping the sand around the pattern, turning the drag upside down exposing the bottom of the pattern.

Roman. Reference to a typographic style of incised or embossed thick and thin letterforms, commonly used for names or initials on the reverse of castings in the mid-nineteenth century. In open-faced Roman, the thick part of the letterform was outlined.

Rosette. A design ornament resembling a rose in shape or color; a roundel filled with leafy forms encircled like petals of a blossom.

Runner. In the casting process, that portion of the gating system that carries molten metal from the sprue-well to the in-gate.

Sadiron. A solid flat-iron. The name derives from an archaic definition of "sad" which meant "heavy, weighty or ponderous." Sadirons came into general use in the eighteenth century. The entire iron was heated until detachable handles were invented. Then one lug could be heating while another was in use.

Scab; Scabbing. Rough or uneven blotches on the surface of castings; molding imperfections caused by the movement of sand when hot metal enters the mold; usually the result of tamping the sand too close, or actually striking the pattern.

Scalloped. A decorative treatment achieved by repetition of curves, or angular shapes, often on a border, rail, support or edge.

Scroll Handle. A curving trivet handle shaped in an open loop with the ends joining the platform and curling outward.

Shake-Out. The dumping of the flask after the metal has been poured and the casting has solidified.

Slab-Serif or Egyptian. In reference to a typographic style of letterforms with square serifs; being thick and thin in the heavy styles, and having more uniform weight in the lighter styles.

Slag. The waste residue which contains impurities from the fuel and metal that is dumped from the furnace or cupola after the iron smelting process.

Slitting Mill. An industrial plant specializing in making rods or strips from sheet metal.

Slick. A small hand tool used to patch and smooth sand molds.

Slurry. A thin mixture of clay and water added to molding sand to increase its strength. Another reference mentions the use of slurry to capture the fine detail of patterns in the "lost wax" process of casting.

Smelting. To melt and fuse iron ore; to extract the metal from the ore while in a molten state.

Smoothing. When an existing trivet is to be used as a pattern, it is burnished, filed, and repaired where necessary; the process is called "smoothing."

Snap Flask. A small flask, hinged at one corner with a latch at the opposite corner, used for making light castings. After tamping, the flask is removed leaving the mold in a block of sand. This same flask can be used to make additional molds.

Spade. A style of trivet or iron which is pointed at the front and hooked or flat at the rear; resembling the shape of the digging instrument called a spade.

Spider. A hand-wrought trivet designed for use in the hearth with a long handle and extended legs.

Splayed. In reference to trivet supports that slant outward from the platform; spread out, sloped or beveled.

Sprue. The metal which solidifies in the downspout between the pouring basin and the sprue heel (where the spout connects to the casting). The downspout channel is made with a sprue-pin.

Sprue-Cutter. A hollow, brass, elongated, tapered cone used to cut a downspout by pressing and rotating the cutter.

Sprue-Pin; Sprue-Plug. The solid, tapered, cylindrical cone with a tapered end used to make a downspout.

Sprue-Pot; Button. A turnip-shaped tool used to widen the opening of the downspout to catch and pool the molten metal when pouring the mold.

Squeeze; Squeezer. To mechanically tamp the sand in the flask; the machine which does the automatic tamping.

Squeeze-Board. A board used by the molder which goes on top of the cope or drag; counterpart to the bottom-board; sometimes called a "mold board" when used on the drag.

Stamp. A mark, initials, symbol or name incised or embossed onto a product. Blacksmiths often marked their work with initials or a symbol. Manufacturers identified their products with a name or stock number.

Stamped Metal. Design cut or formed into light gauge sheet metal made of tin, brass or steel using enormous pressure. On stamped metal trivets the platform design often was decorative open-work, and the feet were made by extensions of the platform bent down to form supports. Other supports were made by stamping them into the platform on three sides and bending them down. Sometimes male and female dies were used to stamp an embossed or debossed surface on the face of a trivet.

Stand. A platform with more than three supports used to hold hot irons or other utensils and protect surfaces from heat or dampness; iron rests often were referred to as "stands."

Steel. Refined pig-iron containing carbon as an essential component made in three grades and malleable under certain conditions. Mild steel is low in carbon; hard steel is high in carbon, up to 1.7 per-cent, and the grade between is called middle steel.

Stock Number. Foundry or manufacturer's identification number on patterns. Numbers were used for inventory, stock or catalogue listings.

Strike Bar. A straight bar of iron or wood used to level the sand and clean the cope and drag edges.

Swab. A sponge-like tool made of fibrous material, dipped in water and squeezed by the molder to moisten the joint between the mold and pattern prior to removing the pattern from the mold.

Swastika. A symbol or ornament in the form of a Greek cross with the equilateral arms bent at the middle in right angles. Most have squared terminals with constant width. Some versions, called "Chinese Swastica," are curvilinear with tapering arms and rounded terminals.

Tassel. A fibrous pendant ornament ending in a knotted or bound tuft of loose threads. In Victorian design it was often symbolic of funeral trappings. The stylized tassels used in trivet designs are often mistaken for brooms.

Taster. A small iron spoon used in tasting food during preparation.

Tea, Coffee and Table Stands. Usually small, round or square unhandled stands with short feet primarily designed for small pots, plates or serving dishes.

Tea Tiles. Round or square stands with ornamental tile insets in wood, wire or metal frames. The more elaborate tea tiles incorporated music boxes inside or had a bell to ring for the maid.

Tole. In reference to a style of folk decoration practiced by early Americans of Germanic descent. Normally done with a brush and paint, but sometimes with stencils. Stylized floral, bird and animal designs were applied to tin, pottery or wood. The practice has been revived as a craft.

Tooled. Shaped by machinery. In reference to the pre-made, shaped feet or legs mainly used on handcrafted brass or copper plate iron rests. Some of these ornamental legs were undoubtedly tooled on a lathe, others were cast. Most had a threaded shaft at the top which was screwed through the platform, then either cut off or pounded down as a rivet. After the legs were inserted and secured, the surface was polished. Some cast-iron supports were gilded or brass plated.

Trammel. An adjustable pothook attached to the hearth or fireplace crane.

Triskelon. A figure or ornament composed of three branches, usually curved and radiating from a center. The three-legged triskelon taken from a Greek vase is commonly associated with the Isle of Man.

Trivet. A three-legged stand used for hearth cooking or to raise hot or wet vessels above table or counter surfaces.

Victorian. In reference to an eclectic, ponderous, ornate style associated with the period of British Queen Victoria's reign, 1837 to 1901.

Waiter. A small metal table used in conjunction with the parlour fireplace; usually with four to six legs.

Wedge. The wedge-shaped tool used for making the downspout. Wedges were used by molders for a variety of purposes, such as to hold the cope and drag firmly together, to insert under the mold board, and provide space for grasping the drag to turn it over.

Well. In reference to pattern-making and casting, the reservoir into which the downspout carried molten metal. From the well, the liquid metal ran through runners to gates and into the mold cavity.

White Metal. An alloy of lead, tin and antimony used by pattern-makers to make an intermediate pattern, which was the pattern between the smoothed trivet or wood, plaster, wax or clay model and the metal production pattern.

White Iron. A grade of pig-iron favored by plate mills; high in carbon content.

Whitesmith. An iron smith who finished his work by polishing as distinct from one who forged it.

Winter. A term used by Paley to describe a small metal table usually made of iron or brass with a platform resting on a shaft set into a three-or four-footed base. The shaft often had a set-screw so the height of the platform could be adjusted. The table was used near or in the fireplace.

Wrought. Reference to the process of shaping iron by hammering it into shape with tools. Wrought iron is a commercially refined form of iron which is tough, malleable and relatively soft; also called "bar-iron."

IX. BIBLIOGRAPHY OF REFERENCES

Books

An American Sampler: Folk Art from The Shelburne Museum, National Gallery of Art, 1987.

Berney, Esther S., *A Collector's Guide to Pressing Irons and Trivets*; Crown Publishers, New York, New York, 1977.

Binder, Fredrick Moore, *Coal Age Empire;* Pennsylvania Historical and Museum Commission, Harrisburg, Pennsylvania, 1974.

Boland, Simpson, *The Iron Founder;* John Wiley & Sons, New York, New York, 1893.

Boucher, Jack E., *Of Batsto and Bog Iron*; The Batsto Citizen's Committee, Batsto, New Jersey, 1964, 1970, 1973.

Bridgeport Brass Company, *Seven Centuries of Brass Making*; Bridgeport, Connecticut, 1920.

Donsco Incorporated 1906-1981; Donsco Corporation, Wrightsville, Pennsylvania, 1981. (Annual Report)

Dosey, William H. and I.C.S. Staff, *Green-Sand Molding*; International Textbook Company, Scranton, Pennsylvania, 1934.

(The) Encylopedia of Collectibles, Telephones to Trivets; Time-Life, Alexandria, Virginia, 1980.

Fundamentals of Metal Casting; Penton Publishing Company, Cleveland, Ohio, 1972.

Garvan, Beatrice B., *The Pennsylvania German Collection*; Philadelphia Museum of Art, Philadelphia, Pennsylvania, 1982.

Glissman, A.H., *The Evolution of the Sad Iron*; published by the author, Carlsbad, California, 1970.

Gombrich, E.H., *The Sense of Order*; Phaidon Press Limited, Oxford, England, 1979.

Grennan, Stimpson Gray, *Foundry Work*; American Technical Society, Chicago, Illinois, 1942.

Hammond, Dorothy, *Confusing Collectibles*; Wallace Homestead, Des Moines, Iowa, 1969.

Hankenson, Dick, *Trivets, Book 1, Trivets, Book 2, Old and Reproductions;* Wallace Homestead Book Company, Des Moines, Iowa, 1972.

Harned, Bill & Denise, *Griswold Cast Collectibles; History and Values*; published by the authors, Edinboro, Pennsylvania, 1985.

Harner, John Z., *Seed Time to Harvest*; The Kutztown Publishing Company, Kutztown, Pennsylvania, 1957.

Hornung, Clarence P., *Treasury of American Design and Antiques*; "A Trivet for the Hot Pot," pp. 497-503. Harrison House; Harry Abrams, Inc., New York, New York, 1986.

Horst, Melvin J. and Smith, Elmer L., *Early Iron Ware*; Applied Arts Publishers, Lebanon, Pennsylvania, 1971.

I.C.S. Reference Library, a series of textbooks prepared for the students of the international correspondence schools and containing in permanent form the instruction papers, examination questions, and keys used in their various courses. Wood Working, Wood Turning, Patternmaking, Greensand Molding, Core Making, Dry-sand and Loam Work, Cupola Practice, and Mixing Cast Iron. Scranton International Textbook Company, Scranton, Pennsylvania, 1905.

Jewell, Brian., *Smoothing Irons, A History and Collector's Guide*; Wallace Homestead Book Company, Lombard, Illinois, 1977.

Kurjack, Dennis C., *Hopewell Village*; National Park Service Handbook Series No. 8, Government Printing Office, 1954, 1961.

Larsson, Gustaf, *Handbook of Geometrical Wood Carving*; E.L. Kellogg & Co., New York, New York and Chicago, Illinois, 1895.

Lasansky, Jeannette, *To Draw, Upset, & Weld*; Pennsylvania State University Press, University Park, Pennsylvania, 1980.

Lantz, Louise K., *Old American Kitchenware 1725-1925*; Thomas Nelson, Everybody's Press, Camden, New York, 1970.

Lewis, David W. and Hugins, Walter., *Hopewell Furnace, Official National Park Handbook*; Division of Publications, National Park Service, Washington, D.C., 1983.

Lifshey, Earl, *The Housewares Story*; National Housewares Manufacturers Association, Chicago, Illinois, 1973.

McClinton, Katherine Morrison, *Antique Collecting for Everyone*; McGraw Hill Book Company, Inc. New York, New York, Toronto, Canada, London, England, 1951.

McNerney, Kathryn, *Antique Iron*; Collector Books, Paducah, Kentucky, 1984.

Meyer, Franz Sales, *Handbook of Ornament; a grammar of art; industrial and architectural designing in all its branches for practical as well as theoretical use.*; The Bruno Hessling Company, New York, Paris and Berlin, 1910.

Norton at 100 Years; 1984 Annual Report, Norton Company, Worcester, Massachusetts, 1984.

Overman, Fredrick, *A Treatise on Metallurgy; Mining and General and Particular Metallurgical Operations with a Description of Charcoal, Coke and Anthracite Furnace, Blast Machines, Hot Blast, Forge Hammers, Rolling Mills, Etc.*; D. Appleton & Company, New York, New York, 1852.

Politzer, Judy, *Tuesday's Children: Collecting Little Irons and Trivets*; published by the author, Carlsbad, California, 1977.

Politzer, Judy, *Early Tuesday Morning: More Little Irons and Trivets*; published by Frank Politzer, Carlsbad, California, 1986.

Schaffner, Cynthia V.A. and Klein, Susan, *Folk Hearts*; Alfred A. Knopf, New York, New York, 1984.

Schiffer, Peter, Nancy, & Herbert, *The Brass Book*, Schiffer Publishing Company, Exton, Pennsylania, 1978.

Simpson, Bruce L., *Metal-Casting Industry*; American Foundrymen's Society, Des Plaines, Illinois, 1948, 1969.

Spretson, N.E., *A Practical Treatise on Casting and Founding*; E. & F. N. Spon, London, England, New York, New York, 1878.

Stoudt, John Joseph, Ph.D., *Pennsylvania Folk Art, An Interpretation*; Schlechter's, Allentown, Pennsylvania, 1948.

Thenot, J.P., *Dessin Lineaire*; Isidore Pesron, Libraire-Editeur, Paris, France, 1845.

Articles

Bagdade, Susan and Al, "Reproduction Trivets No Trivial Matter For Collectors," *Antique Week*, January 18, 1988.

Carrick, Alice Van Leer, "Trivets and Toasting Forks," *House Beautiful*, April, 1928.

Charlton, Mrs. Frank,* "Trivets on the Wall," *The Spinning Wheel*, June, 1956, p. 40.

Darmstaetter, Hugo, "Cast and Wrought Iron Beauty in Trivets and Other Hot Items," *The Spinning Wheel*, September 1950, p. 10-12.

Hankenson, Dick, "Old and New Cast Iron Trivets," *The Spinning Wheel*, June, 1962, p. 16.

Jenkins, Dorothy M., "Trivets,"*Collectors News*, May, 1976, p.6.

Knight, Nancy, "Right as a Trivet," *The American Home*, May, 1947. Included in "The Spinning Wheel Complete Book of Antiques."

Koehler, Margaret H., "Toy Trivets to Treasure," *The Spinning Wheel*, July-August 1969, p.35.

Lancaster Sunday News, "Pennsylvania Dutch Artcraft Thrives in Big and Small York County Plants," February 12, 1950.

Mace, Glenda L., "Trivets Take the Heat," *The Collector*, April, 1988. New York/Pennsylvania.

Menard, Gene, "Trivets," *Hobbies*, October, 1938, p. 63.

Paley, William, *Spinning Wheel*,

"Birds and Animals in Trivets," p. 20, September, 1967. Included in "The Spinning Wheel Complete Book of Antiques."

"Brass Trivets Old and New," p. 60, October, 1969.

"Circles in Trivet Designs," p. 22, June, 1968.

"Flowers and Vine Trivets," P. 30, September, 1973. Included in "The Spinning Wheel Complete Book of Antiques."

"Heart Designs in Trivets," p. 14, May, 1966.

"Is It A Trivet?", p. 14, May, 1972. Included in "The Spinning Wheel Complete Book of Antiques."

"Trees, Leaves and Fruit in Trivet Design," p. 44, November, 1974.

"Trivets From A To Z," p. 40, March, 1971.

"Wire Trivets," p. 54, June, 1970. Included in "The Spinning Wheel Complete Book of Antiques."

Paley, William, *Hobbies*

"Classification of Trivets; Circular Trivets," p. 98, July, 1969.

"Geometric Shapes in Trivets," p. 114, September, 1969.

"Heart Shapes," p. 122, March, 1970.

"Horseshoe Shaped Trivets," p. 48, September, 1971.

"Oval and Elliptical Trivets," p. 98, March, 1972.

"Shield and Spade Shaped Trivets," p. 140, December, 1972.

"Star, Snowflake and Leaf Trivets," p. 102, April, 1973.

"Unusual Features in Gadget Trivets," p. 28, June, 1977.

"Wire Household Utensils," p. 146, April, 1972.

Paley, William, *Antiques Journal*

"Triangular Trivets," p. 22, November, 1973.

Trade Catalogues

The majority of these catalogues are found in either the Winterthur or Hagley Libraries on the Dupont estate in Wilmington, Delaware.

A.C. Williams Company, 48th edition; house furnishing specialties and toys; Ravenna, Ohio, n.d. (after 1900).

A.C. Williams Company; Ravenna, Ohio, 1931.

Allen (W.D.), Manufacturing Company; Chicago, Illinois, 1926.

American Foundry Equipment Company; 1910.

Atlantic Stamping Company; Rochester, New York, 1913.

American Stove & Hollow Ware; Philadelphia, Pennsylvania, 1873-4.

B.C. Bibb Stove Company; Baltimore, Maryland, 1907.

Chesapeake Stove Company; Baltimore, Maryland, 1898.

Clad (V) & Sons; Philadelphia, Pennsylvania, 1905.

Colebrook Iron Company; 1917.

Comstock-Castle Stove Company; 1888.

Dover Stamping Company; Boston, Massachussetts 1869.

Gluck, William; 1901-02.

Grey Iron Casting Company Ltd.; Mount Joy, Pennsylvania, c. 1900.

Hall & Carpenter; Philadelphia, Pennsylvania, 1913.

Haslet, Flanagen & Company; Philadelphia, Pennsylvania, 1900.

Kern, John Jr. & Company; Baltimore, Maryland, 1881-82.

Lisk Manufacturing Company; Canandaigua, New York, 1911.

Logan & Strobridge Iron Company; New Brighton, Pennsylvania, 1877.

Marietta Casting; Marietta, Ohio, 1872.

Merchant & Company; Philadelphia, Pennsylvania, 1902.

Mount Penn Stove Works; Reading, Pennsylvania, 1891.

Murdock Parlor Grate Company; Boston, Massachussetts, 18—.

New Jersey Lamp & Bronze Works; New Brunswick, New Jersey, c. 1900.

Peckham J S & M; Utica, New York, 1889.

Reading Hardware Company; Reading, Pennsylvania, 1876.

Reading Saddle & Manufacturing Company; Reading, Pennsylvania, 1909.

Rochester Stamping Company; Rochester, New York, 1910.

Rohrman & Son; Philadelphia, Pennsylvania, 1860.

St. Louis Stamping Company; St. Louis, Missouri, 1876.

Shannon (J. Jacobs) & Company; Philadelphia, Pennsylvania, 1889.

Sidney Shepard & Company; Buffalo, New York, 1873, -86, -90, -90.

Sidney Shepard & Company; Buffalo Stamping Works; Buffalo, New York, c. 1890.

Sterling Wheelbarrow Company, Cat. 32; Milwaukee, Wisconsin, 1916.

Thomas, Roberts Stevenson Company; Philadelphia, Pennsylvania, 1897.

Vogel, William & Brothers; Brooklyn, New York, 1880.

U.T. Hungerford Brass and Copper Company; New York City, 1915.

Walker (F.A.) & Company; Boston, Massachussetts, 1860.

Wheaton & Hickcox; Worcester, Massachussetts, 1855.

Whitehall Stove & Agricultural Works; 1859.

Williamson C.T.; Newark, New Jersey, 1883.

Wire Goods Company; Worchester, Massachussetts, 1919.

Woods Sherwood & Company; 1878.

Wrightsville Hardware Company; Wrightsville, Pennsylvania, c. 1920.